GENDER QUOTAS FOR COMPANY BOARDS

GENDER QUOTAS FOR COMPANY BOARDS

Marc De Vos
Philippe Culliford
(eds.)

intersentia
Cambridge – Antwerp – Portland

Intersentia Publishing Ltd.
Trinity House | Cambridge Business Park | Cowley Road
Cambridge | CB4 0WZ | United Kingdom
Tel.: +44 1223 393 753 | Email: mail@intersentia.co.uk

Distribution for the UK:
NBN International
Airport Business Centre, 10 Thornbury Road
Plymouth, PL6 7 PP
United Kingdom
Tel.: +44 1752 202 301 | Fax: +44 1752 202 331
Email: orders@nbninternational.com

Distribution for the USA and Canada:
International Specialized Book Services
920 NE 58th Ave. Suite 300
Portland, OR 97213
USA
Tel.: +1 800 944 6190 (toll free)
Email: info@isbs.com

Distribution for Austria:
Neuer Wissenschaftlicher Verlag
Argentinierstraße 42/6
1040 Wien
Austria
Tel.: +43 1 535 61 03 24
Email: office@nwv.at

Distribution for other countries:
Intersentia Publishing nv
Groenstraat 31
2640 Mortsel
Belgium
Tel.: +32 3 680 15 50
Email: mail@intersentia.be

The content of this book is up to date as at 31 December 2013.

Gender Quotas for Company Boards
Marc De Vos and Philippe Culliford (eds.)

ISBN 978-1-78068-229-7
D/2014/7849/71
NUR 825 / 827

British Library Cataloguing in Publication Data. A catalogue record for this book is available from the British Library.

SETTING THE SCENE

Since the creation of what would eventually become the European Union, gender equality has been an important principle of EU law, both as a market principle and as a social right. Numerous directives and an important body of cases have implemented these principles across all EU Member States. EU equality law is mostly formal in its approach of non-discrimination, while exceptionally embracing a more substantive approach that favours overall outcomes over individual merit and equality of opportunity. The position of women in company boards has increasingly received attention from that substantive angle.

Gender quotas for company boards indeed address the highest rungs of the economic ladder from the perspective of guaranteeing a minimal target of gender diversity *per se*. While this move has gained traction in various European countries and at the EU level as such, its interaction with general non-discrimination law is far from straightforward, as *M. De Vos* demonstrates in this book. Moreover, the basic premises of improved corporate governance and company performance that underpin many of the quota initiatives are themselves not beyond doubt, as *H. De Wulf* points out in his introductory chapter.

Notwithstanding these caveats, the opinion that it is positive for companies to have more women in their board of directors has grown in all the countries that have participated in this project.[1] However, it also clear that the evolution in public opinion varies significantly from country to country. Public opinion in Iceland, for instance, is more critical of company boards that do not meet gender equality standards than public opinion in Spain, as we learn from the articles of *A. Kovalainen* for Finland and *R. Pala Laguna* for Spain.

Not all European countries have (as yet) embarked upon formal law making to boost gender diversity in the board room. There is a wide and sometimes also complementary experience with soft law under the guise of corporate governance codes and various recommendations, the scope of which often extends beyond that of any formal quotas. Several contributions to this book describe the nature and impact of soft law approaches in their respective countries, while others trace the emergence of hard law rules with a similar purpose.

---

1 Belgium, Finland, France, Germany, Iceland, the Netherlands, Norway and Spain.

There is, indeed, a growing tide of imposed and formal quotas to boost gender diversity in board rooms in several European countries. This book describes many of the recent initiatives in that regard, both inside the European Union and beyond. The European Commission, with Commissioner Reding at the political forefront, has claimed its stake in the quotas debate by offering a template for an EU Directive that would generalize and coordinate efforts to impose gender diversity at company boards across the European Union. *A. Stein* presents both the preparation and the contours of an initiative that seeks to balance a clear-cut political agenda for more female representation with the overall gender neutrality archetype of the EU law of which the Commission itself is the institutional guardian.

Gender quotas for company boards are a controversial subject. The contributions to this book do not avoid the debate and provide the reader with clear insights, whether they are societal, legal, or economic. As *B. Waas* mentions in his article, the human right to property and the freedom of association are at first sight obstacles against imposing gender quotas on the boards of directors of private companies. Quotas are difficult to square with an anti-discrimination vision rooted in individual fairness and merit, rather than in group membership. This tension exists and persists well beyond the level of EU discrimination law, as *B. Gressy* illustrates for France.

Wherever the reader stands on the topic, the topicality of gender quotas for company boards is beyond doubt. This book seeks to offer timely information and analysis, both on the broader and cross-country dimensions of corporate governance, economic performance, and EU law, and on the domestic agenda in eight relevant European countries. The contributors to this book not only come from different countries but also partially from different fields. We have indeed strived to integrate the various cross-disciplinary perspectives that are required to fully appreciate the topic but that often remain partially out of view in the single-dimension approaches that dominate academic research. In order to respect the specifics and authenticity of each discipline, we have deliberately chosen to respect the diversity in research and reference styles.

Ours is certainly not the last word on a topic that remains in full swing in a period where many policy and law makers are reconsidering some basic rules of the capitalist economy. Nor does it pretend to offer a fully comprehensive analysis of all the potentially relevant issues. But it will offer the interested reader a broad and honest perspective that integrates various angles and allows for cross-country comparisons. May it contribute to an informed and pragmatic societal debate.

Marc De Vos and Philippe Culliford

CONTENTS

CHAPTER 1
DO GENDER QUOTAS CONTRIBUTE TO BETTER CORPORATE GOVERNANCE?

Hans De Wulf*

I. INTRODUCTION: AN EFFICIENCY PERSPECTIVE

The different contributions to this book approach gender quotas from different angles: some contributions contain the facts and figures on the number of female directors, others discuss legislative developments at the European level and in several individual countries, or look into the question whether gender quotas are compatible with the legal principle of equality and non-discrimination. This contribution will leave all that completely out and will focus instead on the effects mandatory quotas for female board membership may have on corporate governance in commercial, for profit corporations.

The wish to improve corporate governance practices at the corporate level is only one of the possible rationales one may put forward to increase female boardroom participation.[1]

If, for instance, one argues that the number of women on boards should be increased because this corresponds to the wishes of the majority of the population or at least of the electorate, this is essentially an attempt to legitimise quotas on democratic grounds. There is quite a bit of survey-based evidence that

* Ghent University, Financial Law Institute.

1 For an overview of some of the most important justifications invoked in policy debates to support increases in board diversity – where diversity is measured more broadly than just gender diversity – see J. Fanto, L. Solan and J. Darley, "Justifying board diversity", 89 *North Carolina Law Review*, 2011, 901–936. For an article noting that, at least in the U.S., proponents of board diversity have recently stressed the business case, and arguing that this is a mistake, see L. Fairfax, "Board diversity revisited: new rationale, same old story", 89 *North Carolina Law review* 2011, 855 (the author bases her argument partly on her finding that the (re)new(ed) emphasis on the business efficiency of boardroom diversity has not actually led to greater diversity in US boardrooms).

for instance the majority of German citizens is in favour of higher rates of female board membership.[2]

One may also invoke ethical reasons in support of quotas, arguing that it would be "just" if a higher percentage of board members were women. Of course, a specific theory of justice would be needed to support this assertion, otherwise a yardstick to measure whether any progress has been or could be made in the quest for justice by introducing quotas would be totally lacking. One could for instance invoke Aristotelian ideas about distributive justice, which essentially boil down to the idea that everybody should be given his or her just dessert, based on qualities a person already has: if you have to decide which young kid should receive a top of the range flute, a rich one who has great musical talent and is perhaps already an accomplished flute player or a poor one with an intense desire to become a good flute player, Aristotle would probably have answered that the rich kid merits to receive the flute, because it is most useful for him: it complements his talents. In the same vein one could argue that more women should get board seats if their personal qualities make them as suitable as male candidates for a board seat or, in other words, that a specific female candidate should be chosen on meritocratic grounds if she has more of the qualities needed in a board member than male competitors for the job.

Efficiency reasons could of course also be invoked to support (or oppose) more women on boards. Efficiency-based theories rely on some form of cost-benefit analysis to decide what decision (e.g. board quotas or not) should be taken.

In this contribution, we will mainly adopt this efficiency approach, neglecting other approaches like the political or moral ones. More specifically we'll look at the available evidence – mainly gathered by economists – concerning the question whether higher rates of female boardroom membership have contributed or at least could potentially contribute to better corporate governance.

This of course immediately raises the question what the meaning of "better corporate governance" could be.

II. WHAT DO WE MEAN BY "BETTER CORPORATE GOVERNANCE AT BOARD LEVEL"?

When someone says that some policy measure or legal rule like female quotas improves corporate governance, this can have essentially two possible meanings.

---

2 See the surveys referred to in G. Bachmann, "Zur Umsetzung einer Frauenquote im Aufsichtsrat", *ZIP* 2011, 1131, footnote 9.

It may indicate that the person thinks that the rule increases the value of the firm, as measured through traditional valuation techniques. For listed firms, economist will usually check this by looking at the evolution of stock prices, but often some accounting measure like return on equity (ROE) or Tobin's Q will be used. In probably all countries that have introduced mandatory rules, including quotas, to increase female boardroom participation, these rules are only applicable to listed companies and there is therefore some justification in focusing our review of the literature on research concerning listed companies. There is very little research (in this area) on non-listed companies anyway.

A second meaning of "better corporate governance" may be that a rule or practice improves certain processes and practices within the company so that the company functions better in some way or another. Since corporate governance is mainly concerned with so-called agency conflicts, i.e. potential conflicts between the different stakeholders whose input is needed to have a functioning firm[3], we could say that female quotas contribute to better corporate governance when they contribute to increased control over and a better management of agency conflicts within firms.

Since quotas are introduced at board level, the central question for us is whether they at least potentially contribute to a better functioning of the board. In order to answer that question, we must first determine what the important tasks of the

[3] More precisely, one may define agency conflicts as conflicts and tensions that arise between people (or groups of people) who want to collaborate, pursuing a common goal, but at the same time have diverging interests concerning the way the cooperation is structured. For instance, most functioning firms need input from shareholders and creditors, who provide the financial means of the firm, which often can only produce goods or services with the help of employees it hires and these employees often need to be managed by a separate group of managers, who are monitored (on behalf of shareholders, possibly also of creditors) by a board of directors, usually appointed by the shareholders. All these stakeholder groups function together in one firm, and want the firm to be successful, but different preferences lead different stakeholders to different valuations (positive or negative) of certain decisions that "the firm" makes. This is the essence of the agency conflict. Economists tend to focus on differences in risk appetite between stakeholders as the source of agency conflicts. For instance, it is assumed that managers are as a rule more risk-averse than shareholders, because the typical manager in a listed firm will have invested almost all his human capital in one single firm, and his human capital will be severely impaired when the firm becomes insolvent, whereas the typical shareholder would be well-diversified and would therefore prefer the firm to undertake more risky projects which may generate higher returns on equity if they are successful and will not dramatically impact the fortunes of the shareholder when they fail, precisely because the investor is well diversified.
The foundational texts on agency conflicts are Michael C. Jensen and William H. Meckling, "Theory of the Firm: Managerial Behavior, Agency Costs and Ownership Structure", *Journal of Financial Economics*, Vol. 3, issue 4, 1976; and E.F. Fama and M.C. Jensen, "Separation of Ownership and Control", *Journal of Law and Economics*, Vol. XXVI, June 1983.

board are. Here, most people would agree on a list of functions that looks more or less like this[4]:

- The board must select and if necessary dismiss top management and set its remuneration.
- It needs to monitor management (see below).
- The board is an important connection of the firm to the outside world, including the stakeholders and therefore board members have an important task in representing the company in a suitable way to the outside world, but must also help the company to internalise the expectations stakeholders and society at large have of the company[5].
- The board must report, through the general meeting, to shareholders on developments (financial and otherwise) of the company since at least traditionally, the board was seen as performing its functions mainly for the benefit of the shareholders.
- Whereas the board normally does not manage the company, it may intervene in management in crisis situations, not only be sacking managers or redistributing powers, competencies and budgets, but also by taking crucial decisions itself (e.g. whether to enact a poison pill to defeat a public takeover bid that the board sees as hostile to the interests of the company).

The monitoring function of the board, as it has come to be called over the past few decades, involves at least the following tasks:

- Approving and where necessary change the budget of different departments, divisions, management teams (and setting financial limits above which separate board approval is required for certain decisions).
- The board must approve (or reject) overall strategy as developed by management, also in view of what the board sees as acceptable levels of risk for the corporation.
- The board must oversee the development by management of a system of internal controls, designed to catalogue and harness to an acceptable level all kinds of risks to which the company is exposed (compliance and other risks).

4 See e.g. L. Van den Berghe and A. Levrau, "Evaluating boards of directors: what constitutes a good corporate board?", *Corporate governance: an international review* 2004, 46; H. De Wulf, *Taak en loyauteitsplicht van het bestuur in de naamloze vennootschap*, Intersentia, Antwerp-Oxford, 2001, 17–88.

5 This is a function of the board that is stressed in the so-called "resource dependence" literature, see for an introduction about this and other theoretical frameworks to analyse boards H. De Wulf, *Taak en loyauteitsplicht van het bestuur in de naamloze vennootschap*, Intersentia, Antwerp-Oxford, 2001, 17 ff. and H. Hung, "A typology of the theories of the roles of governing boards", *Corporate governance: an international review* 1998, 101–111, both with further references to the fundamental literature. E.g., if pollution by corporations was not an issue in the 1950s but is so today, one function of the board is to make sure that the company devotes enough attention to the issue of environmental impact of the company's activities.

- Management must report to the board at regular intervals on all important developments within the company; on these occasions the board may and must where appropriate ask critical questions of management and may try to steer management policy through giving advice to managers – the so-called "sounding board" function of the board.
- In case of (serious) differences of opinion within top management, the board should mediate to resolve these issues and should where necessary replace managers or give them another function.

We may conclude that if we want to find out whether female board quotas and other measures to increase female boardroom participation contribute to good governance, we must ask ourselves whether these policy measures have a positive impact on firm value or/and have a positive impact on the way the board performs at least one of its aforementioned tasks.

The short answer is that, contrary to what all kinds of interest groups allege in one sense or the other – pro or anti quotas – we do not really know.

III. IMPACT OF QUOTAS ON FIRM PERFORMANCE: FINANCIAL PERFORMANCE AND BOARD PERFORMANCE

A. METHODOLOGICAL PROBLEMS, AND WHY IT WOULD BE COUNTERINTUITIVE TO FIND A LINK BETWEEN DIRECTOR GENDER AND PERFORMANCE

There is only a limited number of empirical studies on the impact of female participation rates[6] at board level on firm performance. A large number of the studies that are available, especially of the studies most cited in the media, have not been published in top scientific journals, indeed, many studies have not been published in scientific journals at all, but only in the form of reports issued by certain organisations, including consultancy firms like McKinsey but also organisations like Catalyst that at least partially act like lobbying groups.

As a result, the methodology employed has sometimes not been clearly described and was not subjected to scientific peer review. Sometimes only the conclusions of the research are published and no information on methodology is published.

---

6 In this text, by "female participation rates", we mean the percentage of board members (or in certain contexts board committee members) in a specific board that is female. The expression does not refer to actual participation in board meetings or board discussion, in other words has nothing to do with actual boardroom involvement of women.

In some articles or reports, the results themselves are presented in a very vague or general way, making it difficult to assess their meaning and value.

Of course, as is the case with a very large part of empirical research, research concerning board diversity has to deal with the problem of distinguishing correlation from causation. This is self-evident, but needs repeating, because in our area, some of the more unnuanced reports do not heed much attention to the issue: if, for instance, firms with a higher percentage of women on board than a control group perform better as far as total firm value or operating efficiency is concerned, this a very interesting finding, but not as such proof that increasing the percentage of women on boards leads to better economic results in firms.

As always, the results of statistical research need to be subjected to a sanity check: one must always ask what could potentially explain certain correlations that have been established. If no logical explanation is forthcoming, extra care needs to be taken with the results.

A good example of assertions allegedly based on empirical research that, on closer inspection, undermine the credibility of a whole project, is the finding reported in the British Davies Report (2011)[7] that female directors are more holistic in their approach (whatever that may mean) and pay more attention to detail than male directors.[8] (Fairly) interesting, until one reads, hidden in a footnote, that this result was obtained based on a poll of 1071 Britons (and not on research of actual director behaviour nor on a poll of directors or managers). In other words, this passage in the Davies Report simply reflects existing prejudices about female qualities among the British population.

Fortunately, research on our topic is proliferating, so more reliable insights into the question of the effect of female quotas on corporate governance should become possible.

It seems a reasonable assumption to start from that it would be surprising to find a (causal) link between the composition of the board of directors and firm value.[9] As explained, boards, at least in larger corporations, do not have a management but merely a monitoring function[10] and it seems reasonable that in addition to firm-external factors, management decisions are the main drivers behind

7 *Women on Boards,* 2011, 36 p., available at https://www.gov.uk/government/uploads/system/uploads/attachment_data/file/31480/11-745-women-on-boards.pdf (hereinafter referred to as "Davies Report").

8 Davies Report (previous footnote), p. 7, text accompanying footnote 6.

9 Among many making the point, see e.g. S. Nielsen and M. Huse, "The contribution of women on boards of directors: going beyond the surface", 18 *Corporate Governance: an international review,* 2010, at 137.

10 See the overview in Adams et al. (2010).

fluctuations in firm value. In any case, a direct impact of better or worse monitoring by the board outside crisis situations such as hostile takeover bids or looming insolvency would be a surprising finding, since it is highly doubtful that the quality of monitoring has a direct impact on such variables as operating efficiency, profits or turnover. This does not of course mean that the establishment of a connection between monitoring quality and firm value should be excluded *a priori*, only that *a priori* it is a less likely hypothesis.

On the other hand, the composition of the board could arguably be considered by some investors as a proxy, an indirect indicator, of features of the board which these investors cannot observe directly but to which they attach considerable importance, e.g. a certain kind of attitude towards risk; a stress on consensual rather than quicker but dictatorial decision-making processes. In other words, and as has been argued in other contexts, board composition may well have a signalling function towards investors.[11] Many people, including, one may assume, investors, seem to harbour the working hypothesis that women have, on balance, a different attitude than men towards risk, the time horizon to be employed in decisions making and the decision making processes that are to be valued or rejected.[12] If enough investors do indeed *believe* that increases in the female participation rate lead to a better functioning of the board, this may of course result in higher (stock market) valuations for firms with more women on their board, even in those cases where higher female board membership does not in fact contribute to better board processes.

A comparison with research on the impact of board independence as measured by the percentage of independent directors on firm value may be helpful.[13] There has been quite a bit of research on this topic and the different but related topic of the impact of non-executive directors. Most of the research fails to find a connection between the percentage of independent board members and firm value or other financial indicators of firm success. A much-cited study by Bhagat and Black even finds a negative correlation between the number of independent directors and firm value.[14] There is, however, more research that lends support to

11 See L. Broome and K. Krawiec, "Signaling through board diversity: is anyone listening?", *University of Cincinnati Law Review* 2008, 431.

12 Presentation by Prof. Lutgart vanden Berghe, Executive Director of Guberna, during a hearing in the Belgian Parliament, 18 November 2011, slide 2 (ppt presentation on file with the author).

13 In addition to this research, research on the relationship between other aspects of board composition and firm performance has tended to yield inconclusive results; for a brief overview and discussion with further references, see R. Adams, B. Hermalin and M. Weisbach, "The role of boards of directors in corporate governance: a conceptual framework and survey", 48(1) *Journal of Economic Literature*, 2010, 58–107.

14 See the econometric studies of S. Bhagat and B. Black, "The non-correlation between board independence and long-term performance", 27 *Journal of Corporate Law*, 2002, 231; see also

the hypothesis that a higher level of independence at board level gives rise to a higher level of certain governance interventions by the board that are usually deemed desirable, such as more CEO turnover when the firms performs relatively badly as far as stock price or other financial indicators are concerned; slower growth of top management compensation, etc.

While this body of research on the impact of independent directors does of course not at all prove that more female (non-executive) directors would not have an impact on firm value either, it is at least compatible with the hypothesis that, since directors as such do not manage the company, they have little impact on its value, whatever their features (independent or not, female or not, young or old, ...), unless these features are perceived to presumably lead to another pattern of action (sacking the CEO or not e.g.) in crisis situations. Interestingly and compatible with this hypothesis, Shrader et al.[15] found that the proportion of female *managers* was positively correlated with performance measures such as ROE, ROA and ROIc, but such positive relationship was lacking at the level of female *directors*. Similarly, more recent research in Canada by Francoeur and others did find a positive correlation between the prevalence of female top managers and some financial metrics, but no relationship between female directors and financial performance.[16]

In the US, some research has been devoted to the impact of racial diversity within boards on firm value and performance. In general, no correlation with firm performance could be found. A study by Dobbin and Jung (2011) found that the disclosure by listed firms of an explicit racial diversity policy at board level, had a negative impact on stock price. The authors suggested this could be explained by the finding, based on interviews with institutional investors, that these feared that "too much" attention to policies such as diversity would distract the firm from focusing exclusively on creating shareholder value.[17] Also, Dobbin and Jung argue that greater diversity within the board leads to greater difference of opinion among directors which would negatively affect decisiveness.[18]

S. Bhagat and B. Black "The uncertain relationship between board composition and firm performance", 54 *The Business Lawyer* 1999, 921.

15 C.B. Shrader, V.B. Blackburn and P. Iles, "Women in management and firm financial performance: an exploratory study", 9(3) *Journal of Managerial Issues* 1997, 355–376.

16 C. Francoeur, R. Labelle and B. Sinclair-Desgagné, "Gender diversity in corporate governance and top management", 81 *Journal of Business Ethics* 2008, 83–95.

17 F. Dobbin and J. Jung, "Corporate board gender diversity and stock performance: the competence gap or institutional investor bias?", 89 *North Carolina Law Review*, 2011, (809), 833.

18 F. Dobbin and J. Jung, "Corporate board gender diversity and stock performance: the competence gap or institutional investor bias?", 89 *North Carolina Law Review*, 2011, 809.

B. OVERVIEW OF SOME OF THE RESEARCH ON BOARD GENDER COMPOSITION AND FIRM PERFORMANCE

Let's now look in some more detail at some of the empirical research on the impact of increased presence of women on firm value.

As is apparent from Table 1 below, taken from a recent working paper by Joecks, Pull and Vetter,[19] the results are mixed[20]: of the 18 studies cited, 7 find a positive link between female boardroom participation and some kind of performance measure, the other studies find no link or even a negative link. These divergent results may be the outcome of, among other potential factors, different populations, different countries, different industries, different times and time frames at which the research was performed, but they make it hard, in any case, to draw firm conclusions. As indicated, several studies find simply no relationship, neither negative nor positive between board gender composition and financial metrics.[21] Another factor which may explain differences in results is the use of different performance measures: some studies focus on Tobin's Q[22], others on ROI (return on investment), ROE (return on equity), ROIC (return on invested capital), ROS (return on sales) or ROA (return on assets) or some combination of these.[23]

One problem that the vast majority of serious academic empirical studies of all kinds of aspects of the functioning of boards has to deal with, is that board

---

19 J. Joecks, K. Pull and K. Vetter "Gender diversity in the boardroom and firm performance: what exactly constitutes critical mass?" Working paper, department of Economics, Tübingen University, 22 February 2012, available at SSRN: http://ssrn.com/abstract=2009234.

20 Another review of much of the research on the topic can be found in what explicitly is a review article, namely S. Terjesen, R. Sealy and V. Singh, "Women directors on corporate boards: a review and research agenda", *Corporate Governance: an international review* 2009, 320–337.

21 E.g. T. Miller and T.M. del Carmen, "Demographic Diversity in the Boardroom: Mediators of the Board Diversity-Firm Performance Relationship", 46 *Journal of Management Studies* 2009, 777 (no impact on ROI or return on sales); for Denmark: C. Rose, "Does Female Board Representation Influence Firm Performance? The Danish Evidence", 15 *Corporate governance: an international review* 2007, 404 (Tobin's Q); N. Smith, V. Smith and M. Verner, "Do Women in Top Management Affect Firm Performance? A Panel Study of 2500 Danish Firms", 55 *International Journal of Productivity and performance management* 2006, 569 (various performance measures).

22 The ratio between the market value of a company and the replacement value of its assets. This is seen as an indicator of the efficiency of management in deploying the assets of a company.

23 (Legal) people unfamiliar with these concepts can be referred to standard textbooks on corporate finance/financial economics or to Wikipedia, Investopedia and other internet sources that give some basic explanation of these concepts. It should be noted that in spite of their apparent clarity and simplicity, even sophisticated researchers sometimes use slightly different definitions of a concepts like ROE, making comparisons of the results of their research even more difficult.

structure is endogenous.[24] That is, there is a danger of reverse causality, of a loop of causality. For instance, a correlation between increases in the number of female directors and firm performance may not necessarily mean that women contribute to better performance. Not only may there be another, unexplored explanatory variable[25], it may well be that better-performing firms attract more women. Of course all serious empirical research controls for factors like firm size and industry, but endogeneity is far harder to get rid of, even with the most sophisticated approaches.[26]

Another difficulty for research on the influence of female boardroom participation on firm performance is that, if a board has any influence at all on firm performance, it is most likely to result from the impact the board has on strategy. The impact of strategic decisions is, however, only felt over the longer run, and it is notoriously difficult to establish correlations let alone causal links between variables and firm performance over the longer run, if only because the longer the time frame studied, the greater the likelihood that confounds confuse the statistical picture.[27]

Finally, it should be noted that there is hardly any empirical research on the effect specifically of gender quotas on firm performance. What little research there is on gender and firm performance almost always looks at the influence of women in general at board level, without distinguishing between situations where these women were appointed as a result of quotas or not. This means that even when a positive correlation is found between more women on board and better firm performance in a system without quotas, these results are not certain to hold once quotas are introduced: it could be that those women selected without he pressure of quotas are primarily selected because of their competence – which may well exceed that of the average male director, who is perhaps more often than his female counterparts selected for other reasons, such as belonging

24 Classic studies of the issue are B. Hermalin and M. Weisbach, "Endogenously Chosen Boards of Directors and Their Monitoring of the CEO", 88(1) *American Economic Review*, 1998, 96–118 and B. Hermalin and M. Weisbach, "Boards of Directors as an Endogenously Determined Institution: A Survey of the Economic Literature", 9 (1) *Federal Reserve Bank of New York Economic Policy Review*, 2003, 7–26.

25 In our context, A. Hillmann, C. Shropshire and A. Cannella, "Organizational predictors of women on corporate boards", 50 *Academy of Management Journal*, 2007, 941 argue that firm size, industry type, firm diversification strategy and links with other boards all have a significant explanatory value for board gender diversity. If this is true – and one study is of course far from sufficient to prove such matters – then any study about board diversity that does not control for all of these factors risks finding spurious correlations.

26 See also, in our context, D. Rhode and A. Packel, "Diversity on corporate boards: how much difference does difference make?, Rock Center for Corporate Governance working paper series-no 89, September2010, available at ssrn.com/abstract=1685615, at 6.

27 Cf. M. Lückerath-Rovers, "Women on board and firm performance", April 2010, 5–6.

to the right male network – whereas women that are added to boards in an environment where mandatory quotas exist, may well have characteristics that make them less suitable for board membership, so that they have no positive effect on board or firm performance.[28] In fact, in policy debates and in interviews with both male and female directors, this kind of argument often surfaces: quotas, it is argued by some, are undesirable because a stigma will attach to those women – "tokens"[29] – who are perceived to have been nominated only because the law requires it of the company, and some female directors, it is argued, will indeed simply be appointed because of the law without having the necessary qualities.[30]

When reading empirical research on our topic, one should also pay due attention to the fact that some research focuses exclusively on female *boardroom* participation rates – which are at the heart of our topic – whereas other contributions deal only with the number of women at the top *executive* level below the board, and still other research pertains to both boardroom and top management participation at the same time (making it next to impossible to draw any conclusions specifically about the potential effects of boardroom quotas which by definition do not directly affect the number of women in top management positions).

---

28 To be perfectly clear: I'm not saying this hypothesis is true. I'm only saying that it is a hypothesis which should also be empirically tested and that for reasons such as those expressed in this hypothesis, it would be methodologically wrong to simply extrapolate results obtained in a non-quota system to systems where the law contains mandatory quotas.

29 "Excuustruus" is the popular Dutch expression.

30 In this sense, among many examples, Michèle Sioen, Interview in Belgian daily *De Tijd*, 5 september 2012, p. 5. Mrs Sioen holds multiple directorships and was recently chosen as president of the "VBO/FEB", the Belgian Federation of Enterprises, the most important organisation representing the interests of large Belgian firms/employers. In the interview Mrs. Sioen argues, among other things, that by 2020 there will not yet be enough women available with both the right qualifications and enough experience to fill 40% of board seats at listed companies, as the EU proposes; she also argues that in her experience the differences in boardroom behaviour between male and female directors are minimal and far less important than differences between individuals regardless of their gender. In an interview published on the same page of *De Tijd*, Mr. Vandermeiren, the male CEO of Elia (a large electricity distributor) disputes the last point: in his view women have other approaches to risk, think more long term, are more careful about reputation and are better at taking care of external communication. He believes there are more than enough women with the right qualifications and is in favour of quotas because he believes directors are still too often selected among the (outdated but still important) "old boys networks" with their own sense of male humour and communicating. A search of press databases such as Mediargus or Factiva would yield dozens of viewpoints by directors similar to those held by Mrs. Sioen and Mr. Vandermeiren.

Table 1. Overview of the literature (chronological)[31]

Author(s), Year	Gender diversity measure (explanatory variable)	Performance measure (dependent variable)	Data base (n, country, years)	Main result
Mahadeo et al. (2012)	women's ratio	ROA	371 directors of 39 companies listed on the Stock Exchange of Mauritius (2007)	positive link
Ahern and Dittmar (2012)	women's ratio	Tobin's Q	248 Norwegian public-limited firms (2001–2009)	negative link
Lindstaedt et al. (2011)	women's ratio	ROA, ROE, price to book value	160 German companies of the DAX family (2002–2010)	positive link for firms with a high ratio of female employees and for B2C business
He and Huang (2011)	Blau Index	ROA	530 US manufacturing firms (2001–2007)	negative link
Torchia et al. (2011)	no. of women; four groups: (1) no, (2) one, (3) two, (4) three + women	innovation (self-reported)	317 Norwegian companies (2005/2006)	three + women are positively related to innovation
Böhren and Ström (2010)	women's ratio	Tobin's Q, ROA, ROS	203 firms in Norway listed on the Oslo Stock exchange (1989–2002)	negative link
Haslam et al. (2010)	dummy (women on the board: yes / no); women's ratio	ROE, ROA Tobin's Q	126 British companies included in the FTSE 100 index (2001–2005)	no link (ROA and ROE); negative link with at least one woman on board (Tobin's Q)
Lückerath-Rovers, (2010)	women's ratio	ROE, ROS, ROIC	99 Dutch companies (2005–2007)	positive link (ROE)
Adams and Ferreira (2009)	dummy (women on the board: yes/ no); women's ratio	ROA, Tobin's Q	1939 US firms based on IIRC (1996–2003)	negative link

31 Reproduced with permission from J. Joecks, K. Pull and K. Vetter "Gender Diversity in the Boardroom and Firm Performance: What Exactly Constitutes a Critical Mass?" 118 *Journal of Business Ethics 2013*, 61-72, available at SSRN: http://ssrn.com/abstract=2009234.

Author(s), Year	Gender diversity measure (explanatory variable)	Performance measure (dependent variable)	Data base (n, country, years)	Main result
Miller and del Carmen Triana (2009)	Blau Index	ROI, ROS	326 US Fortune 500 firms (2003)	no link
Campbell and Mínguez-Vera, (2008)	dummy (women on the board: yes/ no), women's ratio, Blau and Shannon Index	Tobin's Q	68 Spanish companies (1995–2000)	dummy not significant; otherwise: positive link
Rose (2007)	women's ratio	Tobin's Q	more than 100 Danish companies listed on the Copenhagen Stock Exchange (1998–2001)	no link
Randöy et al. (2006)	women's ratio	ROA, stock market value	154 Danish, 144 Norwegian, 161 Swedish firms (2005)	no link
Smith et al. (2006)	women's ratio	gross profit, net sales, contribution to margin sales, operating income/net assets, net income after tax/net assets	2,500 Danish firms (1993–2001)	positive link depending on education of women and performance measure
Carter et al. (2003)	dummy (women on the board: yes / no), women's ratio	ROA, Tobin's Q	638 US Fortune 1000 firms (1997)	positive link (Tobin's Q)
Erhardt et al. (2003)	minorities' and women's ratio	ROA, ROI	112 US Fortune 1000 firms (1998)	positive link (demographic diversity included)
Shrader et al. (1997)	women's ratio	ROS, ROA, ROI, ROE	200 US firms (from Wall Street Journal) (1992)	negative link
Siciliano (1996)	women's ratio	social performance, total revenue to total expenses, donations	240 YMCA organizations (1989)	no link with total revenue to total expenses, positive link with social performance, negative link with donations

Source: Joecks, Pull, Vetter (2012).

Before having a closer look at some of this serious academic research, it may be worth to pay some attention to what are probably[32] the two most cited studies in discussions of the topic in the European press and among politicians, namely the McKinsey studies and the research by Catalyst.[33]

In studies from 2007 and 2010, McKinsey found stronger financial performance at European companies with at least three women in top executive positions.[34] The positive results were largest concerning EBIT (Earnings before tax and interest) and growth in stock price. The authors argue this is probably a proxy for better overall organisation at the firms involved, resulting in an EBITDA[35] and market capitalisation that are both twice as high than with less well organised firms. It should be stressed that this research did not relate to board composition. Even though the studies are often cited in discussions of the efficiency of female quotas, no conclusions can be drawn from them in this respect. The studies do lend support for the important but different thesis that an increase in the number of female *top executives* to at least three has a positive impact on financial performance. Note that, as argued before, it is a priori far more likely that executives have influence on firm performance than non-executives. Most if not all legislation or recommendations about female board quotas pertains, like e.g. the Belgian legislation, to board membership in general, without distinguishing between female executive and non-executive directors. When companies have to increase the number of female directors in a relatively short period, it is far more likely that they do so by appointing extra non-executives than by nominating extra executives, for which they would have to create a useful top management function. In other words, when increased female presence at board level is the result not of "organic" growth of the number of female top executives who then

32 I have done no citation research on this through Google or press databases like Factiva. It is simply my anecdotal impression based on my own reading. Also very often cited is the British Davies report, but that is not a study as such but a policy document.

33 For criticism of the methodology and the lack of clarity about it in both the Catalyst and McKinsey studies, see e.g. M. Lückerath-Rovers, "Women on board and firm performance", 17 (2) *Journal of management and Governance* 2013, 491–509; citations in our (this) text are however to the pages of the working paper version, April 2010, available at SSRN: http://ssrn.com/abstract=1586832, p. 10–12 for the criticism of Catalyst and McKinsey, with further references to other critical reviews.

34 See www.mckinsey.com/client_service/organization/latest_thinking/women_matter for all the McKinsey reports on the issue. The 2007 report is McKinsey&Company, *Women matter. Gender diversity, a corporate performance driver*, 2007, 24 p. The 2010 report is McKinsey&Company, *Women matter 2010. Women at the top of corporations: making it happen*. 2010, 22 p. There is a 2012 follow-up report (*Women matter. Making the breakthrough*) which focuses on strategies firms may employ to successfully get more women into top management positions, based on the research McKinsey did at 235 European companies. In 2012, McKinsey also issued a report specifically on the Belgian situation, called *Women matter. Making the breakthrough in Belgium* (all available on the website mentioned at the beginning of this footnote).

35 Earnings before interest, tax, depreciation and amortisation.

go on to become executive or non-executive directors, it is unlikely that the number of female executive directors will increase in a meaningful way even when the total number of female directors does increase significantly.

In an influential 2007 study[36], Catalyst found that companies with a "higher" number of women on their boards generated sales profits 42% higher than companies with less female directors, a 66% higher return on investment (ROI) and a 53% higher return on equity (ROE). The results did not hold, however, for the financial sector. A "higher" number of women directors was defined in this study as boards with either at least three female members, or where 30% of the board consisted of women.

In a 2011 follow-up study[37] (which looked at the period 2004–2008), Catalyst found that:

- *"Companies with the most women board directors (WBD) outperform those with the least on ROS by 16 percent.*
- *Companies with the most WBD outperform those with the least on ROIC by 26 percent.*
- *Companies with sustained high representation of WBD, defined as those with three or more WBD in at least four of five years, significantly outperformed those with sustained low representation by 84 percent on ROS, by 60 percent on ROIC, and by 46 percent on ROE."*

One of the glaring weaknesses of the Catalyst studies is that they simply compare two or three groups of companies (depending on the number of women on their boards), without, as far as we can see from the published results, controlling for other possible influences on firm performance like industry or firm size.

Among economists, event studies that study the stock price reaction to a certain event over a short period of time (one day, three days) are common. These certainly yield interesting hard data, but my guess is that at least most non-economists, would tend to draw fewer conclusions, at least at the level of governance research, from these event studies than is common among economists. More specifically, even though certain events lead to short term stock price spikes or drops, this seems to say very little about the value or desirability of the event: it

---

36 Catalyst, *The Bottom line: corporate performance and women's representation on boards*, 2007, available at www.catalyst.org/knowledge/bottom-line-corporate-performance-and-womens-representation-boards The published version of the study consist of only two pages. The 2007 study was preceded by a more extensively published 2004 study on the impact of gender diversity in general, called *The Bottom line: connecting corporate performance and gender diversity*, also available at www.catalyst.org/knowledge.

37 Available at www.catalyst.org/knowledge/bottom-line-corporate-performance-and-womens-representation-boards-20042008.

only says something about market sentiment.[38] In any event, it is worth noting that Ellis and Keys found significant positive abnormal returns on the date on which measures promoting workforce diversity, including the appointment of an additional female director were announced.[39] This indicates that financial markets tend to view female appointments as something positive, which was also the conclusion of a study which reported positive stock market reactions to the appointment of female directors in Spanish listed firms[40] and one that registered a positive 2.3% increase in share value over the two days after the appointment of a female director (between 1988 and 2001) in Singaporean firms[41] – although a confound may be that those women that are suggested for appointment at all are simply so superior in quality as directors that the results may not be interpreted as a positive reaction to the nomination of female directors, but simply as a positive reaction to the striking quality of the proposed candidates. Lee and James, on the other hand, found a negative stock market reaction in their sample to the appointment of a new CEO, and this negative reaction was significantly larger when the new CEO was a woman.[42] The authors offer as an explanation that markets see the appointment of a new CEO as an event that creates uncertainty, and this uncertainty would then apparently be deemed larger when the new CEO is female. What all these event studies had in common was that they simply measured the stock market reaction to the appointment of female directors or executive. It may be more informative, in order to help exclude confounds, to compare the stock market reaction to the appointment of female with the reaction to the appointment of male directors in the same company. That is exactly what Adams, Gray and Nowland did in a 2011 working paper on Australian companies, where they found that "*the average reaction for female appointees is roughly 2 percent higher than for male appointees even after controlling for other appointee characteristics, such as independence, expertise and qualifications. This suggests that the gender of directors matters per se*".[43]

---

38 For remarks about some of the methodological problems raised by events studies concerning board gender composition, see Adams, Gray, Nowland, *infra* note 43 at 5.

39 K.M. Ellis and P.Y. Keys, "Stock Returns and the Promotion of Workforce Diversity", Working paper, University of Delaware, 2003. We have not personally seen and read this working paper and cannot find a reference to a later publication; but is often cited, for example by Adams and Ferreira, *infra* note 49 or by Terjesen et al. *infra* note 41.

40 K. Campell and A. Minguez Vera "Female board appointments: short-and long-term effects", 14(1) *Journal of Management & Governance*, 2010, 37.

41 Study by Ding and Charoenwong cited by S. Terjesen, R. Sealy and V. Singh, "Women directors on corporate boards: a review and research agenda", *Corporate Governance: an international review* 2009.

42 P.M. Lee and E.H. James, "She'-E-Os: Gender Effects and Investor Reactions to the Announcements of Top Executive Appointments", 28 (3) *Strategic Management Journal* 2007, 227–241.

43 R. Adams, S. Gray, J. Nowland, "Does Gender Matter in the Boardroom? Evidence from the Market Reaction to Mandatory New Director Announcements", 2 November 2011, available at SSRN: http://ssrn.com/abstract=1953152.

Some researchers seem to suggest that, rather than having a proven positive impact on firm performance, women tend to serve on the boards of better-performing firms[44]; this could perhaps be explained by financially successful firms being in a better position to afford the "luxury" of focusing on diversity, or by female candidates for directorships being able to exploit the relative scarcity of female candidates to only accept nominations at firms that already perform well.[45] The latter theory is at odds, however, with research which purports to show that, at management level, female managers tend to hold more precarious[46] management positions than their male counterparts, sometimes described as the "glass cliff" phenomenon.[47] If the latter theory is correct, it could be used to argue that it is more difficult, on average, for women top managers or directors to contribute positively to firm performance, since they start, in many cases, from a more difficult position; hence, one could argue, even a weak finding of positive female influence on performance could be an indication of a much greater positive contribution, since women start from a lower baseline. Opponents of this view could argue, conversely, that it should be easier to generate a positive influence on performance when the firm starts with low performance indicators. To help settle this question, studies should be undertaken which do not study the relationship between female boardroom participation and firm performance simply by comparing firms with more with forms with fewer female directors, but by looking at the impact changes in the number of female directors within a certain firm have on firm performance. But we should remain aware that the glass cliff theory remains far from proven, as attested by research by Adams, Gupta and Leeth[48] which found that in the US, women tend to be appointed as CEO when firm performance is relatively good. Perhaps this can be seen as confirming that US firms in the period 1992–2004 felt they could only take the relatively unusual step of appointing a female CEO when times were good.

---

44 It should be mentioned that some studies try to tackle the issue of reverse causation, e.g. Campbell and Minguez Vera test whether performance is a predictor of diversity, with a negative result, whereas they had found a positive effect of diversity on Tobin's Q: K. Campell and A. Minguez Vera "Female board appointments: short-and long-term effects", 14(1) *Journal of Management & Governance*, 2010, 37.

45 K.A. Farrel and P.L. Hersch, "Additions to corporate boards: the effect of gender", 11 *Journal of Corporate Governance*, 2005, 85–106.

46 In the sense of: at firms that are doing less well financially, sometimes sliding towards insolvency.

47 M.K. Ryan and S.A. Haslam, "The glass cliff: evidence that women are over-represented in precarious leadership positions", 16 *British Journal of Management* 2005, 81–90; M.K. Ryan and S.A. Haslam, "Glass cliffs: exploring the dynamics surrounding the appointment of women to precarious leadership positions", 32(2) *Academy of management review* 2007, 549–572.

48 S.M. Adams, A. Gupta and J. Leeth, "Are female executives overrepresented in precarious leadership positions?", 16(2) *British Journal of management* 2008, 81–90.

In what is one of the most rigorous empirical studies concerning the influence of women on boards, financial economists Adams and Ferreira[49] found that, "*in a sample of US firms, (...) female directors have better attendance records than male directors, male directors have fewer attendance problems the more gender-diverse the board is, and women are more likely to join monitoring committees. These results suggest (according to Adams and Ferreira) that gender-diverse boards allocate more effort to monitoring.*"

When Adams and Ferreira looked at specific monitoring influence in some of the areas that have traditionally been the object of empirical corporate governance research, they found, among other things, that that chief executive officer turnover – i.e. CEOs leaving their post, either voluntarily or after being dismissed – was more sensitive to stock performance in firms with more gender-diverse boards. In other words, when there are relatively more female members, the CEO is probably sacked more quickly when the stock price underperforms. Adams and Ferreira also found that directors receive more equity-based compensation in firms with more gender-diverse boards. This form of compensation is often intended to be performance-related and therefore one can argue that, if this correlation is also causal, women directors seem to insist more on performance-related pay, which at first sight is a sound corporate governance practice.[50]

To the dismay of quite a few non-academic commentators, however, the overall conclusion of Adams and Ferreira on female board influence and on mandating quotas is negative: "*the average effect of gender diversity on firm performance is negative. This negative effect is driven by companies with fewer takeover defences. Our results suggest that mandating gender quotas for directors can reduce firm value for well-governed firms.*" In other words, while increased female presence on boards may as a rule have a positive effect on the board taking seriously its monitoring duty, increasing the number of female directors in firms that are already well governed may have a negative impact on overall firm performance (as measured by financial indicators). As is the case with the vast majority of empirical research based on regression analysis in the field of corporate governance, the as such excellent study by Adams and Ferreira nevertheless contains some questionable assumptions. In order to distinguish between well-governed and less well governed firms, for instance, they use the amount of takeover defences as an indicator. They assume that if a firm has installed fewer anti-takeover defences this is probably because it thinks it need not fear unwarranted takeovers since it is

---

49 R. Adams and D. Ferreira, "Women in the boardroom and their impact on governance and performance", 94 *Journal of Financial Economics* 2009, 291–309.

50 Of course, the reader will know that performance-related pay is extremely controversial these days, especially because since the financial crisis of 2007, it is often argued that performance related pay formed an incentive for traders and some top executives at financial institutions to take unwarranted risks. We cannot enter this debate here.

already well run. There may be some truth to this, but taking it as a "scientific" criterion to distinguish well-governed and less well-governed firms is of course very debatable, even though many Anglo-American economists seem to routinely accept the validity of this and similar criteria.

Adams and Ferreira's finding that women cause the board to devote more attention to its monitoring tasks is supported by several other less academically rigorous studies. Canadian research cited by the Conference Board finds that an increase of the number of women on a board leads to increased attention to adherence to codes of conduct and the rules on conflicts of interests; to the development of more precise criteria to measure strategy implementation; and to a greater stress on non-financial performance indicators.[51]

The headhunting consultancy Heidrick & Struggles reported that women directors are more assertive in enforcing self-evaluation by the board and taking seriously its monitoring task.[52] In the same vein, both Scandinavian and Israeli[53] academic research found that women directors take preparing themselves for board meetings so that they appear on the scene with enough information, more seriously than do their male counterparts.

In a 2011 working paper, Deszo and Ross[54] report results that indicate that leadership style attributes that are apparently more typical of women, contribute positively to firm performance – as measured primarily through Tobin's Q – when the women are appointed at top management level below the level of CEO. But the same authors find a negative impact of female CEOs, which they tentatively ascribe to the idea that CEOs need different leadership capacities than other top managers. This latter result is compatible with the finding by Lee and James[55] that the stock market reacts negatively (in a sample of US firms) to the appointment of a female CEO.

---

51 Conference Board of Canada, report by V. Anastopoulos, D. Brown and D.L. Brown "Women on boards: not just the right thing... but the 'bright' thing", 2002, 17 p. available at www.conferenceboard.ca/e-library/abstract.aspx?did=374 or at www.europeanpwn.net/files/women_on_boards_canada.pdf (last consulted at October 21 2013).

52 As reported in the Davies report, p. 10, without any reference in a footnote to publication or even title of this study, which we could not find in the public domain.

53 D. Izraeli "Women directors in Israel" in R. Burke and M. Mattis (eds.), *Women on Corporate Boards of Directors: International Challenges and Opportunities*, Kluwer Academic Publishers, Dordrecht, The Netherlands, 2000, 75–96. M. Huse and A.G. Solberg, "Gender-related boardroom dynamics: How Scandinavian women make and can make contributions on corporate boards", 21(2) *Women in Management Review*, 2006, 113–30.

54 C.L. Dezso and D.G. Ross, "Does Female Representation in Top Management Improve Firm Performance? A Panel Data Investigation", 9 March 2011, Robert H. Smith School Research Paper No. RHS 06-104. Available at SSRN: http://ssrn.com/abstract=1088182.

55 P.M. Lee and E.H. James, "She'-E-Os: Gender Effects and Investor Reactions to the Announcements of Top Executive Appointments", 28 (3) *Strategic Management Journal* 2007, 227-241.

C. DOES GREATER GENDER DIVERSITY AT BOARD LEVEL LEAD TO BETTER BOARD PROCESSES?

As already illustrated by the research of Adams and Ferreira, even if female directors do not contribute to better financial performance, they may, potentially, still have a positive impact on the way the board performs its functions by, for example, making sure that the board takes its monitoring duty at heart or meetings are better prepared.

The UK Higgs review confirmed opinions often voiced in the press as well as in the pub, that boards consisting of both men and women may bring a broader perspective to issues raised at board level than boards with only one gender or dominated by one gender group.[56] And after a workshop at the Davos World Economic Forum asked the question whether it would have made any difference if Lehman Brothers had been Lehman Sisters[57], it became conventional wisdom in some circles that in a financial sector dominated by women, the financial crisis probably would not have happened or that, at least, fewer risks would have been taken at banks.

However, as e.g. Huse and Solberg have explained[58], it remains extremely difficult to piece together from stories people tell and from knowledge about gender differences in various fields of enquiry reliable facts about the impact female board members may have on boardroom behaviour and board processes. One way of finding out whether women and men make different contributions in boards consists of interviewing board members, but a huge difficulty here is avoiding both socially desirable answers or simply answers that reflect the prejudices of the persons being interviewed.

There seems to be at least substantial evidence that is not interview-based that women, on average, deal with risks in a different way than men and are generally

56 Higgs Review, *Review of the role and effectiveness of non-executive directors*, 2003, available at: http://webarchive.nationalarchives.gov.uk/+/www.dti.gov.uk/bbf/corp-governance/higgs-tyson/page23342.html.

57 See among many reports about this workshop e.g. K. Bennhold, "Where would we be if women ran Wall street?", *NY Times* February 1 2009. See echoes by Harriet Harman, at the time deputy leader of the British Labour Party, and by the IMF's Christine Lagarde at www.independent.co.uk/news/uk/home-news/harriet-harman-if-only-it-had-been-lehman-sisters-1766932.html (4 August 2009) and Dealbook (*NY Times*), 11 May 2010 "Lagarde: what if it had been Lehman sisters", http://dealbook.nytimes.com/2010/05/11/lagarde-what-if-it-had-been-lehman-sisters/?_r=0.

58 M. Huse and A.G. Solberg, "Gender-related boardroom dynamics: how Scandinavian women make and can make contributions on corporate boards", 21(2) *Women in Management Review*, 2006, 113–30. See also M. Huse, "Women directors and the 'black box' of board behaviour", in Vinnicombe, Singh, Burke, Bilimoria and Huse, *Women on Corporate Boards of Directors: International research and Practice*, Edward Elgar, Cheltenham, 2008.

more risk-averse when it comes to financial risk.[59] According to a survey-based[60] study by Adams and Funk, female and male directors (in Sweden) differ systematically in their core values and risk attitudes, but in ways that differ from gender differences in the general population; they find that women directors are *more* prone to take risks than men, not less...[61] So even here, it seems, the more research is done, the more uncertainty is created.

It is often alleged that "groupthink" as a consequence of groups of decision-makers that are too homogenous, has a negative impact on the quality of the decisions: boards that are too uniform would not recognize the uniformity of their own thinking.[62] More women on boards would then bring more diverse perspectives. Zelechowski and Bilimoria argue that such negative group dynamics can be prevented by adding at least three female directors to a board.[63] Some argue that difference of opinion is more readily accepted in more diverse groups, which, if true, would be conducive to open, productive debates about the heart of the matter.[64] Also, if a company adopts a diverse board, this may signal to its employees and other stakeholders that it attaches importance to equal opportunity and stakeholder interests[65] – although without hard proof of the contrary, I personally believe very few stakeholders know anything about gender composition of the board, which would mean that the potential signaling effect is lost.

Such positive findings are, almost inevitably, countered by research that purports to show that more diversity leads to more boardroom tension and poorer intra-director communication.[66] Still other research finds that there are remarkably few differences, at least in Canada, between male and female directors, in that female directors would value the creation of shareholder value as much as their male counterparts.[67]

---

59 E.g. N.A. Jianakoplos and A. Bernasek, "Are women more risk averse? Attitudes toward financial risk", 36 *Economic Inquiry*, 1998, 620.

60 They asked about 40 questions of all 1796 directors and CEOs of Swedish public companies in 2005; 628 individuals responded, covering all but 36 (= about 12%) of all public Swedish companies.

61 R. Adams and P. Funk, "Beyond the Glass Ceiling: Does Gender Matter?", 58(2) *Management Science* 2012, 219–235.

62 M.L. Maznevski, "Understanding our differences: performance in decision-making groups with diverse members", 47(5) *Human Relations* 1994, 531–52.

63 D. Zelechowski and Bilimoria, "Characteristics of women and men corporate inside directors in the US", 12(3) *Corporate governance, an international review* 2004, 337–42.

64 E. Mannix and M. A. Neale, "What Differences Make a Difference? The Promise and Reality of Diverse Teams in Organizations", 6 *Psychological Science in the Public Interest* 2005, 31.

65 L. Broome and K. Krawiec, "Signaling through board diversity: is anyone listening?", *University of Cincinnati Law Review* 2008, 447.

66 F. Dobbin and J. Jung, "Corporate board gender diversity and stock performance: the competence gap or institutional investor bias?", 89 *North Carolina Law Review*, 2011, 809.

67 P. Bradshaw and D. Wicks, "Experiences of white women on corporate boards in Canada: compliance and non-compliance to hegemonic masculinity" in Burke/Mattis (eds.), *Women*

It is quite often alleged, also in academic literature, that women devote more attention to stakeholders, but hard evidence is often not provided. Exceptions could be Matsa and Miller, who document that companies affected by the Norwegian boardroom gender quota laws increased relative labour costs and employment.[68] Cohen and Huffman show that the gender wage gap for non-managerial workers is lower the greater the representation of women in management.[69] Adams/Gray/Nowland see this as confirming that female directors may attach more importance to stakeholder interests-read: employee interests versus only shareholder interests in the short run.[70]

D. CRITICAL MASS THEORY: THE MAGIC NUMBER OF THREE FEMALE DIRECTORS

The different results of various empirical studies concerning the influence of women in boards may also be due to the fact that proportionately small numbers of women, below a certain threshold of the total number of directors, may of course have less or perhaps even no influence on dependent variables compared to studies in which most of the sample consists of boards where there is a certain critical mass of women.

Kanter's theoretical work on gender critical mass is probably the best-known and most important elaboration of this idea.[71] Apart from uniform groups,

---

on Corporate Boards of directors: international challenges and opportunities, Kluwer, Dordrecht, 2000, 197–212.

68 D. Matsa, and A. Miller, "A Female Style in Corporate Leadership? Evidence from Quotas," 2011 forthcoming *American Economic Journal: Applied Economics*, available at SSRN: http://ssrn.com/abstract=1636047.

69 Ph. Cohen and M. Huffman, "Working for the Woman? Female Managers and the Gender Wage Gap", available at www.genderprinciples.org/resource_files/Working_for_the_Woman-_Female_Managers_and_the_Gender_Wage_Gap.pdf.

70 R. Adams, S. Gray, J. Nowland, "Does Gender Matter in the Boardroom? Evidence from the Market Reaction to Mandatory New Director Announcements", 2 November 2011, available at SSRN: http://ssrn.com/abstract=1953152 at 4.

71 R.M. Kanter, "Some effects of proportions on group life: skewed sex ratios and responses to token women", 82(5) *The American Journal of Sociology*, 1977, 965–990. Kanter elaborated her ideas in a 1977 book which we did not consult, *Men and Women of the Organization*, New York, Basic Books, 1977. The abstract of Kanter's article, cited above, is as follows: *"Proportions, that is, relative numbers of socially and culturally different people in a group, are seen as critical in shaping interaction dynamics, and four group types are identified on the basis of varying proportional compositions. "Skewed" groups contain a large preponderance of one type (the numerical "dominants") over another (the rare "tokens"). A framework is developed for conceptualizing the processes that occur between dominants and tokens. Three perceptual phenomena are associated with tokens: visibility (tokens capture a disproportionate awareness share), polarization (differences between tokens and dominants are exaggerated), and assimilation (tokens' attributes are distorted to fit preexisting generalizations about their social type). Visibility generates performance pressures; polarization leads dominants to heighten*

where all members have the same sex, Kanter distinguished between skewed, tilted and balanced groups. She argues that groups will be skewed when only up to 20% of the group is of the other sex than the dominant group. This may lead, in her view, to the gender minority members being mere "tokens" and the effects of their gender being neutralised through assimilation or, conversely, leading to higher visibility of these tokens and their presence having a polarizing effect on the group as a whole, so that the group as a whole performs less well than when these "token members" would not have been present. Kanter expects female presence to have a potentially beneficial effect only in tilted or balanced groups. A group is tilted towards male dominance when it contains between 20 and 40 percent women, it is balanced when both gender groups form between 40 and 60 percent of the total group. Kanter's theory was not based on empirical research[72], but seems broadly compatible with later empirical research concerning boards which seems to suggest that female influence will be felt, and will be beneficial, if women make up at least 30% of a board (without, one presumes, being so dominant that the group becomes skewed) which often seems to correspond to at least three female directors. Research by Joecks et al. on German supervisory boards, which consist exclusively of non-executives who, in firms with more than 500 employees, are partly chosen by employees, found that firms with a supervisory board skewed towards men had a significantly lower ROE than those with "tilted boards" who are in turn outperformed (as far as ROE is concerned) by balanced supervisory board(i.e. boards with more than 40% but less than 61% women on them).[73] One remarkable aspect of this study is that, as indicated and as the authors stress, it dealt with supervisory boards, of which most observers would assume that they have even less impact on firm performance in general than unitary boards that also contain executives, or the all-executive *Vorstand* of German and Austrian companies.

Other research, by Konrad et al. and by Torchia et al. also suggests that having at least three women directors on the board is critical, as do the McKinsey and Catalyst studies discussed earlier. The Konrad and Kramer study[74] was not based on pure quantative data but on interviews and discussions with 50

---

their group boundaries; and assimilation leads to the tokens' role entrapment. Illustrations are drawn from a field study in a large industrial corporation. Concepts are extended to tokens of all kinds, and research issues are identified."

72 Even though in her article we cited in the previous footnote she did study one firm empirically.

73 J. Joecks, K. Pull and K. Vetter, "Gender Diversity in the Boardroom and Firm Performance: What Exactly Constitutes a 'Critical Mass'?" 118 *Journal of Business Ethics* 2013, 61-72.

74 A.M. Konrad, V. Kramer and S. Erkut, "Critical mass: the impact of three or more women on corporate boards", 37(2) *Organizational Dynamics* 2008, 145–164; The study was also presented in A.M. Konrad and V. Kramer, "How many women do boards need?", 84 (12) *Harvard Business Review* 2006, 22.

women directors, 12 CEOs (9 male), and seven corporate secretaries (one male) from *Fortune* 1000 companies.[75] According to the authors' interlocutors, women more often brought a collaborative leadership style to the boardroom, with more attention to listening and "win-win problem-solving" while at the same time not shying away from tough questions, which, it was said, were more often asked by women than by men. The authors contend that the presence of women at boardroom level makes it less likely that difficult issues will be brushed under the carpet and that boardroom discussion would better reflect the perspectives of a broader range of stakeholders than in an all-male board. It seemed to be crucial that the "magic number" of at least three female directors was obtained, not only to give weight as such to the positions taken by women (one presumes, however, that the female directors do not always take the same position) but also to avoid the impression, apparently prevalent in boards with only one female director, that her point of view was a typically "woman's point of view".

The research by Torchia et al. builds on earlier research which lends support to the thesis that more diverse, less homogenous boards have a positive influence on firm innovation.[76] Looking at Norwegian firms, they find that innovativeness increases at firm level as soon as a critical mass of at least three female directors is reached.

It may be mentioned that this importance attached to the magic number three is in line with earlier psychological research on group dynamics which seems to show that perception/the expression of opinions by a person is influenced by others within the group who outnumber the dissenter by a factor of three, whereas adding more members to the majority does not seem to have additional influence.[77]

---

75 There is of course an important gender bias to this study, with all 50 "ordinary" directors that were interviewed being female. It seems questionable that their female perspective was balanced by the fact that 9 out the 12 CEOs who cooperated were male.

76 Defined by the authors as "a company's commitment to create and introduce new products, processes and organizational systems".

77 Founding father of this research topic is S.E. Asch, "Effects of Group Pressure upon the Modification and Distortion of Judgement", in H. Guetzkow (ed.), *Groups, Leadership and Men*, Carnegie Press, Pittsburgh, PA, 1951, pp. 177–190; S.E. Asch, "Opinions and Social Pressure", *Scientific American* 193(5), 1955, 31–35. See further references to other research in this area in Torchia et al. In one of Solomon Asch's experiments, a person was asked to tell which of two lines was the longer one. All others in the room, who were, unbeknownst to the minority person, in fact collaborators of Asch, intentionally gave the wrong answer. It seemed that as soon as three persons gave the wrong answer, there was a measurable influence of the majority's perception on the answer given by the lone minority person. This and similar experiments do not, of course, directly support the converse hypothesis, which is the one relevant for us, namely that as soon as one has a three person minority, this will be able to "stand its ground" against a large majority, but it is compatible with it.

If this "critical mass" view would turn out to be correct, it could be used to eliminate as irrelevant the results of an early (1997) study by Shrader et al.[78] which found a negative link between the number of women in top management and financial performance as measured by ROE, ROI, ROA and other measures: most firms in their sample (U.S. firms mentioned in the Wall Street Journal in 1992) had at most one top female executive.

On the other hand, relatively recent research by Lückerath-Rovers on 99 Dutch listed companies which compares a group of companies with no female board members at all with a group with at least one female director, finds that companies with at least one woman on the board significantly outperform all-male boards as far as ROE is concerned. This result holds when there is only one female board member.[79] As the author herself stresses, her results do not prove causation and she indicates that it is not self-evident why even one woman could make a difference. She speculates that having women on the board might be an indication of a more innovative and modern corporation, where all "employees are motivated to excel because they all see they can reach the top"[80] and that such companies are more successful (higher ROE) because they devote more attention to all their stakeholders and to using the qualities of all their employees.

E. SPECIFIC QUOTAS-RELATED RESEARCH

The vast majority of empirical studies we are aware of study the relationship between female board presence and some kind of performance variable. There are very few studies that explicitly study the effect of quotas on board performance. Hence, little can be said on the effects of gender quotas as such on firm performance. More specifically, even if female presence above a certain threshold is found to have positive effects on firm performance, we do not know whether such results would hold in those cases where female presence is to a large extent the result of gender quotas rather than of voluntary company appointments. Research by Ahern and Dittmar indicates that women who are appointed to boards as a result of the Norwegian quotas legislation tend, on average, to be younger and have less CEO experience than their male

78 C.B. Shrader, V.B. Blackburn and P. Iles, "Women in management and firm financial performance: an exploratory study", 9(3) *Journal of Managerial Issues* 1997, 355–376.

79 M. Lückerath-Rovers, "Women on board and firm performance", 17(2) *Journal of management and Governance* 2013, 491–509; citations in our (this) text are, however, to the pages of the working paper version, April 2010, available at SSRN: http://ssrn.com/abstract=1586832.

80 M. Lückerath-Rovers, "Women on board and firm performance", working paper April 2010, available at SSRN: http://ssrn.com/abstract=1586832, 18.

counterparts, but also have a higher level of education.[81] As far as we know, there is no hard evidence that experience as a CEO or greater age have a positive impact on one's performance as a board member, but common sense suggests that some experience of what life is like at the top level of a corporation should, as longs as it does not outweigh objectivity in judgment and create a pro-management bias, be a good thing for board members. If the results from Ahern's and Dittmar's study can be extrapolated outside of Norway, this could be seen as support for (which is something else than conclusive proof of) the views that a. female directors appointed as a result of quotas are different in background from other directors b. there may be a dearth of supply of female candidates with useful top executive experience c. women appointed as a result of quotas have a negative effect on firm performance, – Ahern and Dittmar found negative effects on Tobin's Q – whereas women who are appointed by firms without legislative pressure might have a more positive impact (since there are studies showing that women have a positive effect on performance, especially above the 30% or 3 female directors level).

Nygaard[82] contests the findings of Dittmar and Ahern. He finds positive stock market reactions to the appointment of female directors in Norwegian firms as a result of the quotas law, at least in those firms where non-executive directors can make a positive contribution because they are not hindered by too big information asymmetries *vis-à-vis* management. In firms where such information asymmetries are prevalent, he finds a negative reaction, but this is not statistically significant. He suspects that the different results of Dittmar and Ahern are due to a sort of selection bias in their sample, which, he argues, focused on relatively young firms, where board members, including the female ones, tend to be younger (and therefore less experienced). One question raised by Nygaard's research is whether his results are truly gender-related: perhaps the positive stock market reaction he sees in firms without important information asymmetries are simply due to a positive evaluation by the stock market of the appointment of additional non-executive directors who stand a reasonable chance of being effective in monitoring the executives, whether they are female or male.

81 K.R. Ahern and A.K. Dittmar, "The changing of the boards: the impact on firm valuation of mandated female board representation", 127 *The Quarterly Journal of Economics*, 2012, 137–197.

82 K. Nygaard, "Forced Board Changes: Evidence from Norway" working paper March 9, 2011, NHH Dept. of Economics Discussion Paper No. 5/2011, available at SSRN: http://ssrn.com/abstract=1793227.

IV. ARE QUOTAS NECESSARY TO CREATE GROWTH IN THE NUMBER OF FEMALE DIRECTORS?

A. THE EFFECT OF QUOTAS

It is clear that "natural growth" in the number or rather percentage of female directors is quite insufficient to reach parity between male and female directors or even a 30% level of female board participation within a generation. It used to be argued by some that one of the main factors explaining the lack of female directors was that fewer women than men had a university degree; the expectation then was that since as many women as men now go to university in Europe, the gender gap in boards would gradually decrease and eventually disappear. This idea has clearly not been borne out and the position is now untenable.

In Germany, supervisory boards (*Aufsichtsrat*), which consist entirely of non-executive directors, contain clearly more women than the executive board: 10% of members versus only 3.7% for the executive board (*Vorstand*). In companies with more than 500 employees, 1/3 of the members of the supervisory board must be elected by employees, in companies with more than 2000 employees the figure is 50%. It appears that of the female non-executive board members, 74% have been chosen by employees.[83] These figures strongly support the idea that employees are more willing to appoint female directors than shareholders. This is compatible with the view – which it does not prove – that "male clubby networks" explain why so few women are appointed: women who are not "one of the boys" because they do not belong to the social circles of leading shareholders and directors or managers, do not get the same chances as men who do belong to the social environment in which the existing male directors circulate.

If one wants more female *executive* directors, more women will have to reach top executive management positions. Interestingly, in the UK the "supply" of women in top executive positions is larger than the number of women that grow into a board position, in other words, increases in the number of top executive positions do not seem to be followed by a proportional increase in the number of female directors. Allegations that there is insufficient supply of top executives are, at least for the recent past, hard to square with this finding. On the other hand, research in the UK on the FTSE100 companies shows that these usually have only three executive directors: the CEO, CFO and a third one. Since very few CEOs and CFOs are female, there seems to be only a small

83 For all these figures, see M. Weckes, "Geschlechterverteilung in Vorständen und Aufsichtsräten in den 160 börsennotierten Unternehmen (Dax-30, M-Dax, S-Dax, tec-Dax) zum 31. Januar 2011", report of the Hans Böckler Stiftung, available at www.boeckler.de.

supply of female top executives who could take up non-executive positions in other companies.[84]

The Norwegian experience proves that quotas do – rather obviously – have an impact on female boardroom participation rates and, more importantly and less obvious, that they can lead to results where soft law and voluntary action did not.

In 2002, only 6.8% of all board members in Norwegian listed companies were female. In 2002, a law was enacted which determined that by 2005, 40% of all directors would have to be female. The law did not contain meaningful sanctions, however. When 2005 arrived, only 24% of directors appeared to be female. This led to a change in the law, whereby the sanctions for not reaching the desired quota were made very severe, namely forced dissolution of the company. This resulted in 40% female board members in 2009 and 44% in 2011.[85]

A side effect of the Norwegian legislation has been that the size of boards of Norwegian companies has increased.[86] Most corporate governance literature on the topic argues that small boards, containing at most 12 people, are preferable over large boards where meaningful debate is less easy to accomplish. It is therefore not surprising that some authors have argued that the quotas legislation has disrupted the functioning of boards that had a good composition prior to the enactment of the quotas act. It should also be noted that the Norwegian legislation has not led to more female executive directors. It's the number of female NEDs that has increased. Also, the number of female CEOs in Norway seems to be stuck at 5%[87], without any perceptible influence of quotas-legislation.

In Spain, a 2007 law sets a goal of 40% female boardroom participation. This non-binding legislative goal has proven to be only mildly successful, certainly it has had far less impact than the Norwegian mandatory rules: the number of female directors at listed companies was 5.2% in 2006, before the law was enacted, and had increased to only 10% in 2010.[88] Of course, cultural factors may also be in play, but it is nevertheless certain that a mandatory law on the Norwegian model would by definition have had a much bigger impact.

---

84 See the Davies Report, p. 15.

85 M. Lückerath-Rovers and S. Paans, "De haalbaarheid van het quota wetsvoorstel", *Ondernemingsrecht*, 2011, 161, same figures in the Davies Report, p. 22.

86 At least according to the Davies Report, p. 26, where no precise figures are provided.

87 According to a press report, see Clark, "getting women into boardrooms, by law", *International Herald Tribune*, 28 January 2010, 1. According to the Davies Report, p. 26, the figure is only 2% female CEOs in Norway.

88 R. Pande and D. Ford, "Gender quotas and female leadership: a review", Background Paper for the World Development Report on Gender, 2011, 35, available at www.hks.harvard.edu/fs/rpande/papers/Gender%20Quotas%20-%20April%202011.pdf.

Another issue is that, if an increase in the number of female directors amounts to increase in the number of non-executives in general, this could, potentially, lead to a decrease in the amount of sector-specific expertise that is represented in the typical board. Many would regard such an evolution as undesirable. Since the financial crisis has convinced many commentators that several financial institutions that got into trouble had too few directors with relevant banking or financial experience, an increase in the percentage of directors with no sector-specific expertise is the opposite of what many governance experts want. But because relatively few women become top executives, few women have the relevant expertise to which so much importance is attached these days.

B. ARE THERE VIABLE ALTERNATIVES FOR QUOTAS?

The Norwegian experience suggests that quotas can be very effective in increasing the percentage of women on boards. But they are, of course, a controversial technique. Some lawyers argue that they are incompatible with fundamental principles of equality and non-discrimination.[89] It is therefore legitimate and useful to ask whether there are other policy instruments that could be good alternatives for quotas.[90]

At least every listed company already publishes the composition of its board. If it also explicitly indicates how many women are members, this may help lobby groups or institutional investors who attach importance to these data and who want to use their clout to exert some pressure on companies that in their view have an insufficient number of female directors.

A second step could consist of clearly disclosing the selection criteria for new directors that the company will use. These criteria could of course contain a gender component. If many companies published this information and it often contained a gender element, this could also signal to headhunters that many companies want to increase the number of female directors, so that these headhunters take this into account. It is sometimes alleged that many headhunting firms often tend to look to the same rather narrow group of people when they are looking for new directors and that these traditional circles are dominated by men.

---

89 On this topic, see the contribution of Marc Devos to this volume.

90 For an empirical investigation into what policies listed companies in Belgium, Spain, Norway, Ireland adopt, and announce in their annual reports, to promote both gender diversity in the workforce and at board level, see D. Ahern and B. Clarke, "Listed Companies' Engagement with Diversity: A Multi-Jurisdictional Study of Annual Report Disclosures", August 1, 2013, ECGI – Law Working Paper No. #221, available at SSRN: http://ssrn.com/abstract=2306932.

Some firms devise and disclose an explicit diversity policy, be it at the level of the firm as a whole or at board level (or both). A committee or at least some people within the firm could then be tasked with the follow up of this diversity policy: does it have any effect and is it in fact implemented? If not, how can this be remedied? Does it lead to an increase of diversity in general and more female board members in particular?

As part of their diversity policy, some firms may want to include specific gender quotas which they impose on themselves on a voluntary basis. They would then normally follow up on the evolution of female boardroom participation and could and normally would explain in their annual reports or similar documents whether the objectives (the suggested quota) are obtained or not, and if not, what the reasons for this could be and how the firms intends to remedy this situation.

The Australian experience suggests that such softer, disclosure-based can be an effective approach in increasing the number of female directors. In 2009 only 5% of newly elected directors were women. In 2010, an obligation was introduced for listed companies to publish their policy concerning gender balances at board level. This resulted in 27% of new directorial appointments being women.[91]

V. CONCLUSION: QUOTAS PROBABLY CONTRIBUTE TO JUSTICE AND EQUITY, EVEN THOUGH GENDER-BALANCED BOARDS MAY NOT BE MORE EFFICIENT THAN ALL-MALE ONES

In social science and especially economics, hard statistical evidence in favour or against a certain policy is often very hard to come by. It's no different with research concerning the impact on firm or board performance of gender quotas. Not only is there very little research specifically on the effects of gender quotas on firm performance, the more prevalent but still limited research on the effects of female board members offers no conclusive evidence one way or the other.

Still, it is somewhat strange and at first sight hard to justify that women, who are not a minority in the population as a whole, occupy less than 15% of board seats in western countries outside Scandinavia. Unless one assumes that prior top management experience is required for a board member to be effective – in which case there may indeed be a supply problem[92] – there seem to be too few

---

91 See Davies Report, p. 27.

92 D. Zelechowski and Bilimoria, "Characteristics of women and men corporate inside directors in the US", 12(3) Corporate governance, an international review 2004, 337–42 indicate that

women on boards. Is such prior executive experience required? This article did not look into the question, but academic literature often argues that it is not a prerequisite for a useful role as a director and it is, moreover, clear that a large number of male non-executive directors have no such experience either.

Mandatory quotas are, of course, very helpful in speeding up female boardroom participation. It is also clear that non-mandatory quotas or other forms of soft law or self-regulation are not nearly as effective in increasing the proportion of female directors. One incontestable fact is that "natural" growth rates are, without the stimulus of at least soft law or self-regulation, far too slow to achieve any meaningful progress within a period of 20 to 30 years even now that in western Europe and the US women attend university and enter professional careers at at least the same rate as men.

Since science provides no clear-cut answers allow me to finish, for what it's worth, with my personal conviction: in spite of a huge professionalization of director selection since the 1990s, men realise that women often do have a slightly different approach to boardroom meetings; and most men socialize more with other men than with women (there is no lack of occasions where mixed companies meet; but there are still quite a few environments in which men forge social bonds without many women involved, watching and actively participating in sports being a prime example). Therefore a large number of men probably prefer to select other male candidates as new directors. In this sense, the old boys network is probably not dead yet.[93] Quotas are an efficient way of riding roughshod over these informal networks. These networks and the fact that there are fewer female top management executives probably conspire against serious increases in the number of women on boards. If quotas want to avoid increasing inefficiency at board level by "dropping" "token women" into the board, thereby creating the danger that the presence of this rare woman or two has an antagonizing or stigmatizing effect, the lessons of critical mass theory, even though it's far from scientifically proven, should be taken at heart and the number of female directors should be at least three. The problem remains, though that, based on the stories I occasionally hear from directors and complaints one reads in the newspapers, there seems to be a genuine worry

---

such a supply problem may well exist, since they find that female independent directors in their sample hold fewer corporate titles and executive positions and the broader one's already existing connections in the corporate world, the more chances of being selected for a directorship. See also the evidence cited in D. Rhode and A. Packel, "Diversity on corporate boards: how much difference does difference make?, Rock Center for Corporate Governance working paper series-no 89, September 2010, available at ssrn.com/abstract=1685615, at 15–16 (III.B).

93 This was also one of the conclusions of the Davies Report, p. 17, based on the feedback they got during their consultation process.

among directors that it is difficult to find enough women with what is deemed to be relevant executive experience. The lack of female top executives, could, however, potentially be remedied by quotas as well: since it's the board that selects top management (in those companies where it's not the other way round), more female directors may lead to more female top managers[94], even though it is likely that more women than men with the capacity to become top executives are hindered by their own attitudes and by the way society is organised to apply for the position. In order to solve the latter problem, we should all read and implement what Sheryl Sandberg says in her excellent book[95], rather than just buying it and leaving it unread.

To conclude, contrary to what is often argued by proponents of increased female board membership, the evidence that this would contribute to increased board or firm efficiency is very thin. But since there is hardly any evidence that increases of the number of women on boards would have any detrimental effect either, the burden of proof is on those who would want to defend the position that we need less female boardroom participation than workforce participation. Unless it can be proven that women simply do not want these top positions, the proponents of that thesis would probably be defending a hopeless case. Since other measures than quotas do not seem to create any meaningful effects within an acceptable time frame (less than 20 years), we should probably vote for them. There is one last snag though: what if all those non-academic directors are right who allege that as yet there are too few women with the right capacities, and that women appointed as a result of quotas run a high risk of being stigmatized, which would contribute to less effective relationships among board members? Well, even though there is as yet no firm evidence in favour of quotas, there is no firm evidence against them, the stigmatizing effect is likely to be less important when at least 25% of the board is female (= 3 directors, usually) and like we've just argued, quotas could have the effect of creating a larger future supply of top female executives who could go on to become directors.

---

94 In the US, this seems to be what research by Catalyst has found, see Advancing women leaders: the connection between women board directors and women corporate officers, 2008, at 6 (available at www.catalyst.org/knowledge/advancing-women-leaders-connection-between-women-board-directors-and-women-corporate): firms with two or more female directors in 2001 had 30 percent more female officers in 2006 than firms with only one female director in 2006 even when in 2001 they had the same or similar levels of female officers. Interestingly, Adams and Kirchmaier (R. Adams and T. Kirchmaier, "Making It to the Top: From Female Labor Force Participation to Boardroom Gender Diversity", 22 December 2012, ECGI – Finance Working Paper No. 347/2013, available at SSRN: http://ssrn.com/abstract=2192918) have found that female labour force participation is significantly related to the representation of women on boards; this is strong support for the thesis that it is necessary to increase female management positions in order to foster more female directorships.

95 Lean In: Women, Work and the Will to Lead, Knopf, New York, 2013.

ANNEX

STUDIES REFERRED TO IN TABLE 1

ADAMS, R.B. and FERREIRA, D.: 2009, "Women in the boardroom and their impact on governance and performance", *Journal of Financial Economics* 94, 291–309.

AHERN, K.R. and DITTMAR, A.K.: 2012, "The changing of the boards: The impact on firm valuation of mandated female board representation", *The Quarterly Journal of Economics* 127, 137–197.

BÖHREN, Ö. and STRÖM, R.Ö.: 2010, "Governance and Politics: Regulating Independence and Diversity in the Board Room", *Journal of Business Finance & Accounting* 37 (9), 1281–1308.

CAMPBELL, K. and MÍNGUEZ-VERA, A.: 2008, "Gender Diversity in the Boardroom and Firm Financial Performance", *Journal of Business Ethics* 83(3), 435–451.

CARTER, D.A., SIMKINS, B.J. and SIMPSON, W.G.: 2003, "Corporate governance, board diversity, and firm value", *The Financial Review* 38(1), 33–53.

ERHARDT, N.L., WERBEL, J.D. and SHRADER, C.B.: 2003, "Board Director Diversity and Firm Financial Performance", *Corporate Governance* 11 (2), 102–111.

HASLAM, S.A., RYAN, M.K. KULICH, C. TROJANOWSKI, G. and ATKINS, C.: 2010, "Investing with Prejudice: The Relationship Between Women's Presence on Company Boards and Objective and Subjective Measures of Company Performance", *British Journal of Management* 21, 484–497.

HE, J. and HUANG, Z.: 2011, "Board informal hierarchy and firm financial performance: Exploring a tacit structure guiding boardroom interactions", *Academy of Management Journal* 54(6), 1119–1139.

LINDSTAEDT, H., WOLFF, M. and FEHRE, K.: 2011, "Frauen in Führungspositionen-Auswirkungen auf den Unternehmenserfolg", *German Federal Ministry of Family,* Senior Citizens, Women and Youth 08/2011.

LÜCKERATH-ROVERS, M.: 2010, "Women on Board and Firm Performance", *Journal of Corporate Governance*, 1–30.

MAHADEO, J.D., SOOBAROYEN, T. and HANUMAN, V.O.: 2012, "Board Composition and Financial Perfor-mance: Uncovering the Effects of Diversity in an Emerging Economy", *Journal of Business Ethics* 105, 375–388.

MILLER, T. and DEL CARMEN TRIANA, M.: 2009, "Demographic Diversity in the Boardroom: Mediators of the Board Diversity-Firm Performance Relationship", *Journal of Management Studies* 46(5), 755–786.

RANDÖY, T., OXELHEIM, L. and THOMSEN, S.: 2006, "A Nordic perspective on corporate board diversity", *Nordic Innovation Centre*, 1–32.

ROSE, C.: 2007, "Does female board representation influence firm performance? The Danish evidence" *Corporate Governance* 15 (2), 404–413.

SHRADER, C.B., BLACKBURN, V.B. and ILES, P.: 1997, "Women in management and firm financial perfor-mance: an exploratory study", *Journal of Managerial Issues* 9(3), 355–376.

SICILIANO, J.I.: 1996, "The Relationship of Board Member Diversity to Organizational Performance", *Journal of Business Ethics* 15, 1313–1320.

SMITH, N., SMITH, V. and VERNER, V.: 2006, "Do women in top management affect firm performance? A panel study of 2500 Danish firms", *International Journal of Productivity and Performance Management* 55(7), 569–593.

TORCHIA, M., CALABRÒ, A. and HUSE, M.: 2011, "Women Directors on Corporate Boards: From Tokenism to Critical Mass", *Journal of Business Ethics* 102(2), 299–317.

CHAPTER 2

GENDER QUOTAS AND EU DISCRIMINATION LAW

Marc De Vos*

I. INTRODUCTION AND PURPOSE

A book dedicated to the emergence of gender quotas in company boards in the European Union needs a chapter on the contentious and complex relationship between quotas and the overarching EU law of non-discrimination in employment. Gender quotas, in one way or another, are a form of benign discrimination aiming to correct labour market and corporate realities that fly in the face of the policy aims that quotas seek to promote.

Our purpose is limited and specific: we seek to establish the *acquis* on gender quotas as a form of positive action/discrimination addressed in case law of the European Court of Justice (ECJ) related to the key EU law provisions prohibiting sex discrimination in employment. We will not develop this inquiry further into the similar realm of human rights law or national constitutional law, even though both these angles may well be additionally relevant.

Our premise is the natural relevance of the EU gender discrimination *acquis* for the purpose of any legislation on gender quotas in company boards, whether European or national. Indeed, the principle of non-discrimination on grounds of sex is a general principle of EU law and a transversal EU goal, making it a primary, directly applicable and supreme touchstone for any legislation in the employment field.[1] As such, the *general* analysis that follows, in its attempt to combine both the principles of EU non-discrimination law and the potential aims of gender quotas at large, is a self-evident reference tool to assess the validity of the *specific* case of gender quotas in company boards.

---

* Ghent University Law School. Chapter finalized per 1 July 2013.

1 See the overview and references in C. Barnard, *EU Employment Law*, Oxford, OUP, 2012, Part III, 253 *et seq.*

In what follows we will retrace the steps of the limited case law available, after contextualizing the broader issue of positive action and positive discrimination in EU discrimination law (II). Our careful reconstruction of the available ECJ case law ends with a clear but restrictive framework for gender quotas under EU gender discrimination law (III). Upon concluding, we will briefly touch upon a new strand of recent case law on *age* discrimination that deviates from the gender model in being more accommodating to positive discrimination, potentially heralding an alternative framework for assessing gender quotas as well (IV).

II. EQUALITY, POSITIVE ACTION, AND DISCRIMINATION IN EU LAW

A. FORMAL AND SUBSTANTIVE EQUALITY

Anyone seeking to understand the precise nature of the relationship between "quotas" and "non-discrimination" in EU sex discrimination law, must return to the basic building blocks of so-called "positive action" measures – of which quotas are an extreme example – and their position in EU discrimination law.

"Positive action", particularly in the field of gender, has been a problematic issue for decades. On the *societal and political level* it has strongly divided opponents and proponents who both claim to defend a truly equal society. From a *legal perspective*, the European Union's experience with positive action has been at times fitful and always controversial, especially through see-sawing visions at the European Court of Justice.

The legal difficulties surrounding "positive action" primarily relate to the combination of non-discrimination and positive action. A good understanding of the legal issues surrounding "positive action" therefore requires an analytical insight into the principle of non-discrimination and its relation to positive action.

The story of the European Union's equality and non-discrimination law is not one of clear-cut and comprehensive statutory construction. Rather, it is essentially one of step-by-step organic development through an ever expanding array of case law and secondary legislation without an overarching conceptual framework. Over several decades various authors have tried to fill this theoretical void and develop a suitable *equality model* by tapping into international or historical examples or by falling back to alternative disciplines such as ethics, philosophy, and sociology. None of these scholastic attempts has ever fully succeeded.

With a large degree of simplification, two major models of equality and its legal protection can be discerned. One the one hand there is a "formal", "liberal" or "symmetrical" approach that is based on "individual justice" and "the merit principle". This model focuses on equality for individuals, formal neutrality, and procedural justice. On the other hand there is the "substantive", "asymmetrical" or "group justice" approach. This model in varying degrees focuses on group characteristics and (dis)advantages, group impact, actual results, material equality and desired outcome. Somewhere in between those two poles lies the middle ground of "equality of opportunities" which combines elements of both.[2]

The European Court of Justice (hereinafter: ECJ) for half a century has consistently defined discrimination as the *"application of different rules to comparable situations or the application of the same rule to different situations"*.[3] This definition is seen as a manifestation of a formal, procedural approach to equality, in line with the European Union's core economic principles. The first tenet of the definition indeed promotes formally equal treatment in comparable situations, irrespective of outcome. From that perspective, the primary emphasis of EC equality law lies on *formal equality*.[4]

There are three main weaknesses to formal equality: it requires comparison with a comparator in order to establish discrimination, it is essentially passive and static and does not assure any particular outcome, and it disregards the inherent collective dimensions of inequality such as group membership, entrenched inequality or societal realities. *Substantive equality* addresses many of these weaknesses: it does not require a comparator, it focuses on outcome and addresses group dimensions. However, a pure substantive approach runs the risk of interchanging quality for quantity while reinforcing divisions or reintroducing individual inequality through the backdoor.

---

2 For a general overview and discussion see, inter alia, G. Barret, "Re-examining the Concept and Principle of Equality in EC Law", in P. Eeckhout and T. Tridimas (eds.), *Yearbook of European Law 2003*, Oxford University Press, Oxford, 2004, 117–153; M. Bell and L. Waddington, "Reflecting on inequalities in European equality law", (2003) 28 *ELR* 349–369; S. Fredman, *Discrimination Law*, Oxford, Oxford University Press, 2002, 1–26; R. Fullinwider, *The Reverse Discrimination Controversy*, Rowan and Littlefield, 1980.

3 See, e.g., *Government of the Italian Republic v. Commission of the European Economic Community*, C 13/63, [1963] ECR 165; *Racke v. Hauptzollamt Mainz*, C 283/83, [1984] ECR 3791; *Finanzamt Köln-Alstadt v. Roland Schumacker*, C-279/93, [1995] ECR I-225, 259; *A v. Commission*, Case T-10/93, [1994] ECR II-179; *Milk Marque and National Farmers' Union*, C-137/00, [2003] ECR I-7975; *Spain* v *Commission*, C-304/01, [2004] ECR I-7655.

4 G. de Búrca, "The Role of Equality in European Union Law", in A. Dashwood and S. O'Leary, The Principle of Equal Treatment in EC Law, London, Sweet and Maxwell, 1997, 24–29; C. Tobler, *Indirect Discrimination: a case study into the development of the legal concept of indirect discrimination under EC law*, Antwerp, Intersentia, 2005, 26–28.

It is a testimony to the ECJ's intellectual creativity and to the EU's flexibility that EU law has been able to address formal equality's shortcomings without abandoning it and the individual justice it stands for:

- The comparator has all but disappeared with the prohibition of potential discrimination.
- Outcome and collective dimensions have come into the frame with the prohibition of indirect discrimination and a strategy commonly known as *"positive action"*.

Positive action, therefore, is associated with a more substantive, result-based notion of equality. Since EU law at the same time integrates formal equality in its core definition of discrimination, the resulting combination is a balancing act. The European Union's equality and non-discrimination law cannot be squarely placed into any one of the conceptual equality camps. A blend of form and substance lands the EU's equality concept in the middle ground of "equality of opportunity", a grey zone with few conceptual bearings where positive action is seen to contribute to *effective equality of opportunity for individuals and groups alike.*

B. POSITIVE ACTION

In light of the scholarly distinction between formal and substantive equality, positive action under EU law can be described as *a process to introduce a dynamic, result oriented approach that internalizes group dimensions into an equally static and individual formal equality model.*

While positive action has as a common denominator its ambition to alter group representation in a given environment, it can be conducted in myriad ways. Building on McCrudden's classification, several categories of increasing intensity can be identified[5]:

- Consciously examining, identifying and *eradicating any discriminatory or distorting practices.* This might be labelled "positive fairness" and can result in systematic *mainstreaming.*
- *Facially neutral target policies* that seek to increase the proportion of members of the underrepresented group by using criteria that do not overtly discriminate, e.g. focusing on a geographical area or on the unemployed.
- *Outreach programmes* that do use group affiliation and seek to accelerate the inclusion of the underrepresented group, either through targeted *support*

5 C. McCrudden, "Rethinking Positive action", (1986) 15 *Industrial Law Journal* 219, 223–225.

(information, training, education, advertising, the creation of lobby groups etc.), or through targeted *sensitisation*. This might be labelled "positive mobilisation".
- *Facially biased diversity policies* that seek to increase the proportion of members of underrepresented groups through soft targets that do not resort to actual preferential treatment.
- *Accommodation programmes* that seek to reduce barriers by offering *personal* accommodation for members of certain *groups* and which therefore combine both group consideration and personal merit.
- *Actual preferential treatment* through reverse discrimination: favouring members of the underrepresented group over members of the dominating group.
- *Redefinition of "merit"* by making group affiliation a relevant job qualification. This is in fact a rather theoretical proposition.[6]

Irrespective of its substance, the *author or origin* of positive action may also differ. Positive action may be organized or supported by the state or a governmental authority, it may be voluntarily decided by public actors or private actors such as companies, or it may be imposed as remedial action by courts in certain jurisdictions. And while the *purpose* of positive action may vary infinitely it is important to distinguish between *backward-looking positive action* that seeks to compensate for past discrimination and pro-active, *forward-looking positive action* that aims at redistributive justice.

The typology above should not in any way be interpreted formalistically. What matters is to appreciate the immense diversity of "positive action" processes. That diversity yields two immediate conclusions. The first conclusion is *terminological confusion*. The variety of possible measures is not reflected in the single denomination of "positive action". There is an unhelpful tendency to reduce "positive action" to controversial or downright discriminatory processes. The second conclusion is that there is plenty of room for *real and effective positive action that does not collide with formal equality and non-discrimination*. In that respect, positive action really need not necessarily be the divisive and political issue it has become. In what follows, the focus will rest on the contentious tip of the iceberg: the borderline issues between formal equality, non-discrimination and positive action. It is there where quotas emerge.

6 It boils down to plain preferential treatment unless group affiliation constitutes a genuine occupational requirement, in which case its deliberate introduction for equality reasons is theoretical.

C. POSITIVE DISCRIMINATION

Under the EU's formal equality approach, discrimination turns on a differential treatment, in a comparable situation, that is causally linked with a prohibited ground. Positive action measures that do institute such differential treatment thus constitute discrimination and become *positive discrimination*.

Positive discrimination is sometimes referred to as "benign" or "reverse" discrimination in the sense that its positive focus on substantive equality renders it benign or tries to reverse a historically entrenched situation. However, a "negative" motive or intention is no prerequisite for discrimination in a formal equality concept that favours neutrality and therefore defines discrimination through *objective comparisons* and an *objective causal* link between the contested treatment and the protected characteristic.[7] No matter how "positive" or "benign", discrimination therefore remains discrimination under EU law as a matter of principle. The question, then, becomes to what extent EU law is prepared to condone "positive" discrimination *by way of exception*.

Positive "discrimination" in need of justification, of course, cannot be deduced from mere differential treatment alone. Under EU law any claim that deduces discrimination from differential treatment presupposes that the purported victim is in a *sufficiently comparable* situation as the beneficiary. A claim of discrimination under the Union's formal equality model indeed requires a *comparator*, either real or potential. Therefore, there can be no conflict with equality law where a contested positive action measure in fact lacks the requisite comparator.

This self-evident principle was illustrated in the *Abdoulaye* case. The ECJ was asked whether the principle of equal pay in what is now Article 141 TEC precludes the making of a *lump-sum payment exclusively to female employees who take maternity leave*. The Court recognized that the prohibition of pay discrimination does not preclude such a payment if male and female workers are indeed in different situations because of the concrete occupational disadvantages inherent in maternity leave, which the payment is designed to offset. As always, is it is for the national court to determine whether this is the case.[8] *Abdoulaye* illustrates that a formal approach to equality is not without its substantive merits either.

---

7 C. Bayart, *Discriminatie tegenover differentiatie: arbeidsverhoudingen na de discriminatiewet, arbeidsrecht na de Europese ras- en kaderrichtlijn*, Larcier, Gent, 2004, 281–284; E. Ellis, *EU anti-discrimination law*, Oxford University Press, Oxford, 2005, 103.

8 Case C-218/98 *Abdoulaye* [1999] ECR I-5723, 16–20.

D. POSITIVE ACTION AND INDIRECT DISCRIMINATION

Indirect discrimination deduces discrimination against an individual from the *factual impact* (actual or potential) of a contested criterion, provision or practice on the *group* of which the individual is a member.[9] In that respect positive action and the prohibition of indirect discrimination share a common focus on substance rather than form, and on the group rather than the individual. Besides this conceptual resemblance the relationship between indirect discrimination and positive action is essentially twofold.

First, the Union's prohibition of indirect discrimination does *not* entail a blanket obligation of positive action to avoid the disproportionate impact of on their face neutral criteria, provisions or practices. This was emphatically underscored by the ECJ in *Bilka*. The ECJ faced the question whether the then Article 119 TEC on pay discrimination (now Article 157 TFEU) *obliges* the employer to take into account the impact of family responsibilities on female workers. The Court summarily discarded compulsory positive action:

> "an obligation such as that (…) goes beyond the scope of article 119 and has no other basis in community law as it now stands"[10]

The Court's off-hand rejection is understandable. It is of the essence of indirect discrimination that impact as such only raises a presumption of discrimination, which can then be countered by offering an objective justification that meets the requirements of proportionality. Any assumption of compulsory, impact aimed positive action through the prohibition of indirect discrimination therefore clearly goes beyond the scope of that prohibition.

However, to the extent that Union law *prohibits unjustifiable indirect discrimination* it effectively demands the avoidance of such discrimination. A limited *duty of positive action is therefore implicit in any prohibition of indirect discrimination*. In any event, it is clear that the mere existence of the prohibition of indirect discrimination is likely to induce awareness and hence proactive positive action from actors who will be naturally keen to avoid the risk of indirect discrimination through impact in their organization.

Second, a positive action measure which for the non-promoted group entails the disproportionate impact characteristic of indirect discrimination, will itself presumptively constitute a case of indirect discrimination. One is then in the presence of reverse *indirect* positive discrimination, the justification of which –

9 The deduction operates as a *presumption of discrimination* that can be justified.
10 Case C-170/84 *Bilka* [1986] ECR 1607.

as for any case of indirect discrimination – depends on the traditional test of legitimate aim and proportionality.

That is the lesson of *Schnorbus*, where the ECJ had to judge a national provision giving priority for admission to the civil service to persons who have completed compulsory or civilian service. The Court quickly established that this positive action measure constituted indirect sex discrimination since, under the relevant national legislation, women are not required to do military or civilian service. It went on to scrutinize and accept the preferential treatment, stressing both its limited duration and its aim to counterbalance the effects of the delay experienced in the progress of their education by applicants who have been required to do military or civilian service.[11]

Similarly, in *Badeck* and *Abrahamsson*, the ECJ acknowledged that positive action may be organized by filtering selection criteria in such a way that, although formulated in terms which are neutral as regards sex and thus capable of benefiting men too, in general favour women. In the final analysis the contested positive action was rejected because its criteria were not clearly tailored to prevent or compensate for the occupational difficulties of the promoted group.[12]

While the outcome of these cases was different, they all show the ECJ's willingness to entertain the purpose of a Member State's positive action scheme as a possible justification for its indirect discrimination. From this perspective, the "positive" nature of the discrimination, while it cannot exclude the qualification as discrimination, may yet help in justifying it. It should be noted that all three cases deal with indirect discrimination through state systems.

III. POSITIVE ACTION, QUOTAS, AND THE *ACQUIS* IN EU GENDER DISCRIMINATION LAW

A. ARTICLE 2(4) OF THE ORIGINAL EQUAL TREATMENT DIRECTIVE

The first provision in EU legislation in the field of gender-based positive action measures was Article 2(4) of the Equal Treatment Directive 76/207, which held in its original wording:

> "This Directive *shall be without prejudice* to measures to promote equal opportunities for men and women, *in particular by removing existing inequalities* which *affect women's opportunities in the areas referred to* in Article 1(1)" (emphases added).

---

11 Case C-79/99, *Schnorbus* [2000] ECR I-10997.

12 Case C-158/97, *Badeck* [1999] ECR I-1875; Case C-407/98, *Abrahamsson* [2000] ECR I-5539.

B. POSITIVE ACTION AND POSITIVE DISCRIMINATION

From its earliest case law the ECJ has recognized that Article 2(4) could potentially serve as a basis, not only for mere positive action measures that do not amount to preferential treatment that interferes with formal equality, but also for apparently discriminatory measures. In *Commission v. France* the ECJ stated that:

> "the *exception* provided for in Article 2 (4) is *specifically and exclusively designed* to allow measures which, *although discriminatory in appearance*, are in fact *intended to eliminate or reduce actual instances of inequality* which may exist in the reality of social life".[13]

In its later case law, the Court has continued to contrast positive discrimination with formal equality, seeing the potential authorisation of the former as part of a partially *"restricted concept"* of the latter. The aim of Article 2(4) is:

> "(...) to *achieve substantive, rather than formal, equality* by reducing de facto inequalities which may arise in society."[14]

The ECJ therefore squarely sticks to formal equality as the mother principle of EU discrimination law, allowing reverse discrimination only as its exception under the contrasting concept of substantive equality. The story of the case law is the gradual discovery of the limits of this exception.

C. OPTIONAL NATURE, OBJECTIVE CONTENTS, AND PURPOSE

Article 2(4) of the original Equal Treatment Directive declared itself "*without prejudice* to measures to promote equal opportunities". This clearly did not *impose* positive action, as the ECJ pointed it out in *Bilka*. Asked whether Article 119 TEC on pay discrimination (now Article 157 TFEU) *obliges* the employer to take into account the impact of family responsibilities on female workers, the Court summarily discarded any notion of compulsory positive action throughout Union law, adamantly stating that:

> "an obligation such as that (...) goes beyond the scope of article 119 *and has no other basis in community law as it now stands*"[15] (emphasis added).

---

13 Case C-312/86 *Commission v. France* [1988] ECR 6315, par. 15, emphases added.

14 Case C-407/98 *Abrahamsson* [2000] ECR I-5539, 48; Case C-319/03, *Briheche* [2004] ECR I-8807, 25, emphasis added.

15 Case C-170/84 *Bilka* [1986] ECR 1607.

The ECJ has also been careful to scrutinize the *objective contents and purpose* of measures that want to pass as positive action under Article 2(4) of the Equal Treatment Directive. In *Commission v. France* the ECJ ruled out a French legislation that generally authorized the preservation of special rights for women in collective bargaining. The Court stressed that Article 2(4) only allows for measures which are "intended to eliminate or reduce actual instances of inequality which may exist in the reality of social life".[16] A generalized preservation of special rights for women, as in the French legislation in question, is therefore overbroad and fails as a matter of principle.

Griesmar allowed the ECJ to clarify the objective contents of positive action measures. The Court was called to evaluate a service credit provided to female civil servants in respect of each of their children for the purposes of calculating a pension. This credit was not provided to male civil servants. It appeared that the grant of the credit was unrelated to maternity leave or to the disadvantages which a female civil servant incurs in her career as a result of being absent from work during the period following the birth of a child. It was merely a standard monetary advantage at the time of retirement and did not *objectively address occupational difficulties that women encounter during their careers*. As such, the resulting discrimination against male workers in the comparable situation of having assumed child rearing responsibilities could not be justified as a positive action measure.[17]

The need for positive action measures to objectively address the career difficulties of the promoted group was further emphasized in *Abrahamsson*, where the Court was called upon to judge a Swedish scheme aimed at promoting university positions for female candidates over male candidates. The ECJ rejected the scheme, *inter alia* because the preferential treatment of female candidates was not based on "clear and unambiguous criteria such as to prevent or compensate for disadvantages in the professional career of members of the under-represented sex."[18]

For a measure to be acceptable as "positive action" for women in employment and occupation it must therefore *at least objectively, be based on clear and unambiguous criteria, address specific career inequalities and help women to conduct their professional life on a more equal footing with men*. It now remains to be seen what restrictions the Court imposes on measures that do meet this objective standard.

---

16 Case C-312/86 *Commission v. France* [1988] ECR 6315, par. 15, emphasis added.
17 Case C-366/99 *Griesmar* [2001] ECR I-9383.
18 Case C-407/98 *Abrahamsson* [2000] ECR I-5539, 49–50.

D. THE EVOLUTION TOWARDS A PROPORTIONALITY TEST

The *substantive limits* of the original Equal Treatment Directive's positive action provision were developed in a series of cases. In *Commission v. France* the ECJ opted both for an extensive and a restrictive approach, stating that:

> "the *exception* provided for in Article 2 (4) is *specifically and exclusively designed* to allow measures which, *although discriminatory in appearance*, are in fact *intended to eliminate or reduce actual instances of inequality* which may exist in the reality of social life".[19]

Article 2(4) is branded as an exception to the non-discrimination principle, ostensibly permitting preferential unequal treatment of women. However, this liberal reading is immediately restricted to measures which are *"specifically and exclusively designed"* to eliminate or reduce actual inequalities. As we have seen, a generalized preservation of special rights for women, which the French legislation authorized in collective bargaining, fails to meet this standard.

Commission v. France clearly demanded positive action measures that amounted to positive discrimination to be *narrowly tailored to the accepted goal of eliminating or reducing actual inequality.*

This approach was further pursued and refined in *Kalanke*, where the Court confronted a German quota system which automatically favoured women if the candidates for a particular official post were in a tie-break situation and thus equally qualified. An automatic preference for women is detached from demonstrable inequality. This was the linchpin which brought AG Tesauro to reject what he labelled reverse discrimination designed to confer results rather than removing obstacles. The Court duly followed, explicitly favouring equality of opportunities over equality of results and stressing the necessary strict interpretation of Article 2(4) as a derogation from the neutrality principle in non-discrimination.[20]

Kalanke exemplified a formal and individualistic approach to non-discrimination in which the room for positive discrimination becomes critically confined. The Court's logic appeared to require actual inequality *in the particular case* for positive discrimination to become acceptable. This approach effectively closed the door for group based positive discrimination and generated upheaval among experts and lobby groups. It was, albeit obliquely, partly abandoned in

---

19 Case C-312/86 *Commission v. France* [1988] ECR 6315, par. 15, emphasis added.

20 Case C-450/93 *Kalanke* [1995] ECR I-3051.

the subsequent cases *Marschall*[21] and *Badeck*.[22] The Court now allowed a national rule favouring equally qualified female candidates for promotion over male candidates in sectors where females are under-represented:

> "if such a rule *may counteract the prejudicial effects on female candidates* of the attitudes and behaviour and *thus reduce actual instances of inequality which may exist in the real world*" (emphases added).

The Court exchanges a purely individualistic approach for a balanced group approach that *allows individual decisions of positive discrimination to be justified on the basis of group inequality*. It formally distinguishes its new line from the one adopted in *Kalanke* by focusing on the *conditional nature* of the positive discrimination at hand:

> "a measure which is intended to give priority in promotion to women in sectors of the public service where they are under-represented must be regarded as compatible with Community law if *it does not automatically and unconditionally give priority to women* when women and men are equally qualified, and the *candidatures are the subject of an objective assessment which takes account of the specific personal situations of all candidates*."[23]

The requirement of an objective assessment comparing the intended individual beneficiary and the victim of a collective positive action measure was further expanded by the Court in the already mentioned *Abrahamsson* case. There the ECJ had to consider a Swedish regulation on universities which enabled preference to a candidate of the under-represented sex who, although sufficiently qualified, did *not* possess qualifications equal to those of other candidates of the opposite sex. The absence of equal qualification implied a greater deviation from the individual merit principle and one which the Court was unwilling to swallow in the absence of objective criteria clearly tailored to prevent or compensate for the occupational difficulties of the promoted group. Moreover, the scheme lacked an objective assessment taking into account the specific personal situations of all the candidates, which made it a priori unacceptable.[24]

Abrahamsson could be formally distinguished from *Marschall* and *Badeck* in its preferential treatment, without objectively tailored criteria, of less qualified female candidates, just as *Marschall* and *Badeck* could be formally distinguished from *Kalanke* in their use of a savings clause that made the positive discrimination conditional. It is clear, however, that the Court sooner or later

21 Case C-409/95 *Marschall* [1997] ECR I-6363.
22 Case C-158/97 *Badeck* [1999] ECR I-1875.
23 Case C-158/97 *Badeck* [1999] ECR I-1875, par. 23, emphasis added.
24 Case C-407/98 *Abrahamsson* [2000] ECR I-5539.

would have to abandon its case-by-case balancing act for a more comprehensive test. It admitted as much when it considered the *Abrahamsson* scheme "in any view, to be disproportionate to the aim pursued" and squarely attempted an overall proportionality test in *Lommers*. The ECJ returns to its premise, initially espoused in *Commission v. France*, which sees positive discrimination as an exception to the non-discrimination principle and states:

> "(...) according to settled case-law, in determining the scope of any derogation from an individual right such as the equal treatment of men and women laid down by the Directive, due regard must be had to the principle of proportionality, which requires that derogations *must remain within the limits of what is appropriate and necessary in order to achieve the aim in view* and that the *principle of equal treatment be reconciled as far as possible with the requirements of the aim thus pursued*".[25]

Applying this traditional proportionality logic to the facts at hand, the Court validates a scheme set up by a Ministry to tackle proven extensive under-representation of women within it under which, in a context of proven insufficiency of proper, affordable care facilities, a limited number of nursery places made available to its staff is reserved for female officials alone while male officials still have access to them (i) in cases of emergency and (ii) on the same conditions as female officials if they take care of their children by themselves.

It is important to note that the explicit development of the proportionality test in *Lommers* does not turn back the clock for the previous rulings. On the contrary, the analyses developed in earlier cases such as *Marschall* and *Badeck* should be seen as an *illustration of the proportionality test*. The Court was quick to point this out in the *Briheche* case and continues to reject positive discrimination that gives automatic and unconditional priority to certain categories of women.[26]

E. ARTICLE 157(4) TFEU – EQUAL TREATMENT DIRECTIVE 2006/54/EC

1. *Textual observations*

Since the Treaty of Amsterdam the elimination of gender inequality and the promotion of gender equality have been enshrined as a central EU goal and as a Member State obligation. This renewed active approach to gender equality also transpires in the modified treaty article on pay discrimination, now Article 157 TFEU, of which the fourth section holds that:

---

25 Case C-476/99 *Lommers* [2002] ECR I-2891, par. 39, emphasis added.

26 Case C-319/03 *Briheche* [2004] ECR I-8807, par. 24 *et seq.*

"With a view to *ensuring full equality in practice* between men and women in working life, the principle of equal treatment shall not prevent any Member State from maintaining or adopting measures providing for *specific advantages* in order to make it *easier for the underrepresented sex to pursue a vocational activity or to prevent or compensate for disadvantages in professional careers*" (emphases added).

Article 157(4) is still the only TFEU provision that explicitly refers to positive action, although gender is now only one of the many outlawed grounds for discrimination. Its emphasized wording potentially puts Article 157(4) ahead of the old Article 2(4) of the Equal Treatment Directive in several ways.

The reference to "ensuring full equality in practice" owes more to a substantive equality model than to a formal one. The concept of "equal opportunities", central to the original Article 2(4) of the Equal Treatment Directive and to the findings in *Kalanke* and *Marschall*, is not used. At the least equal opportunity is recognized as necessary to the achievement of "full equality in practice". It is however unclear whether positive action should still be treated as an exception to the principle of equal treatment or as an independent element on the path towards the achievement of real equality of opportunity. The "shall not prevent" passage is indicative of the former rather than of the latter.

The authorization of "specific advantages" does seem to indicate new direct avenues for positive action. Finally, by admitting positive measures that both "prevent or compensate" the TFEU combines a compensatory and a proactive approach beyond the initial Equal Treatment Directive's emphasis on merely "removing existing inequalities".

While the text of now-Article 157(4) TEC thus appeared to widen the scope of positive action in comparison to the initial Equal Treatment Directive, it now remained to be seen how the ECJ would handle the new framework. In this respect, the Court's approach should logically also apply to the *Consolidated Equal Treatment Directive* whose positive action provision has been deliberately modified to assure uniformity with the now-Article 157(4) TFEU.[27]

2. *ECJ case law*

To our knowledge, the ECJ so far has only had to deal with cases that initially arose under Article 2(4) of the original Equal Treatment Directive. As a result,

[27] Article 3 Directive 2006/54/EC on the implementation of the principle of equal opportunities and equal treatment of men and women in matters of employment and occupation (recast) states: "Member States may maintain or adopt measures within the meaning of Article 141(4) of the Treaty with a view to ensuring full equality in practice between men and women in working life."

the Court has only addressed the new phraseology of Article 157(4) TFEU indirectly and as *obiter dictum*. This has precluded the Court from adopting a clear and unambiguous position.

The Court has not been without stimulus from Advocates-General to use the now-Article 157(4) TFEU to expand the scope of authorized positive action. Both AG Saggio in *Badeck* and AG Poiares Maduro in *Briheche* advocated that the then-Article 141(4) TEC should imply broader discretion to adopt positive action measures, either independently or through a harmonized reading of Article 2(4) of the original Equal Treatment Directive. It is revealing that the ECJ has so far refused to erect a different level of scrutiny through 141(4) and has merely, albeit cursorily, integrated Article 141(4) in a natural and harmonious development of its scrutiny through the original Equal Treatment Directive.

In the *Abrahamsson* case mentioned above, the ECJ capped its rejection of the contested scheme under Article 2(4) of the Equal Treatment Directive with the off-hand remark that:

> "even though Article 141(4) TEC allows the Member States to maintain or adopt measures providing for special advantages intended to prevent or compensate for disadvantages in professional careers in order to ensure full equality between men and women in professional life, it cannot be inferred from this that it allows a selection method of the kind at issue in the main proceedings which appears, on any view, *to be disproportionate to the aim pursued*."

As we have seen, this proportionality test was later confirmed and developed in *Lommers for the sole purpose of Article 2(4) of the original Equal Treatment Directive*. Both Articles 2(4) and 141(4) are therefore approached through the prism of proportionality. There is no indication of an increase in the legitimate scope for positive action.[28] The Court appears to envelop both positive action provisions in the same approach without recognizing any significant difference in substantive scope.

This line was continued in *Briheche*, where the Court again stopped short of following a separate Article 157(4) track with the statement that it cannot allow measures "which prove in any event to be disproportionate to the aim pursued". In the same case the Court reiterates its traditional view of positive action as a *limited derogation to formal equality*.[29] This is again noteworthy since Article 157(4) TFEU was claimed by some to mark the advent of a substantive approach to equality in EU law. The Court apparently remains to be convinced,

28 L. Waddington and M. Bell, "More equal than others: Distinguishing European Union Equality Directives", (2001) 38 *Common Market Law Review* 587, 601.

29 Case C-319/03, *Briheche* [2004] ECR I-8807, par. 25 and 31.

confirming instead uniformity in that the derogatory Article 2(4) of the original Equal Treatment Directive aims:

> "(...) *in accordance with Article 141(4) EC*, to prevent or compensate for disadvantages in the professional career of the persons concerned."[30]

In short, whereas the current case law from the ECJ certainly recognizes the separate co-existence of Article 2(4) of the original Equal Treatment Directive and of Article 157(4) TFEU, it has so far failed to indicate, let alone decide, that different articles also imply different levels of scrutiny. On the contrary, all indications tend towards a uniform approach of "proportionality" that does not significantly depart from the earliest cases. If anything, the impact of Article 157(4) has been to clarify the necessary aim of authorized positive action measures in the sense that these measures must, "in any event, contribute to helping women conduct their professional life on an equal footing with men".[31]

F. THE GENDER *ACQUIS* AND QUOTAS: A VERY THIN LINE TO TOE

Given the wide variety of positive action measures, as seen above, it should be stressed that the existing case law only deals with a small fraction of the spectrum. This is of course entirely normal, since only those positive action measures that entail some form of actual positive discrimination are potentially problematic from the perspective of equality law.

Secondly, it is equally telling for the reality of positive discrimination in the EU that the Court – to our knowledge – so far has not had the opportunity to develop doctrine in the field of *private sector* positive action for gender. All but one irrelevant case concerned public employers[32] which in almost all of the cases applied positive action measures embedded in national legislation.

With these caveats in mind, the *acquis* of positive action case law can be summarized as follows.

First and foremost, the ECJ sticks to a restrictive approach in which group based positive action, especially positive discrimination, is seen as an *exception to be narrowly tailored to its justification* (*Commission v. France, Abrahamsson, Briheche*).

---

30 Case C-319/03, *Briheche* [2004] ECR I-8807, par. 25.

31 Case C-366/99 *Griesmar* [2001] ECR I-9383, par. 64. In the same vein, C-104/09, *Alvarez*, 30 September 2010.

32 The irrelevant case being Case C-79/99, *Schnorbus* [2000] ECR I-10997, which was solved as a case of indirect discrimination.

Second, although all the current case law deals with facts that arose under the original Equal Treatment Directive, the ECJ in several occasions has shown manifest hesitation to adopt a wider scope of positive action under Article 157(4) TFEU or the equivalent Article 3 of the recast Equal Treatment Directive. Whereas the ECJ certainly recognizes the difference in wording between the two provisions, it has so far indicated an *integrated approach under a proportionality test that does not appear to contain any significant difference* (*Abrahamsson, Lommers, Briheche*).

The concept of "proportionality" traditionally entails three separate tests: *legitimacy, effectiveness*, and *necessity*. The existing case law is centred on legitimacy while stating but barely scratching the surface of the other two criteria.

Legitimacy is accepted where measures that result in individual positive discrimination are aimed at remedying a *proven imbalance* between the sexes. The ECJ seems not particularly concerned with the origin of the imbalance, loosely admitting positive discrimination in response to the "prejudicial effects on women in employment which arise from *social attitudes, behaviour and structures*" (*Kalanke, Marschall*). Positive discrimination therefore should not necessarily seek to compensate for past discrimination as such. The required imbalance should not necessarily have adversely affected the beneficiary of the positive measures.

What *level of imbalance* is required for positive discrimination to be legitimate has never been squarely asked to the ECJ. The Court has dealt with a variety of imbalances without ever having to judge their merits directly. However, it is clear that the aim of positive action measures should be to *eliminate and correct the causes of reduced opportunities of access to employment and careers* and to improve the ability of the underrepresented sex to compete on the labour market and pursue a career on an equal footing (*Commission v. France, Griesmar, Lommers, Alvarez*). Moreover, such positive discrimination measures should *objectively serve the stated aim and rely on objective and transparent criteria* (*Commission v. France, Abrahamsson, Griesmar*).

This is an important double restriction of the potential legitimacy of positive discrimination measures in gender. The *aim* that can potentially justify such measures is essentially codified into the TFEU and the Recast Equal Treatment Directive: it is to "*make it easier for the underrepresented sex to pursue a vocational activity or to prevent or compensate for disadvantages in professional careers.*" Any other policy aim that cannot be squared under this codification will make the positive discrimination illegal *per se* as long as the ECJ maintains formal equality as the rule and treats substantive equality through reverse discrimination as the exception in need of justification. Moreover, in verifying whether a positive discrimination actually pursues the said aim, the Court insists on criteria that serve it in an objective and transparent fashion. From that perspective, merely seeking to redress gender imbalances for the sake of more gender diversity cannot pass. What is needed instead is a careful identification of the roots of career disadvantages in a particular case, answered with compensatory or promotional action that objectively and transparently addresses these. Diversity for the sake of diversity is not an acceptable platform for positive discrimination that runs afoul of gender neutrality.

Furthermore, any positive discrimination should, in accordance with the principle of *proportionality*, remain within the limits of what is appropriate and necessary in order to achieve the aim in view, *reconciling the principle of equal treatment as far as possible with the requirements of the aim thus pursued* (*Abrahamsson*, *Lommers*, *Briheche*). The emphasis on "appropriateness" and "necessity" is likely to generate crucial discussions about *effectiveness* and *cost/benefit analysis* in positive action. The Court has as yet to clearly state its level of commitment into assessing the actual effects of positive discrimination measures, but it has refused to accept measures that, while ostensibly benefiting women, are in fact liable to perpetuate a traditional distribution of the roles of men and women by keeping men in a role subsidiary to that of women in relation to the exercise of their parental duties (*Alvarez*).

In the same vein, if neutrality is supposed to be principle that can only be abandoned for discrimination out of necessity, every discussion on the legitimacy of positive discrimination measures will inevitably get sucked into an endless quest for possible alternative policies to serve the same aim with no or less discriminatory effect. If necessary does mean necessary, the adoption of positive discrimination measures *per se* leaves little to zero room for policy discretion and can only be accepted as a measure of last resort. Only the choice to actually pursue a policy to prevent or compensate for disadvantages in professional careers is then genuinely within the realm of policy discretion, whereas the tool of positive discrimination can only be landed upon by default, after considering and eliminating all possible alternatives that are less discriminatory.

Whereas the conceptual bearings of the Court's scrutiny seem clear, the extent to which these bearings will actually be followed and applied remains very much unclear. The relative dearth of case law still leaves much room for concrete development of the described proportionality test. Conceptually, the position of the ECJ creates a formal and very tight straightjacket for national policy makers that want to consider positive discrimination in gender. Whether the Court will stick to this rigorous scrutiny or instead demonstrate more flexibility under the all-encompassing umbrella of "proportionality" still remains to be seen. We do know, however, that *proportionality in selection is not fulfilled when the preferential treatment is automatic and unconditional* and does not include an objective assessment of all personal circumstances of all the candidates, allowing for gender neutrality to prevail if the circumstances so demand (*Kalanke, Marschall, Badeck, Briheche*). Hard selection quotas are therefore *in principle* suspect and the ECJ has so far only conditionally admitted soft quota in a tie-break situation.

IV. CONCLUSIONS AND PERSPECTIVES FOR GENDER QUOTAS IN COMPANY BOARDS

The legal framework for positive action and positive discrimination is multi-layered. It combines elements of both international law and European human rights law, of European Union law, and of national law, often including national constitutional law. All these sources approach the interaction of equality and positive action/discrimination in their own way. Legal complexity is further compounded by the enormous variety of measures which can be labelled as "positive action".

Our analysis has focused entirely on positive action and positive discrimination in EU gender equality law. It has shown that, notwithstanding minor textual differences, the positive action provisions in both primary and secondary EU law are essentially similar, in the mould of what is now Article 157(4) TFEU. Article 157(4) TFEU itself has – to our knowledge – not (yet) been used by the ECJ to allow more room for positive action than under Article 2(4) of the original Equal Treatment Directive. Positive action that establishes some form of positive discrimination is still construed as an exception to the principle of formal equality.

The delineation of this exception is done through the prism of *proportionality*. But this particular proportionality test is serious scrutiny. The existing case law, however sparse, brings forward stern requirements that narrowly tailor the scope and heavily reduce the potential for Member-States to use the tool of gender quotas as a policy choice. In fact, when held up against the mirror of the existing case law, many of the current initiatives for gender quotas in company boards slide into legal limbo, or worse.

- *First*, the ECJ has repeatedly shown itself to be allergic to *automatic* quotas that impose certain percentages of gender representation and concomitant gender preference by definition and that do not allow for a comparison that can tilt the balance in favour of the other sex on the basis of personal merit. On this basis alone, some of the national legislations imposing hard gender quotas in company boards appear to be seriously flawed.

- *Second*, any justification of positive discrimination such as gender quotas turns on a clear identification of the legitimate *aim* pursued and of the *objective and transparent connection* of the discriminatory quota criteria to that aim. Moreover, current EU gender discrimination law essentially restricts and codifies the authorized aim to that of addressing the career disadvantages of the underrepresented sex whose members can benefit from the positive discrimination.

  From this double vantage point as well, many of the attempts to impose gender quotas appear to be potentially problematic. Scrutinizing the legal history of gender quotas for company boards yields an array of goals and justifications: better market functioning (meta), more economic growth (macro), better corporate governance and/or financial performance (micro), and more gender equality (outcome). The first reaction to this policy cacophony is: which aim is it? For the specific aim is the starting point for verifying whether the actual terms of the quota system objectively and transparently connect with and serve the aim that the system is supposed to achieve. Many of the domestic measures for gender quotas in company boards fail to meet the ECJ's requirement of "clear and unambiguous criteria such as to prevent or compensate for disadvantages in the professional career of members of the under-represented sex." While they may generally be inspired by broader labour market or career promotional goals, their operation really boils down to imposing diversity for the sake of more diversity. This is close to anathema under the current case law that sees formal equality and neutrality as the overarching principle and that only allows discrimination for substantive equality when its modalities are objectively and transparently tailored to underlying causes of career difficulties in a given scenario.
- *Third*, even when a specific legitimate aim is demonstrably addressed under a soft quota system that does leave room for individual merit-based exceptions, a formidable obstacle to justification presents itself through the combined requirements of effectiveness, proportionality, and necessity. Although only stated as principles and as yet undeveloped in the current case law, these conditions – when drawn to their logical implications – should impose a rigorous appreciation of the practical effects of any gender quota policy. Do gender quotas in company boards actually improve corporate governance, financial performance, economic growth, and the like? And if they do, is the tool of discriminatory quotas proportional to a beneficial effect that cannot be achieved in any alternative and less discriminatory way? These are exceedingly hard questions to answer. The chapter on corporate governance

in this book at best reveals ambiguous connections between gender diversity and corporate performance, even leaving aside the perennial but nonetheless determining question whether connection actually means causation. If the evidence is only partial and tentative, what level of scientific conclusiveness will be required to convince a court that takes its role as the arbiter and guarantor of equal opportunity and merit-based equality seriously? Clearly, beyond the as yet unacceptable aim of more gender diversity per se, any attempt to justify gender quotas on an economic rationale will be an uphill battle, especially since it also has to establish how *only* quotas could achieve the stated aim, with the exclusion of other alternatives. There will always be potential alternatives. At least the clever lawyer will always be able to suggest one that has not been considered, tried and failed, and that is enough if 'necessary' actually means 'necessary'.

In short, if the existing ECJ case law on quotas and positive discrimination in gender is to be maintained and fully applied to the case of gender quotas for company boards, the potential for such quotas to actually pass muster seems exceedingly small. Of course, the overall test of "proportionality" is inherently flexible. Its application remains essentially in the hands of domestic judges who may be more amenable and open to the domestic political agenda. The mantle of proportionality may also allow the Court of Justice to embrace a more flexible approach without having to alter its principles.

The first indications of increased flexibility can be found outside the sphere of gender, in the field of age discrimination. As is well-known, Article 6 of the General Framework Directive 2000/78 allows Member States to accept that, notwithstanding the prohibition of age discrimination in employment, "differences of treatment on grounds of age shall not constitute discrimination, if, within the context of national law, they are objectively and reasonably justified by a legitimate aim, including legitimate employment policy, labour market and vocational training objectives, and if the means of achieving that aim are appropriate and necessary." This article essentially codifies and enables certain forms of positive age discrimination for labour market policy purposes, under the traditional condition of proportionality. In clear contradistinction to its restrictive interpretation of the similar generic possibility of positive gender discrimination, the Court has shown itself to be flexible in administering this specific exception to the formal neutrality prescribed by its non-discrimination law principles.

In a couple of recent cases that deal with the legitimacy of forms of compulsory retirement or termination of employment upon reaching a certain age threshold, the Court has accepted these types of positive age discrimination on grounds that the choices made – either by the domestic legislator or by social partners through collective bargaining agreements – "do not appear to be unreasonable" and "may be appropriate for achieving the set aims".[33] Without any clarification, the Court embraces an easy and pliable standard of "reasonableness" and potential "appropriateness" for what is nonetheless still the opposite of the formal equality and neutrality upon which its discrimination law rests, in each case giving the domestic legislator or the social partners a free pass.[34] Moreover, the Court has shown itself to be increasingly uninterested in carefully assessing the labour market impact of these discriminatory age policies, accepting their effectiveness as a matter of course.[35]

From the perspective of the case law on positive discrimination in gender, such leniency is unexpected and unwarranted. Perhaps the Court gives greater weight to gender neutrality than it does to age neutrality, using Article 6 of the General Framework Directive as a specific indication of how EU law is less adamant about the latter than about the former. Perhaps the Court is more willing to treat Article 6 as a fully-fledged grant of policy appreciation for the Member States, while treating the generic opening towards positive discrimination more as a restriction in need of careful delineation vis-à-vis the key principle of formal equality. Or perhaps the newer case law on age discrimination heralds a turn towards more leniency in gender as well. No doubt the case of gender quotas in company boards will allow us to test these options before the Court in the not too distant future.

33 See cases C-411/05, *Palacios de la Villa*; C-341/08, *Petersen*; C-45/09, *Rosenbladt*; C-499/08, *Andersen*; C-152/11, *Baxter.*

34 The informed reader will not fail to notice the stark difference with the much more stringent level of scrutiny first embraced by the Court in *Mangold*, its first case on the said General Framework Directive but one that did not prove to be a watershed.

35 See cases C-411/05, *Palacios de la Villa*; C-341/08, *Petersen*; C-45/09, *Rosenbladt*; C-141/11, *Hörnfeldt.*

CHAPTER 3
THE COMMISSION PROPOSAL FOR IMPROVING GENDER BALANCE IN COMPANY BOARDS

Andreas Stein and Rosalinde van der Vlies*

On 14 November 2012, the Commission adopted a proposal for a Directive of the European Parliament and the Council on improving the gender balance among non-executive directors of companies listed on stock exchanges and related measures.[1] It has been highly debated in the political arena with extensive media coverage whether intervention at EU level would be necessary or justified, particularly because several Member States have taken targeted measures at national level to increase the gender balance in company boards.[2] This Chapter aims to explain the need for EU action (Section 1) and the main elements of the Commission proposal (Section 2). Section 3 draws some conclusions.

---

* Both authors are officials of the European Commission. This chapter exclusively reflects their personal views.

1 COM(2012)614 final.

2 France, Italy and Belgium have adopted legislation setting quotas for company boards, including sanctions for non-compliance. Spain and the Netherlands have adopted quota laws without sanctions. Denmark has adopted new legislation in January 2013 pursuant to which companies are required to set target figures for themselves, to implement a policy for gender equality and to report on the status of fulfilment of these requirements; however, the new rules do not impose any mandatory quotas to increase the share of women on the boards of directors. Finland, Greece, Austria and Slovenia have enacted rules covering only the boards of state-controlled companies; Germany's existing legislation affects the gender balance on boards via rules governing workers' representation on boards. Austria, Belgium, Finland, France, the Netherlands, and Spain have developed – either on top of legislative measures or as stand-alone measures – voluntary initiatives such as corporate governance codes or charters that companies can sign. The United Kingdom, Germany, Poland, Sweden and Luxembourg have developed voluntary initiatives. The remaining Member States have taken no action.

I. THE NEED FOR EU ACTION

Gender equality is one of the core objectives of the EU. The Treaty on the Functioning of the European Union (TFEU) states that "in all its activities, the Union shall seek to eliminate inequalities and to promote equality between men and women".[3] The EU has adopted several pieces of legislation to turn equal treatment of women and men into a reality for its citizens in practice both in matters of employment and occupation and beyond.[4] All these directives prohibit sex-based discrimination. They explicitly leave the possibility to Member States to take so-called "positive action" measures with a view to ensuring full equality in practice between men and women in working life but do not prescribe any such measures.[5]

Equality in decision-making is one of five priority areas in both the Women's Charter[6] and the European Commission's "Strategy for Equality between Women and Men 2010–2015".[7] In both documents the Commission has reaffirmed its commitment to working to increase the percentage of women in positions of responsibility. In March 2011, the Commission has adopted a Commission staff working document on "The Gender Balance in Business leadership", highlighting the gender imbalance in economic decision-making positions, in particular on corporate boards. At the same time, Commission Vice-President Viviane Reding called on large companies to make concrete commitments by signing the "Women on the Board Pledge for Europe"[8] and to voluntarily increase women's presence on corporate boards to 30% by 2015 and to 40% in 2020. Despite these efforts to give self-regulation another chance, only 24 companies across the whole EU signed the pledge[9] whilst the average

---

3 Article 8 TFEU, see also Articles 2 and 3 (3) of the Treaty on the European Union and Article 23 of the Charter of Fundamental Rights.

4 Directive 2006/54/EC of the European Parliament and of the Council of 5 July 2006 on the implementation of the principle of equal opportunities and equal treatment of men and women in matters of employment and occupation (recast), OJ L 204, 26.7.2006, p. 23; Directive 2010/41/EU of the European Parliament and of the Council of 7 July 2010 on the application of the principle of equal treatment between men and women engaged in an activity in a self-employed capacity and repealing Council Directive 86/613/EEC, OJ L 180, 15.07.2010, p. 1; Council Directive 2004/113/EC of 13 December 2004 implementing the principle of equal treatment between men and women in the access to and supply of goods and services, OJ L 373, 21.12.2004, p. 37.

5 See Article 3 of Directive 2006/54/EC, Article 5 of Directive 2010/41/EU, Article 6 of Directive 2004/113/EC. As stipulated in the latest provision this can be done through specific measures to prevent or compensate for disadvantages linked to sex.

6 COM(2010)78 final.

7 COM(2010)491 final.

8 See press release. Available from: http://europa.eu/rapid/pressReleasesAction.do?reference=MEMO/11/124.

9 Some further initiatives at the national level – for example by the 30 biggest companies listed on the German DAX index – were taken at least partly in reaction to the threat of regulatory

proportion of women on boards across the EU was less than 14%. Following a public consultation[10] to identify measures to address the persistent lack of gender balance in boardrooms of listed companies, the Commission presented a legislative proposal addressing this issue in November 2012.

This section examines the case for EU action. Paragraph A outlines the objectives pursued by the Commission proposal. Paragraph B looks into the question whether action at the EU level would be justified by assessing compliance with the principle of subsidiarity. Finally, the legal right of the EU to act is dealt with in paragraph 3.

A. OBJECTIVES PURSUED

The aim of the Commission proposal is to accelerate the progress towards a more balanced representation of women and men on boards of listed companies while allowing companies sufficient time to make the necessary arrangements.[11] The reasons underlying the objective of a more balanced representation of women and men on boards of listed companies are manifold.

Firstly, there is the need for fairness and equality of opportunity. The underrepresentation of women on company boards shows that opportunities for career advancement are not equally shared between men and women and it is vital that this issue is addressed. Women account for around 45% of the people employed across the EU.[12] They account for around 56% of the people in tertiary education, and have been accounting for a majority amongst tertiary level graduates for many years.[13] Moreover, research shows that 83% of women in mid-level positions have a strong desire to move up to a higher level in their companies. In spite of being ever more skilled and ambitious, however, women are still strongly underrepresented in the highest decision-making bodies of European companies. 83% of non-executive board members and 90% of executive board members are men.[14] Taking into account the differences between Member States, women occupy a quarter of the seats on boards of large listed companies in Finland, Latvia and Sweden and just over a fifth in France. Yet, there are less than 1 in 10 in Ireland, Greece, Estonia, Italy, Portugal, Luxembourg and Hungary, less than 1 in 20 in Cyprus and around 1 in 30 in

action but did not set common objectives for female representation in the highest decision-making bodies.

10 See http://ec.europa.eu/justice/newsroom/gender-equality/opinion/120528_en.htm.

11 See Article 1 of the Commission proposal.

12 Eurostat, Employment by sex, age groups and nationality [lfsq_egan], 3rd quarter of 2011.

13 Eurostat, Tertiary students (ISCED 5–6) by field of education and sex [educ_enrl5], 2009.

14 Commission data base, October 2012.

Malta. Overall, slight progress has been noted, yet the pace of change remains very slow. Between the final quarter of 2003 and October 2012 the share of women on boards has risen from 8.5% to 15.8%, an increase of 7.3 percentage points in a little over nine years. This represents a slow average rate of increase of around 0.8 percentage points per year. In the more recent past progress has accelerated considerably albeit still at a rather modest pace. Yet, this progress is predominantly explained by the effects of binding legislation adopted in only few Member States[15] and, to a lesser extent, by developments in Member States with an active political discussion or the threat of binding measures.[16] In the majority of Member States the share of women among board directors is growing minimally, stagnating or even shrinking.[17]

At the same time, a more balanced representation of women and men on boards of listed companies would also contribute to countering hidden stereotypes about women and their capacity to successfully perform work related to the executive and supervisory level of decision-making. According to a Eurobarometer survey of 2011, 78% of Europeans think that the European business community is dominated by men who do not have sufficient confidence in women.[18] In a survey interviewing 500 senior women from corporations and professional firms across Europe,[19] two thirds highlighted stereotypes and preconceptions of women's roles and abilities as the most important obstacle they faced, closely followed by a lack of suitable female role models, a lack of relevant management experience, family commitments, and a lack of mentoring opportunities. The Commission proposal would help to circumvent the effects of the existing stereotypes on female candidates, since a respectable representation of women on the boards would serve as a safeguard against the further perpetuation of these stereotypes, and would contribute to eventually eliminating the glass ceiling altogether.

---

15 For example, more than 40% of the increase in female representation across the whole EU in the period October 2010 – January 2012 is explained by the developments in one single Member State, France, where a binding quota was introduced in 2011.

16 Such as the UK where a government-supported voluntary process has been initiated by the Lord Davies report in 2011. The latest update to that report in April 2013 indicated, however, that after an initial success the pace of improvements had slowed down or even come to a halt and that the established target of 25% female representation on FTSE 100 boards may be missed. Against that background Vince Cable, the UK business secretary warned companies about the "real possibility" of quotas. See www.ft.com/intl/cms/s/0/47922fbc-a128-11e2-990c-00144feabdc0.html#axzz2XR1XJn2n.

17 For example, in Sweden, one of the Member States with the highest proportion of women on company boards but no binding measures in place or planned, female representation has slightly fallen since October 2010.

18 Special Eurobarometer 376 (2011), *Women in decision making.*

19 Catalyst, *Women in Leadership: A European Business Imperative,* Catalyst and the Conference Board Europe, 2002. www.catalyst.org/publication/92/women-in-leadership-a-european-business-imperative.

Another problem linked to traditional gender roles and circles is that professional networks often exclude women. It seems that appointments to supervisory boards very much depend on networks and personal contacts.[20] Furthermore, selection procedures for board positions are not sufficiently transparent when it comes to preparing the shortlists of candidates for the election or appointment of board members. For instance, the UK Equality and Human Rights Commission reached the conclusion that the board appointment process remains "opaque and subjective, and typically driven by a corporate elite of predominantly male chairmen who tend to favour those with similar characteristics to themselves".[21] The lack of transparency of appointments for board positions was also highlighted by stakeholders responding to the Commission's public consultation, with some suggesting that companies could contribute to a better gender balance on boards by developing clear job descriptions, profile criteria and transparent selection procedures. The Commission proposal would enhance gender equality on company boards through transparency obligations for selection procedures and reporting obligations.

The other reasons for aiming at more gender balanced boards are linked to the business benefits of a more gender diverse boardroom. An increasing number of studies show a positive correlation between a higher share of women at top levels and a company's organisational performance, as diversity in general improves the quality of decision-making, corporate governance and ethical behaviour.[22] A more diverse boardroom offers wider perspectives that better reflect the customer basis[23] and workforce of companies. It is also widely acknowledged that the presence of women on boards improves corporate governance, because a more diverse boardroom incorporates a wider spectrum of ideas, reduces the level of "group think", offers more thorough assessment of proposed decisions and is superior in terms of risk management. It was further found that female board members have better attendance records, improve the attendance of men and are more involved in monitoring committees.[24] The presence of women

---

20 Derek Higgs, 2003, Review of the role and effectiveness of non-executive directors, see: www.berr.gov.uk/files/file23012.pdf, p. 43.

21 This was also a finding of the 2011 Lord Davies report (https://www.gov.uk/government/uploads/system/uploads/attachment_data/file/31480/11–745-women-on-boards.pdf) which in its Recommendation 6 expressly calls for greater transparency in the recruitment process.

22 Some examples: Smith and Verner, "Do Women in Top Management Affect Firm Performance? A Panel Study of 2500 Danish Firms", *International Journal of Productivity and Performance Management*, 2004, 55 (7), "Women matter" by McKinsey (2007, 2008, 2010); "The Bottom Line: Connecting Corporate Performance and Gender Diversity" by Catalyst, 2007; "Female Leadership and Firm Profitability", Finnish Business and Policy Forum (EVA), 2007, "Groundbreakers, using the Strength of Women to rebuild the World Economy", Ernst & Young, etc.

23 Global Survey conducted by The Boston Consulting Group, 2009.

24 Adams and Ferreira, *Women in the Boardroom and their impact on Governance and Performance*, 2009.

might improve team performance, because more diverse teams consider a greater range of perspectives and therefore reach better decisions. Research also shows that women are more risk-averse.[25] Also, a more diverse board possesses more and better information, it is more likely to engage in constructive dissent,[26] and the company can increase its corporate reputation.[27] Therefore, by appointing women to the boards, companies improve their decision making process and their corporate governance.[28]

Numerous studies have also shown that there is a positive correlation between gender diversity at top management level and a company's financial performance and profitability. Starting in 2001, McKinsey and, in 2004, Catalyst conducted research which found positive results (higher stock values, higher returns on equity and greater profitability) related to female presence on boards of companies. Also, their later research found that the financial performance of these companies was well above the average.[29] Other research indicates that a company led by a female CEO is on average slightly more profitable than a corresponding company led by a male CEO.[30] The great variety and difference of the specific results may be due to the different methodologies used, to different time series analysed, different periods, different data and different types of companies, countries, different ways of measuring firm performance and firm value, omitted variables etc.[31] The existence of a 'business case' has recently been supported by Lord Davies Report assessing the situation in UK[32] by Deutsche Bank Research[33], Crédit Suisse[34] and other organizations.

---

25 Matsa et al., "A female style in corporate leadership? Evidence from Quotas", 2011, see: http://papers.ssrn.com/sol3/papers.cfm?abstract_id=1636047.

26 Broome, Krawiec, "Signaling through Board Diversity: Is anyone listening?", 2008, *U. Cinn.L.Rev.* (2008), 431.

27 Bear et al., "The impact of Board diversity and gender composition on corporate social responsibility and firm reputation", *Journal of Business Ethics*, 2010, p. 207–221.

28 Peni, *Essays on the effects of female executives and experts on Corporate Governance and financial reporting practices*, Universitas Wasaensis 2012.

29 See for instance: DIW Wochenbericht 3, 2012, Managerinnenbarometer 2011; Ernst and Young, *Mixed Leadership*, 2012. However, there is another body of research which came to the result that women on board might have neutral or negative effects on stock price. These pieces of research have used data over a long number of years, see for explanation Dobbin and Jung, "Corporate Board Gender Diversity and stock performance: The competence gap or institutional investor's bias?", *North Carolina Law review*, 2011, p. 809–838.

30 The Finnish Business and Policy Forum EVA published in 2007 a study (*Female Leadership and Firm Profitability*), covering 14,020 Finnish companies; see www.eva.fi.

31 See: Campbell, Minguez-Vera, "Gender Diversity in Boardrooms and Firm Financial performance, 2008", *Journal of Business Ethics*, 2008, p. 435–451 (441); Rhode, Packel, 2010, "Diversity on Corporate Boards: How much Difference does Difference Make?", Rock Center for Corporate Governance, working papers series n. 89, p. 8.

32 "Women on boards", Lord Davies of Abersoch Report, UK, 2011.

33 Deutsche Bank Research (2010), *Towards gender-balanced leadership*, www.dbresearch.com.

34 Crédit Suisse Research Institute, Gender diversity and corporate performance, 2012.

Enhancing female presence in the boardrooms not only affects the women appointed to boards, but also contributes to attracting female talent to the company and ensuring a greater presence of women at all levels of management and in the workforce (the so-called "ripple-effect"). A boardroom sets the tone that trickles down through the whole organization. Female board members can be role models to other women within and outside an organization and can demonstrate a company's commitment to gender fairness, helping companies to attract and retain a broader proportion of staff. Therefore, a higher share of women on company boards can have a positive impact on closing both the gender employment gap[35] and the gender pay gap.[36] Making full use of the existing female talent pool would also constitute a marked improvement in terms of return on education for both individuals and the public sector. 60% of university graduates are women and 60% of the PhDs are completed by women.[37] Educational achievements thus show that women are well trained and have many skills to bring to business. As women do not reach the top levels of business (and other high ranking posts) to an extent corresponding with their education[38], this pool is not exploited fully. Thus some of the society's investment in education is wasted.[39]

B. THE EU'S RIGHT TO ACT

The principle of subsidiarity aims to ensure that decisions are taken as closely as possible to the citizens of the EU.[40] As a rule that presupposes the existence of

---

35 The gender employment gap is referring to the differences in labour market participation between men and women. EU average is 75.8% for men and 62.5% for women (2009).

36 The gender pay gap is the difference between average gross hourly earnings of male and female paid employees as a percentage of average gross hourly earnings of male paid employees. The unadjusted gender pay gap is the figure obtained before adjusting for observed characteristics including individual characteristics such as age, education, the number of children, job tenure and occupation, as well as workplace characteristics such as the economic sector and place of employment or the existence of a collective agreement. It is considered an important indicator in monitoring the inequality in pay between men and women in Europe. The most recent Eurostat figures for the unadjusted gender pay gap, which are provisional and relate to 2011, put it at 167.2% on average in the EU27, slightly less than the 17.6% recorded for 2008.

37 HR today, 3/2010, see: www.femdat.ch/C11/C6/ErfolgdankVielfalt/Document%20Library/Frauenquote.pdf.

38 Rubery et al., *The costs of "Non-Gender Equality": The socio-economic impact of EU legislation on Equality for women*, 2003, Manchester School of Management, prepared for the European Commission page 144.

39 The low utilisation of educated women can be seen as a example of incoherence in policy making regarding the investment in education, see: Rubery et al., 2003, "Equality as productive factor", in Burchell et al., *System of production: markets organisations and performance.*

40 It is defined in Article 5(2) TFEU: "Under the principle of subsidiarity, in areas which do not fall within its exclusive competence, the Union shall act only if and in so far the objectives of

EU competence it governs the extent to which the EU is restrained in exercising its powers. EU action needs to be "necessary" in the sense that the objectives of the proposed action cannot be sufficiently achieved by Member States and should have "added value" meaning that the objectives can be better achieved by action at the EU level.[41]

For the outset, it should be noted that the EU has the competence and the authority to act on gender equality, already since the Treaty of Rome in 1957 which included a provision banning pay discrimination on grounds of sex (now Article 157(1) TFEU). Promoting equality between women and men is one of the EU's main objectives, as reflected in its Treaties (Article 3(3) TEU, Article 8 TFEU, Article 157 TFEU) as well as in the Charter of Fundamental Rights (Article 23). Several pieces of EU legislation have put into practice the principle of equal treatment between women in men in the fields of employment and occupation – including self-employment – but also outside the labour market.[42] The EU has thus already made remarkable progress towards equality between men and women, but effective equality, especially in decision making, has not been achieved. Past efforts by EU institutions over several decades to promote gender equality in economic decision-making, notably to enhance female presence in company boards, by Recommendations,[43] Resolutions[44] and by encouraging self-regulation[45] have failed. As stated above, company boards are still predominantly occupied by men. Projections show that without EU action the female representation on boards of publicly listed companies is expected to evolve from 13.7% in January 2012 to no more than 21% in 2020 for the EU. Only one Member State (France) will have achieved a 40% female representation in boards by 2020 as the result of national binding quota legislation. Only 7 more

the proposed action cannot be sufficiently achieved by the Member States, either at central level or at regional and local level, but can rather, by reason of scale or effects of the proposed action, be better achieved at Union level".

41 See Protocol 2 on the application of the principles of subsidiarity and proportionality. This is supervised by the national parliaments, as laid down in Articles 5 (2) and 12 (b) TFEU, in accordance with the "reasoned opinion" procedure set out in Protocol 2.

42 See footnote 4 above.

43 Council Recommendation of 13 December 1984 on the promotion of positive action for women, Official Journal of 19/12/1984, L 331 P. 0034 – 0035, Council of the European Union, in its Recommendation 1996/694/EC of 2 December 1996 on the balanced participation of women and men in the decision-making process, OJ 10 December 1996, L 319/11.

44 See European Parliament Resolution of 8 March 2011 on equality between women and men in the European Union-2010, P7_TA(2011)0085, Resolution on women and business leadership of 9 July 2011, INI/2010/2115 06/07/2011, T7–0330/2011 and Resolution of 11 May 2011 on corporate governance in financial institutions P7_TA(2011)0223. On 13 March 2012, the European Parliament adopted a report calling on the European Commission to table a legislative proposal to introduce quotas to step up corporate board quotas to 30% by 2015 and 40% by 2020 Rapporteur Sophie in 't Veld, Report Nr 0041/2012.

45 See VP Reding's "Women on the Board Pledge For Europe", calling upon large companies to make concrete commitments to voluntarily increase women's presence on company boards to 30% by 2015 and 40% by 2020.

Member States – Finland, Latvia, the Netherlands, Slovakia, Spain, Denmark and Sweden – are estimated to reach 40% before 2035. Therefore, additional EU action in this area is necessary.

In principle Member States do have the possibility to improve gender balance on boards on their own. However, subsidiarity is not only about the hypothetical possibility of reaching a certain policy objective at the level of Member States, it is also about the level of willingness of Member States to actually use the possibilities at their disposal to really and efficiently achieving that objective. In practice many of them are either doing nothing at all (11 EU countries have neither self-regulation measures nor legislation in place and expressed no intention of introducing them) or their actions are so diverse that they lead to very divergent results as reflected in the current situation where female representation on boards ranges from 4% to 29% across Member States). Even though some Member States may achieve substantial progress this clearly indicates that action by Member States individually will not achieve the objective of a more balanced gender representation on company boards across the EU by 2020 or at any point in the foreseeable future and will be better achieved by measures at EU level.

In accordance with Protocol no. 2 of the Treaty on a European Union "on the application of the principles of subsidiarity and proportionality", any national Parliament or any chamber of a national Parliament may, within eight weeks from the date of transmission of a draft legislative act, send to the Presidents of the European Parliament, the Council and the Commission a reasoned opinion stating why it considers that the draft in question does not comply with the principle of subsidiarity. If one third of national Parliaments (corresponding to 18 votes out of 54) contest a proposal by adopting a reasoned opinion – triggering a so-called "yellow card" – the Commission has to review the proposal and decide whether to maintain, amend or withdraw the act and explain the reasons.

National parliamentary chambers from six Member States[46] challenged the subsidiarity compliance of the proposal but they nevertheless agreed that action is needed to improve the presence of women on company boards in publicly listed companies.

At the same time parliaments in Germany,[47] France[48] and Portugal[49] have adopted opinions which included calls supporting the Commission's proposal

46 Czech Republic [Chamber of Deputies – the lower house], Denmark [single chamber system], Netherlands [upper and lower chamber], Poland [upper and lower chamber], Sweden [single chamber system] and the UK [both chambers].

47 Bundesrat – upper house.

48 Assemblée nationale – lower house.

49 Assembleia da República – single chamber parliament.

for EU legislation. The remaining national Parliaments have concluded subsidiarity checks without issuing a reasoned opinion or decided not to carry out such a check.

The proposal has therefore successfully passed the subsidiarity scrutiny in the national parliaments: only 11 negative votes from 6 Member States were delivered (out of 54 potential votes), much below the threshold necessary for revising the proposal (18 votes out of 54 necessary). It is also noteworthy in that respect that the Committee of Regions, an institution tasked with the representation of the interests of regions and thus particularly well placed to consider subsidiarity issues, has adopted an opinion on 30 May 2013[50] coming out in favour of the Commission proposal and confirming its compliance with the principle of subsidiarity. Finally, a number of the specific elements of the proposal assessed further below[51] ensure not only its proportionality but also a broad margin for Member States to choose the appropriate strategy for enhancing gender balance on company boards which in turn contributes to compliance with the spirit of the subsidiarity principle.

C. LEGAL BASIS

The proposed Directive refers to Article 157(3) TFEU as its legal basis, conferring on the Union the power to adopt binding measures aimed at ensuring the application of the principle of equal opportunities and equal treatment of men and women in matters of employment and occupation.

Some have questioned whether Article 157(3) of the TFEU would be the appropriate legal basis for EU action because setting rules on the gender balance of members of company boards cannot be regarded as "matters of employment and occupation" within the meaning of Article 157(3) TFEU. Under national law, board members are usually not employees, as they do not have contracts governed by national labour law. They are either self-employed or assimilated to that status or have a "sui generis" status under national company law, but they do perform tasks for a company in exchange for remuneration.

It follows from both the existing EU gender equality legislation and the case law of the CJEU that the concepts of "employment and occupation" have a wide meaning and cover gender balance rules for non-executive members of company boards.

50 Http://toad.cor.europa.eu/corwipdetail.aspx?folderpath=ECOS-V/039&id=21915.
51 See point II.E. below.

So far, the legislator has also clearly considered Article 157(3) TFEU as a legal basis enabling the EU to take gender equality measures that go beyond employed work under labour law. For example, the EU gender equality acquis covers all professional activities, irrespective of the status of workers under national law[52], the "access" to these activities "at all levels of the professional hierarchy"[53] and all forms of entrepreneurial activity including the setting-up of a company.[54]

The CJEU has clarified that the *sui generis* nature of the employment relationship under national law is of no consequence as regards whether or not a person is a worker for the purposes of EU law.[55] Therefore, for the purposes of the proposed Directive, it does not matter how one becomes a board member and whether, under national law, the legal status of board members is of *sui generis* nature, as long as EU definition of worker is fulfilled. Furthermore, in *Danosa*[56] the CJEU has clarified that board members should be regarded as "workers" covered by EU law in case these board members, in return for remuneration, provide services to the company which has appointed them and of which they are an integral part, who carry out their activities under the direction or control of another body of that company and who can, at any time, be removed from their duties without such removal being subject to any restriction. Moreover, the Court goes further to suggest that, even where a board member would not fulfil the above-mentioned conditions to be considered a worker under EU law and on that account be protected against gender discrimination, this board member would should be categorised as "a self-employed person", equally protected against gender discrimination.

It can be concluded from both the existing EU gender equality acquis and the case law of the CJEU that company board members – irrespective of what their precise status as worker or non-worker is – are protected against discrimination by the existing *acquis* adopted on the basis of Article 157(3) TFEU. This confirms that the same legal basis should be available for legislative measures

52 Directive 2010/41/EU on the application of the principle of equal treatment between men and women engaged in an activity in a self-employed capacity OJ L 180 of 15.7.2010, p. 1 applies not only to self-employed workers, but also to their spouses habitually participating in the activities of the self-employed worker, i.e. persons not having any formal professional status in many Member States.

53 Directive 2006/54/EC on the implementation of the principle of equal opportunities and equal treatment of men and women in matters of employment and occupation OJ L 204 of 26.7.2006, p. 23.

54 Directive 2010/41/EU OJ L 180 of 15.7.2010, p. 1.

55 Judgment of the Court of 20 September 2007, *Sari Kiiski v Tampereen kaupunki*, ECR 2007 I-07643.

56 Judgment of the Court of 11 November 2010, *Dita Danosa v LKB Līzings SIA*, ECR 2010 I-11405.

specifically aiming at improving gender equality for the same category of professionals.

II. THE MAIN ELEMENTS OF THE COMMISSION PROPOSAL

This section describes the main elements of the Commission proposal. The core of the Commission proposal consists of the 40% objective rule (paragraph I), combined with a preference rule based on merit (paragraph II). Paragraph III focuses on transparency and reporting obligations and paragraph IV assesses the sanctions provision. Finally, paragraph V argues why the Commission proposal complies with the proportionality principle.

A. THE 40% OBJECTIVE FOR NON-EXECUTIVE BOARD MEMBERS

"Quotas" or targets imply preferential treatment in favour of certain categories of persons and can be seen as a model of positive action aiming to compensate for past discrimination.[57] Different regimes can be distinguished. A strict quota reserves a number of places for members of the underrepresented sex, thereby giving absolute preferences. The underrepresented sex should be sufficiently qualified, but not necessarily the best qualified for a particular job. Flexible quotas or result quotas aim to achieve a certain level or representation of both sexes in a relatively defined timeframe but allow for flexibility with respect to the appropriate measure to achieve the target. Soft quotas or aspirational targets leave a wide discretion to those responsible for their implementation both in terms of the specific measures and the timeframe and do not include serious penalties for failure. They are mostly used as an awareness-raising or self-improvement tool.

The proposed Directive sets a quantitative objective of at least 40% for the representation of the underrepresented sex among non-executive directors in boards of listed companies.[58] Listed companies should aim to attain the said percentage at the latest by 1 January 2020. A shorter deadline for achieving the objective (1 January 2018) is set for listed companies which are public

[57] See Communication from the Commission to the European Parliament and the Council on the interpretation of the judgment of the Court of Justice on 17 October 1995 in Case C-450/93 *Kalanke v Freie Hansestadt Bremen* COM(1996)88.

[58] See Article 4(1) of the proposed Directive.

undertakings.[59] Member States exercise a dominant influence over such companies and therefore have more instruments at their disposal to bring about change more rapidly.

Article 4 paragraph 2 of the Commission proposal specifies the method of calculation of the exact number of non-executive director positions necessary to meet the 40% objective. The exact number of board positions necessary to comply with the objective should be the number closest to 40%, whether below or above that threshold, but at the same time listed companies should not be obliged to appoint members of the under-represented sex to half or more of the non-executive board positions in order to avoid excessive constraints. In practice the average size of company boards varies between the Member States (within a range from 5 to 12 board members). In a board with five non-executive directors or supervisory board members at least two have to be women. The number of members of the underrepresented sex necessary to comply with the target is further specified for smaller boards in recital 24 of the proposal.

The level of the objective goes beyond the objective set in a number of Member States and is in line with the ambitious targets set in Norway and France. The objective lies well above the "critical mass" of roughly 30% and below strict parity (i.e. 50%). Several studies have identified the need to create a "critical mass" of women on individual company boards in order to break the glass ceiling and significantly affect company performance. Women are easily marginalised when their presence in a larger group is modest and due to their under-representation they are viewed as a token. Only if the size of the female group increases to the point that it is no longer a token minority, a fundamental and sustainable change in the boardroom can be brought about. As a result, a "critical mass" of women would enhance corporate governance, as women would no longer be seen as outsiders and would be able to influence the content and process of board discussion more substantially. These studies have concluded that the critical mass of women directors is reached when boards of directors have at least one third of women.

Instead of setting a 40% objective for non-executive board members, the Commission proposal also gives Member States the flexibility to set a one third (or 33%) objective covering the entire board including non-executive and

59 These are undertakings over which the public authorities may exercise directly or indirectly a dominant influence by virtue of their ownership thereof, their financial participation therein or the rules which govern it. See Article 2(b) of Commission Directive 2006/111/EC of 16 November 2006 on the transparency of financial relations between Member States and public undertakings as well as on financial transparency within certain undertakings, OJ L 318, 17.11.2006, p. 17.

executive directors,[60] which would still ensure a critical mass of the underrepresented sex but enlarge the scope of the objective.

The quantitative objective is defined in such a way that it respects the different board structures that exist at national level, i.e. a dual ("two-tier") system in which there are separate management and supervisory boards, a unitary ("one-tier") system combining the management and supervisory functions in one single board, as well as mixed systems featuring elements of "one-tier" and "two-tier" systems. Non-executive directors or – in the dual board system – the members of the supervisory board do not have management responsibility – unlike executive directors or members of the management board – but they do have important supervisory functions.

The Commission's impact assessment has confirmed that the proposed target and time-frame are realistic. It is much more generous than the deadlines imposed by national quota laws in place.[61] In most cases, the Commission proposal would require in practice at most 2 or 3 replacements on the boards per company. Companies will have up to 2020 to make those replacements. Most stakeholders actually consider 2020 as a generous deadline, as non-executive mandates usually change on an annual or biannual basis.[62] All the companies have the possibility to tap the sufficiently large existing talent pool in recruitment to their increasingly international boards. For example, in a database put together by the most renowned European business schools there are over 8,000 fully qualified women in the EU who are willing and available to take up non-executive board positions.[63]

The Commission proposal also imposes obligations on listed companies to increase the female share among executive or management board members. In those Member States that do not opt for a 33% objective for all (executive and non-executive) board members they will have to set individual quantitative targets regarding the representation of women and men for these positions that are to be achieved by 2020.[64]

It needs to be underscored that while the objectives set out in the proposal would be binding in that listed companies would be obliged to strive for compliance

---

60 See Article 4(7) of the proposed Directive.

61 E.g., Italy: 2015; France: 2017; Belgium: 2012–2019 depending on kind of company; the Netherlands: immediately, expires in 2016.

62 Individual mandates of current non-executive directors can change every year, in certain countries such as FR or UK those mandates last 2–3 years.

63 See http://ec.europa.eu/justice/gender-equality/gender-decision-making/database/index_en.htm.

64 See Article 5(1) of the proposed Directive.

with them they would not constitute rigid quota obligations with the effect of sanctions being triggered by the mere fact of a company not reaching the objective by the deadline. Rather, the proposal combines the existence of the target with a preference rule and transparency obligations in such a way that only the latter two components are enforceable through sanctions in the event of non-compliance. The following sections explain this mechanism in more detail.

B. THE PREFERENCE RULE

The proposed Directive does not contain an "absolute and unconditional" quota, it is a quantified "flexible result quota", which takes into account the relevant case law of the CJEU on positive action in general and on quota measures in particular.

The CJEU dealt with the issue of positive action in form of quotas on different occasions.[65] In the *Kalanke* case, the CJEU held that national rules which guarantee women absolute and unconditional priority for appointment or promotion go beyond promoting equal opportunities and overstep the limits of the positive action exception enshrined in Article 2(4) of Directive 76/207 (Equal Treatment). The Commission clarified its position on this ruling by stating that the only type of quota system which is, according to this Court ruling, unlawful is one which is completely rigid and does not leave any possibility of taking account of individual circumstances. Member States and employers are thus free to have recourse to all other forms of positive action, including flexible quotas.

In the *Marschall* case, the CJEU argued that the system of preferential treatment may be used "if such a rule may counteract the prejudicial effects on female candidates" of prejudices and stereotypes "concerning the role and capacities of women in working life". The Court explicitly found that "the mere fact that a male candidate and a female candidate are equally qualified does not mean that they have the same chances" due to employers' rational or irrational fears that "women will interrupt their careers more frequently, that owing to household and family duties they will be less flexible in their working hours, or that they

---

65 Case 312/86 *Commission v France* [1988] ECR 6315; C-450/93 *Eckhard Kalanke v Freie Hansestadt Bremen* ECR [1995] I-03051; C-409/95 *Hellmut Marschall v Land Nordrhein-Westfalen* ECR [1997] I-06363; C-158/97 *Georg Badeck and Others* ECR [2000] I-01875; C-79/99 *Julia Schnorbus v Land Hessen* [2000] ECR I-10997; C-407/98 *Katarina Abrahamsson and Leif Anderson v Elisabet Fogelqvist* ECR [2000] I-05539; Joseph *Griesmar v Ministre de l'Economie, des Finances et de l'Industrie et Ministre de la Fonction publique, de la Réforme de l'Etat et de la Décentralisation* [2001] ECR I-09383; C-476/99 *H. Lommers v Minister van Landbouw, Natuurbeheer en Visserij* ECR [2002] I-02891; C-319/03 *Serge Briheche v Ministre de l'Intérieur, Ministre de l'Éducation nationale and Ministre de la Justice* [2004] ECR I-08807.

will be absent from work more frequently because of pregnancy, childbirth and breastfeeding". Since these prejudices and stereotypes often remain well concealed during a decision-making process and cannot be easily proven, preferential treatment may be needed to "reduce actual instances of inequality which may exist in the real world". According to the Court, the system of sex-based preferences at issue did not entail an absolute and unconditional priority for women in promotion as considered inadmissible in *Kalanke* because it contained a so-called saving clause which in each individual case, provided for male candidates who are equally qualified as the female candidates a guarantee that the candidatures will be the subject of an objective assessment "which will take account of all criteria specific to the individual candidates and will override the priority accorded to female candidates where one or more of those criteria tilts the balance in favour of the male candidate". With such a saving clause the system was thus found in conformity with EU law.

In *Badeck* the Court further developed and consolidated its case law and accepted a rule imposing binding quantified targets for women, and giving priority in the selection procedure to women under the following conditions: (1) in the given sector women are under-represented, (2) the preference rule applies only where male and female candidates have equal qualifications, (3) the priority proves necessary for ensuring compliance with the objectives of the women's advancement plan containing the targets in question, (4) no reasons of greater legal weight are opposed, and (5) the rule guarantees that candidatures are the subject of an objective assessment which takes account of the specific personal situations of all candidates.

The Commission proposes a model very similar to that accepted by the Court in the *Badeck* judgment: a binding target for the composition of the board as a whole is accompanied by the preference rule for under-represented sex in selection procedures for individual positions on the board, which applies only in case of equal qualifications and allows for individual assessment of every candidate. As a result of the assessment the balance may be tipped in favour of a male candidate if there are specific reasons for that.[66]

It should be underlined that companies will be able to continue to give vacant board positions to the best-qualified candidates, irrespective of their sex. Only in case of equal qualifications in terms of suitability, competence and professional performance, the proposal requires companies to give preference to the candidates of the under-represented sex. However, even this preference rule established by the proposed Directive is not absolute. Where the candidate of the underrepresented sex is equally qualified, the company can still appoint the

66 See Article 4(3) of the proposed Directive.

candidate of the other sex if there are reasons sufficiently important to override the preference granted to the better qualified candidate of the underrepresented sex although it is clear that in such situations the preference of the candidate of the underrepresented sex should be the rule and the use of the saving clause should only occur in exceptional cases. The proposal requires companies wanting to use this flexibility to show that "an objective assessment taking into account all criteria specific to the individual candidates tilts the balance in favour of the other candidate".

C. TRANSPARENCY AND REPORTING OBLIGATIONS

The 40% objective and the preference rule are inextricably linked to important transparency obligations for companies covered by these rules that complete the innovative combination of elements characterizing the design of the positive action measure in this proposal.

Indeed, the proposed Directive requires listed companies that stay below a level of representation of 40% of members of the underrepresented sex to ensure that the selection procedures they use will be transparent thus giving candidates for board positions of the underrepresented sex a fair chance to get the job. This obligation will directly address one of the drivers of the problem of female underrepresentation in company boards, namely the opaque way that appointment decisions are made by the main shareholders in backroom deals drawing on predominantly male business networks. The proposal requires that those companies make their selection procedures more transparent by (i) establishing clear and gender-neutral selection criteria for non-executive board members from the outside (ii) applying those selection criteria in a transparent manner to assess the candidates and (ii) making the appointments to non-executive board positions on the basis of an objective comparative assessment of the qualifications of each candidate. These rules are intended to move companies to broaden their view and, on the basis of the objective selection criteria freely established by themselves, to look for highly qualified candidates of the underrepresented sex outside the usual circles.

The proposal contains a number of other complementary features which would facilitate the enforcement of the procedural obligations of the Directive, specifically the preference rule, and contribute to greater transparency in the sense of public accountability thus providing further incentives to comply with the 40% objective.

First of all, the Commission proposal includes a general rule on the shift of the burden of proof provision in case it is suspected that the preference rule has not been applied by a company.[67] This provision ensures that that where an unsuccessful candidate of the under-represented sex establishes facts from which it may be presumed that that candidate was equally qualified as the appointed candidate of the other sex, it shall be for the listed company to prove that there has been no breach of the preference rule.

The burden of proof provision as proposed is a standard provision which is included also in the existing EU gender equality and anti-discrimination legislation. This mechanism makes it possible to alleviate, though not remove, that burden on the victim. It consists of two stages. First of all, the victim must sufficiently establish the facts from which it may be presumed that there has been discrimination or in this case of a positive action measure a non-application of the preferential treatment rule that would normally have to be observed. Next, if that presumption is established, the burden of proof thereafter lies with the defendant. This balanced system enables a claimant to more easily enforce the right to equal treatment but prevents proceedings from being brought against the defendant with prospects for success solely on the basis of the claimant's assertions.

In addition to this general burden of proof provision, the Commission proposal comprises a complementary disclosure provision in view of the fact that in practice the information that could substantiate claims of a breach of the preference rule is available only to the company. This provision would oblige companies on the request of an unsuccessful candidate, to disclose the qualification criteria upon which the selection was based, the objective comparative assessment of those criteria and, where relevant, the considerations tilting the balance in favour of a candidate of the other sex.[68]

This additional disclosure obligation implies a right to information held by the person "suspected" of discrimination and would be a novelty compared to the existing gender equality and anti-discrimination legislation.[69] The provision would generally not oblige companies to disclose any personal documents or

---

67 Article 4(5) of the proposal.

68 See Article 4(4) of the proposed Directive.

69 In fact, the Commission tabled a proposal intended to establish a right to information for victims of discrimination in 1988 (see Article 4(b) of the Proposal for a Council Directive on the burden of proof in the area of equal pay and equal treatment for women and men (COM(88) 269 final) submitted by the Commission on 27 May 1988 (OJ 1988 C 176, p. 5). That proposal was withdrawn by the Commission in 1998 (OJ 1998 C 40, p. 7). The final texts of the existing gender equality and anti-discrimination legislation do not contain such a right. According to AG Mengozzi in his opinion of 12 January 2012 in Case C-415/10 *Galina Meister vs Speech Design Carrier Systems GmbH*, the absence of an express reference to a right to information in the existing acquis must be interpreted, not as an oversight on the part of the legislature but, on the contrary, as the manifestation of its intention not to affirm such a right.

data of candidates to the extent that the information can be disclosed in a neutral way, not giving away any personal information of the other candidates. If, nevertheless, there was a limited restriction on the right to respect for private life with regard to the processing of personal data as recognised by Articles 7 and 8 of the Charter of Fundamental Rights, in view of the equal treatment interests at stake which are also recognized as having the status of fundamental rights and fundamental objectives of the EU this would be necessary and in conformity with the principle of proportionality.[70]

The proposed Directive imposes reporting and publication mechanisms to ensure compliance with its objectives and obligations.

As from two years after adoption of the proposed Directive, listed companies will have to report annually to national authorities on the gender representation on their boards, distinguishing between non-executive and executive directors and on the measures taken in view of the 40% rule for non-executive board members and their own individual targets for executive directors. Companies are required to publish that information in an appropriate and accessible manner on their website.[71] This reporting obligation, which will not impose unnecessary administrative burdens on companies, would be an important tool for interested third parties to verify compliance and monitor progress of individual companies in achieving the objectives of the Commission proposal.

Where the 40% rule for the non-executive board members or the individual targets for executive board members have not been reached yet, these reports shall include the reasons for not reaching the objectives or commitments and a description of the measures which the company has adopted or intends to adopt in order to meet the objectives or commitments in the future. These reporting obligations and the accessibility of the reports to the general public should provide an additional strong incentive to attain the objectives as soon as possible.

D. SANCTIONS

The experience with measures existing at national level (especially in Norway, France) shows that the most significant and quickest progress is achieved only by binding measures that are equipped with sanctions. Even legally binding targets that are not accompanied by sanctions (as in the case in some Member States, e.g. in Spain) *de facto* turn into rather aspirational objectives and do not produce

70 Judgment of the Court of 9 November 2010, *Volker und Markus Schecke GbR* (C-92/09) and *Hartmut Eifert* (C-93/09) *v Land Hessen*, ECR 2010 I-11063.

71 See Article 5(2) of the proposed Directive.

the desired results. This is why Article 6(1) of the proposed Directive obliges Member States to provide for sanctions which should be applied in case of infringements of national provisions transposing the Directive. Member States should not only provide for sanctions, they should also ensure that they are applied in practice.

Under the proposed Directive, the mere fact that a listed company does not reach a gender balance of non-executive directors of 40% of members of the underrepresented sex by the stipulated deadline will not automatically lead to sanctions per se, as long as this company complies with the other obligations imposed by the proposed Directive. This is because the 40% rule is not a self-standing result obligation, but an obligation of means, linked with the preference rule and the other procedural obligations. Sanctions should therefore only be imposed on those listed companies that do not have a gender balance of 40% and that do not comply with the obligations under the proposed Directive, notably the requirements for selection procedures including the preference rule for equally qualified members of the under-represented sex, the setting of individual targets for executive directors and reporting.

Member States are required to adopt measures that are sufficiently effective to achieve the objective of the proposed Directive and it is specified, in line with the sanctions provisions in the existing gender equality legislation,[72] that sanctions must be "effective, proportionate and dissuasive". Member States have – in line with the subsidiarity principle – a margin within the limits of this general standards to decide which sanctions regime would be most appropriate in the context of the national legal system.

At the same time, some guidance on how these requirements should be interpreted can be derived from existing case law. In order to guarantee real and effective protection for individuals' EU rights, the CJEU has clarified that sanctions for breaches of such rights must: (a) not render impossible or excessively difficult the exercise of rights conferred; and (b) ensure real equality of opportunity through adequate reparation for the loss and damage sustained.[73]

72 See Article 8(d) of Directive 2002/73/EC amending Council Directive 76/207/EEC on the implementation of the principle of equal treatment for men and women as regards access to employment, vocational training and promotion and working conditions, OJ L 269/15 of 5.10.2002; Article 8(2) of Directive 2004/113/EC implementing the principle of equal treatment between men and women in the access to and supply of goods and services, OJ l 373/37 of 21.12.2004; and Article 25 of Directive 2006/54/EC on the implementation of the principle of equal treatment for men and women in matters of employment and occupation (recast).

73 Judgment of the Court of 14 December 1995, *Jeroen van Schijndel and Johannes Nicolaas Cornelis van Veen v Stichting Pensioenfonds voor Fysiotherapeuten*, Joined cases C-430/93 and C-431/93 ECR 1995 I-04705.

In *von Colson and Kamann*, the CJEU gave some concrete examples of what the concept sufficiently effective measures could mean in a situation of discriminatory refusal of employment, namely "provisions requiring the employer to offer a post to the candidate discriminated against or giving the candidate adequate financial compensation, backed up where necessary by a system of fines.[74]

The remedies must have a real and deterrent effect on the employer (dissuasiveness). Dissuasiveness is closely linked to effectiveness; for example, if an employer knows that an employee will have to be compensated in full for any discriminatory acts they commit, they will consider avoiding such acts more carefully. The CJEU defined the principle of deterrence in *von Colson and Kamann* as: "for the employer a means of pressure which it would be unwise to disregard and which would prompt him to respect the principle of equal treatment".[75] In *Marshall II* the CJEU clarified that in case of discriminatory dismissal, the Member States' choice in determining the appropriate sanction is limited to either reinstatement or financial compensation.[76] Where compensation is chosen as the appropriate sanction, it may not be restricted by fixing a prior upper limit, unless the employer can prove that the only damage suffered by an applicant as a result from discrimination is the refusal to take his/her job application into consideration.[77] If compensation is chosen, it must in any event be adequate in relation to the damage sustained (proportionality). In addition, the principle of equivalence requires that measures giving effect to EU rights must be no less favourable that those applicable to equivalent national rights.[78] These same requirements developed in the area of employment law would have to be observed by Member States in view of the somewhat different context of company law and bearing in mind that the obligation in question, the breach of which would be sanctioned, is not to attain the objective of balanced gender representation but to take the procedural measures aimed to achieve this goal.

Article 6(2) of the proposed Directive mentions two examples of possible national sanctions that would meet the criteria of effectiveness, proportionality and dissuasiveness, namely administrative fines and the nullity and annulment

---

74 Judgment of the Court of 10 April 1984, *Sabine von Colson and Elisabeth Kamann v Land Nordrhein-Westfalen*, Case 14/83 1984 0189, paragraph 18.

75 Judgment of the Court of 10 April 1984, *Sabine von Colson and Elisabeth Kamann v Land Nordrhein-Westfalen*, Case 14/83 1984 0189,.

76 Judgment of the Court of 2 August 1993 *M. Helen Marshall v Southampton and South-West Hampshire Area Health Authority* Case C-271/91 ECR 1993 Page I-04367, paragraph 25.

77 Judgment of the Court of 22 April 1997 *Nils Draehmpaehl v Urania Immobilienservice OHG* Case C-180/95 ECR 1997 I-02195, codified in Article 18 of Directive 2006/54/EC (recast).

78 Judgment of the Court of 1 December 1998 *B.S. Levez v T.H. Jennings (Harlow Pools) Ltd* Case C-326/96 ECR 1998 I-07835.

of the appointment or of the election of non-executive directors. These concrete sanctions are only illustrative examples, not legally binding for Member States. They are inspired by the laws of those Member States which have introduced binding targets in their legislation.

E. PROPORTIONATE INTERVENTION

The principle of proportionality regulates the exercise of powers by the EU. It seeks to set actions taken by the institutions of the Union within specified bounds. Under this rule, the involvement of the institutions must be limited to what is necessary to achieve the objectives of the Treaties. In other words, the content and form of the action must be in keeping with the aim pursued.[79] The Commission proposal contains various elements which ensure that the EU intervention does not go beyond what is necessary to achieve the objective of improving gender balance in the highest decision-making bodies of listed companies throughout the EU.

First of all the proposal is limited to setting common objectives, leaving Member States sufficient freedom to determine how they should best be achieved at national level, taking into account national, regional or local circumstances including national company law and company board recruitment practices. Member States which have been or want to be more ambitous can go beyond the minimum requirements of the proposed Directive at national level.

The proposal does not disproportionately interfere with national company law. It introduces only such changes to national company law that are strictly necessary for the transparency of the selection and appointment process (which in turn is a less invasive measure than an obligation concerning the outcome of that process) and it respects the different board structures across Member States. The proposed Directive does not oblige shareholders to make any particular appointment decisions. They maintain their role, functions and freedom to appoint the board members. As explained above, the proposed Directive aims only to ensure that female candidates are given a fair opportunity to be appointed to the board, in order to attain the 40% objective for non-executive directors, by putting in place more transparent appointment procedures strictly based on qualification criteria defined by the companies themselves and applying a preference rule for equally qualified candidates of the under-represented sex.

The right of shareholders to elect board members is an emanation of the right to property and the freedom to conduct a business. These are fundamental rights

79 See Article 5 of the Treaty on the European Union and Protocol 2 annexed to the Treaties.

but they are not absolute. The Constitutions of Member States and the Charter of Fundamental Rights allow the regulation and the restriction of the right to property in the public interest under certain conditions (e.g. proportionality). Such restrictions already exist both at EU level and at the national level in relation to the election of board members. For example, the EU acquis requires at least one non-executive board member to have specific experience in auditing and accounting. National law stipulates in many Member States that a certain share of non-executive board members have to be employee representatives (in Germany employee representatives make up 50% of the supervisory board members). The obligation to appoint board members who are not chosen by the shareholders at all and who represent employees' instead of shareholders' interests is a much bigger interference with shareholders' rights than a gender objective that leaves shareholders full discretion in choosing board members subject to the condition of a balanced gender composition.

As regards its scope of application, the proposed Directive is limited to publicly listed companies only which are usually the largest and most visible. It does not cover small and medium-sized enterprises (SMEs)[80], for which such measures could represent a disproportionate burden. In addition, as explained above, the proposal establishes quantitative objectives only for non-executive board members, thereby considerably limiting interference in the day-to-day management of the company. As non-executive directors perform mainly supervisory tasks, it is also easier to recruit qualified candidates from outside the company or the specific sector – a consideration which is of importance in particular for areas of the economy where members of a particular sex are especially under-represented in the workforce. However, since the proposed Directive establishes minimum standards, nothing prevents Member States from extending the 40% rule also to executive directors, for which the Commission proposal obliges listed companies in any case to establish their own quantified objectives (unless Member States make use of the option to set an overall 33% objective for all board members).

The proposal also gives Member States the option of exempting companies in which less than 10% of the workforce is of one sex from the requirements set in the proposed Directive. In these companies it may be particularly difficult to find board candidates of the underrepresented sex from within the company.

---

80 SME means a company which employs less than 250 persons and has an annual turnover not exceeding EUR 50 million or an annual balance sheet total not exceeding EUR 43 million, or, for an SME which is incorporated in a Member State whose currency is not the euro, the equivalent amounts in the currency of that Member State, by Commission Recommendation 2003/361/EC of 6 May 2003 concerning the definition of micro, small and medium-sized enterprises, OJ L 124, 20.05.2003, p. 36.

This has a particular importance in relation to companies in which employees are elected to company boards.

The most innovative element of proportionate intervention and also of subsidiarity in the proposed Directive is what is called the "equivalent efficacy" clause.[81] Some Member States have already taken ambitious legislative or non-legislative measures to ensure a more balanced representation of men and women on company boards. Those Member States will not be obliged to replace or adapt those measures. The proposed Directive gives them (or any Member State that will still adopt such measures until the entry into force of the Directive) the possibility of suspending the procedural obligations of the proposed Directive, if they can show that the national measures which are already in place will be equally effective as the Directive's approach in reaching the objective of a 40% share of non-executive board members of the underrepresented sex by 2020. They will have to communicate to the Commission the measures they have taken and the explanation as to how they will achieve the 40% objective. The Commission will assess these alternative measures and report on them in 2017. In any case, the suspension of procedural obligations in relation to the appointments is only temporary: for the Member States that make use of it and do not achieve the 40% objective all the obligations under the Directive would kick in in 2020.[82]

Finally, the Commission proposes only a temporary EU intervention to the extent which is necessary to ensure that participation of female board members in publicly listed companies across the EU attains a sufficiently high level and has a lasting effect in changing business culture and recruitment patterns. This regime needs to stay in place and should stay in place only until a stage is reached where its withdrawal would not lead to a reconstruction of the glass ceiling and the economic and societal benefits of gender balance on company boards can be reaped in a sustainable way without further regulatory intervention. The proposal therefore contains a sunset clause, on the basis of which the proposal Directive will be automatically repealed on 31 December 2028.[83] It is expected that by that time sustainable progress in gender composition of boards throughout the whole EU will have been achieved. In the reports on the application of the proposed Directive every two years as from 2021, the Commission will assess whether the progress made is sufficiently sustainable or whether there is a need to propose an extension of the duration of the Directive.[84]

---

81 See Article 8(3) of the proposed Directive.
82 See Article 9(2) of the proposed Directive.
83 See Article 10(2) of the proposed Directive.
84 See Article 9(4) of the proposed Directive.

III. CONCLUSIONS

The causes for the under-representation of women in business leadership are multiple and call for a comprehensive approach to tackle the problem. They stem from traditional gender roles and stereotypes, the lack of support for women and men to balance care responsibilities with work and the lack of transparency in recruitment and promotion practices to name just a few.

The Commission proposal to improve the gender balance on company boards is a logical next step in line with the long-standing commitment and approach of the EU to promote gender equality. Throughout its history, the EU has contributed to progress towards gender equality through a multitude of measures combining legislation with dedicated funding and action programmes, specific measures for the advancement of women, social dialogue and dialogue with civil society and by promoting gender equality in all the EU's activities.

Experience across Europe has shown that measures fighting the roots of under-representation of women at the highest level of decision-making alone do not lead to change within an acceptable time-frame. The ever-growing number of highly qualified women who overcome all the reconciliation obstacles still do not make it to top management levels. Work on further improving the conditions for women to approach the glass ceiling is certainly indispensable but will not remove the glass ceiling in and of itself. The Commission proposal is a targeted binding yet proportionate and balanced measure that will help break through the glass ceiling which currently prevents women from advancing in their careers. It will force companies to be more transparent in their selection and appointment procedures, providing women with a fair opportunity of making their careers just like men.

However, this initiative will not be the "silver bullet" providing solutions to all the problems of gender equality in the economic sphere. Therefore, the Commission has complemented the proposed legislative measure with a Communication outlining policy measures to fight the roots of gender imbalance, to overcome gender stereotypes and to improve working conditions that promote women's advancement in management.[85]

It is now up to the European Parliament and the Member States in the Council to turn this Commission proposal into a reality, which would be a significant leap forward in 50 years of EU gender equality policy making.

---

85 Communication from the Commission – Gender balance in business leadership: a contribution to smart, sustainable and inclusive growth, COM(2012) 615 final of 14.11.2012.

CHAPTER 4

THE LAW OF 28 JULY 2011 TO GUARANTEE THE PRESENCE OF WOMEN ON THE DECISION-MAKING BODIES OF AUTONOMOUS PUBLIC UNDERTAKINGS, LISTED COMPANIES AND THE NATIONAL LOTTERY*

Philippe LAMBRECHT**

I. INTRODUCTION

1. Adopted by the House of Representatives on 1 June 2011 and by the Senate on 30 June 2011, the law of 28 July 2011 was published in the Belgian *Official Journal* on 14 September 2011. Its objective is to guarantee the presence of women on the decision-making bodies of autonomous public undertakings, listed companies and the National Lottery.

2. After having examined the preparatory work for the law (*below* Chapter I), we will describe the new provisions, which are binding, on autonomous public undertakings, listed companies and the National Lottery (*below* Chapter II).

II. PREPARATORY WORK

A. INITIAL PROPOSAL

3. The law of 28 July 2011 is intended to guarantee the presence of women on the boards of directors of certain autonomous public undertakings and listed

* This Chapter is a translation of an article published in French by the author in Y. De Cordt (dir.), *Actes du colloque du 27 octobre 2011 – Droit des Sociétés – Crides Jean Renauld*, Brussels, Larcier, 2011, 161–190.

** Professor at UCL, Director-Secretary General of the FEB.

companies. For the authors of the various legislative proposals[1] which led to the adoption of the law, it was necessary to remedy the under-representation of women on the boards of directors of certain autonomous public undertakings and listed companies. A political cleavage was apparent from the outset.

4. On the one side, five parties tabled draft bills with a view to imposing legal quotas. The five parties were the PS, sp.a, cdH, Ecolo-Groen! and CD&V.

5. The other parties were more in favour of a corporate governance approach, emphasising that the law of 6 April 2010[2] had made it mandatory for listed companies to publish an annual corporate governance declaration[3] and that the Belgian Code of Corporate Governance, recognised by the government as the Belgian benchmark code[4], was intended to promote diversity in the composition of boards of directors in accordance with Article 2.1 of the 2009 Belgian Code of Corporate Governance. These provisions provide that the composition of the board of directors should be "*based on gender diversity, and diversity in general, as well as the complementarity of competences, experience and knowledge*".

6. A broad parliamentary discussion ensued, which involved hearing numerous experts, including three foreign experts, Mrs Sybilla M. Dekker from Stichting Talent naar de Top, Mrs Mari Teigen from the Oslo-based Institute for Social Research and Mrs Marike Stelinga from the weekly journal *Elsevier*.[5]

---

1 Draft bill amending the law of 21 March 1991 reforming certain economic public undertakings and the Code of Company Law in order to guarantee the presence of women on the decision-making bodies of autonomous public undertakings and listed companies, House of Representatives, 24 September 2010, Doc. 53-0211/001 to 003; draft bill amending the Code of Company Law as regards increasing the number of women on the boards of directors of listed companies, House of Representatives, 13 October 2010, Doc. 53-0381/001; draft bill to promote balanced gender representation on the boards of directors of economic public undertakings and companies whose shares are listed on a stock exchange, House of Representatives, 25 November 2010, Doc. 53-0694/001; draft bill amending the Code of Company Law and the law of 21 March 1991 reforming certain economic public undertakings, House of Representatives, 19 November 2010, Doc. 53-0649/001; draft bill amending the Code of Company Law and the law of 21 March 1991 reforming certain economic public undertakings, House of Representatives, 24 November 2010, Doc. 53-0686/001. For an overview of these draft bills see the report produced, on behalf of the Committee with responsibility for commercial and economic problems, by Mrs Marie-Christine Marghem and Mr Karel Uyttersprot, Doc. 53-0211/004, pages 3 to 13, hereinafter the "Marghem - Uyttersprot Report".

2 Law of 6 April 2010 to strengthen corporate governance in listed companies and autonomous public. undertakings and to amend the system of professional disqualification in the banking and financial sector.

3 Aforementioned Article 3, L. 6 April 2010 introducing a new Article 96, §2 in the Code of Company Law.

4 R.D. of 6 June 2010 designating the Code of Corporate Governance to be respected by listed companies.

5 Marghem - Uyttersprot report, pages 4 and 5 and pages 17 to 91.

7. On 11 January 2011, the Corporate Governance Committee recommended to listed companies that they should transform their boards of directors over a 7-year period in order to achieve a level of representation of at least 30% of directors of each gender, ensuring that:

- *"when new directors are appointed, and until the 30% of representation of each gender has been achieved, it is appropriate to propose – at least – that half of the new directors appointed per progressive period of 3 years, should be women;*
- *the accession of women to boards of directors should be divided insofar as possible between all types of directors;*
- *the increased participation of women should not result in an undue increase in the size of boards of directors;*
- *the board of directors should explain in its management report the measures adopted in order to improve the representation of women;*
- *the board of directors should promote the exercising of the duties of director in all its subsidiaries and external companies by all management members and in particular female members".*[6]

8. The House's Committee with responsibility for commercial and economic problems adopted, on 15 March 2011, a compromise proposed by the parties in favour of the introduction of legal quotas.[7]

B. OPINION OF THE COUNCIL OF STATE

9. At its plenary session of 31 March, the House of Representatives sought the opinion of the Council of State on the proposed compromise. This opinion was rendered on 26 April 2011.[8] It began by describing the object and scope of the draft bill, before developing general and specific observations.

In its general observations, the Council of State distinguished between, on the one hand, the National Lottery and economic public undertakings governed by the law of 21 March 1991 reforming certain economic public undertakings, namely Infrabel, SNCB, bpost and Belgocontrol, and, on the other hand, "public limited companies whose shares are admitted to trading on a regulated market referred to in Article 4 of the Code of Company Law".[9]

---

6 For the full text of the *Corporate Governance Committee's report*, see: www.corporategovernancecommittee.be, heading 2009 Code – Gender diversity.

7 Draft bill amending the law of 21 March 1991 reforming certain economic public undertakings, the Code of Company Law and the law of 19 April 2002 on the streamlining of the operation and management of the National Lottery in order to guarantee the presence of women on the board of directors of autonomous public undertakings, listed companies and the national Lottery, House of Representatives, 24 March 2011, Doc. 53–0211/005.

8 Opinion of the Council of State, 26 April 2011, no. 49.473/AG, Doc. 53–0211/07.

9 Opinion of the Council of State, no. 49.473/AG, *op. cit.*, p. 3.

10. *For the first category,* the Council of State noted that the imposition of a quota *"satisfies the definition of a 'positive action' specified in several national laws, namely that it is a specific measure intended to prevent or compensate for disadvantages linked to gender, with a view to guaranteeing complete equality in practice"*.[10]

Therefore, the proposed system needs to be assessed in the light of the conditions specified by *"the Constitutional Court regarding the compatibility of a "positive action measure" with the principle of equality and non-discrimination"* in its ruling of 12 February 2009. After having specified these conditions[11], the Council of State verified compliance with them in the case in point.

It finds that the three conditions stipulated by the Constitutional Court exist: (1) an obvious inequality (2) whose elimination is the objective to be promoted and (3) a temporary measure).

11. On the other hand, it expressed reservations regarding the fourth condition relative to the absence of unnecessary restrictions on the rights of others.

Obviously, *"(...) the federal legislator intends to limit the public authority's exclusive power of appointment, which in itself does not seem to be open to criticism"*.[12] *"However, even when considered as a limitation that the public authority imposes on itself, the validity of the quota rule must, in terms of proportionality, be assessed in national law with regard to articles 10 and 11 of the Constitution as well as with regard to international and European law, by taking account in particular of case law handed down by the Court of Justice of the European Union."*[13]

However, as the Council of State states in point no. 13 of its opinion: *"The requirement imposed as such to comply with a quota of women or men in the composition of the board of directors of an economic public enterprise or of the*

---

10 Opinion of the Council of State, no. 49.473/AG, *op. cit.*, p. 6, point 6.

11 Constitutional Court, ruling 17/2009, 12 February 2009, grounds B.22.2. and B.23.1 and 2, www.const-court.be
Ground B.22.2. "A positive action measure may only be taken if it satisfies the following conditions:
(1) there must be an obvious inequality;
(2) the elimination of this inequality must be designated as an objective to be promoted;
(3) the positive action measure must be temporary, with the intention that it should be annulled once the objective has been achieved;
(4) the positive action measure must not unnecessarily restrict the rights of others (article 10, §2, of the anti-racism law, article 10, §2, of the general anti-discrimination law and article 16, §2, of the "gender" law)."

12 Opinion of the Council of State, *op. cit.*, p. 8, no 12. However, this did not prevent the Council of State from specifying that "even when considered as a limitation that the public authority imposes on itself, the validity of the quota rule must, in terms of proportionality, be assessed in national law with regard to articles 10 and 11 of the Constitution as well as with regard to international and European law, by taking account into particular of case law handed down by the Court of Justice of the European Union".

13 Opinion of the Council of State, *op. cit.*, pages 8 and 9, no. 12.

National Lottery does not appear in itself to be likely to restrict unnecessarily the rights of others, provided however that:

- *it allows a comparison of the qualifications and merits of candidates of a different gender*[14]*;*
- *it only requires a person of a given gender to be selected if such person's qualifications and merits are comparable to those of one or more other candidates of the opposite gender with whom such individual is in competition and who are, like him or her, considered suitable for the position to be filled.*"

"*The quota rule cannot exempt the public appointing authority from comparing qualifications and merits and its compliance with this obligation must be noted in the justification of its appointment decision.*"

For the Council of State, "*(...) this does not necessarily appear to be the case in the system introduced by the draft bill, which, by fixing an absolute quota to be respected unconditionally, could lead to the appointing authority being forced to choose a person of a given gender solely on the grounds of gender, that is to say regardless of the person's qualifications and merits*".

12. The Council of State continued its examination by reviewing the criteria of validity recognised in the case law of the Court of Justice of the European Union regarding positive actions taken in the public sector to promote a gender balance in the field of employment. It discussed the draft bill's compliance with these criteria.

Referring to grounds 18, 22 and 23 of the Badek ruling of 28 March 2000[15], as well as several earlier rulings[16] and the substantial doctrine[17], it noted that "*the application of this case law to the requirement, without the possibility to derogate from it, to comply with a quota of a third of women to men on a board of directors in the case of both an economic public undertaking and the National Lottery may conflict with the principles of the admissibility of a positive action in favour of*

---

14 Opinion of the Council of State, *op. cit.*, p. 9, no. 13.

15 In a footnote on page17, the opinion of the Council of State refers to: "CJEU, 28 March 2000, no C-158/97, Badeck *et al.*, CJEU case law, 2000, I, p.1875, opinion of A. Saggio".

16 In a footnote on page 18, the opinion of the Council of State refers to: "CJEU, 17 October 1995, no C-450/93, Kalanke/Freie Hansestadt Bremen, CJEU case law, 1995, I, p. 3051, ground 23, opinion of G. Tesauro; CJEU, 11 November 1997, no C-409/95, Marschall/Land Nordrhein-Westfalen, Case law CJEU, 1997, I, p. 6363, ground 33, opinion of F. Jacobs and CJEU 6 July 2000, no C-407/98, Abrahamsson, CJEU case law, 2000, I p. 5539, ground 20".

17 In a footnote on page 19, the opinion of the Council of State refers to: "D. Cuypers and C. Van Vyve, *De criteria voor positieve actie in de rechtspraak van de hoogste rechtscolleges*, in C. Bayart, S. Sottiaux, S. Van Drooghenbroeck (eds.), *Actualités du droit de la lutte contre la discrimination*, Bruges, Die Keure, 2010, p. 272; M. De Vos, *Positieve actie en discriminatie in het Europese en Belgische discriminatierecht*, in C. Bayart, S. Sottiaux and S. Van Drooghenbroeck (eds.), *De nieuwe federale antidiscriminatiewetten*, Bruges, Die Keure, 2008, p. 316."

persons of a given gender as determined by the CJEU (...). Compliance with such a quota may lead, in certain circumstances, to the selection of a director of the required gender for the sole reason that the quota has not been reached. This choice will therefore be made regardless of an objective assessment of the specific, personal situation of all the candidates, as priority has to be given, pursuant to the law, to this candidate even if he or she is under-qualified in comparison with the other candidates because they are of a different gender (...)".[18]

Finally, it suggests that "*to ensure that the implementation of (the) objective (of promoting a better gender balance on the decision-making bodies of economic public undertakings and the National Lottery complies with higher legal norms, it would be advisable to adapt the system specified in the draft bill by accompanying the quota, for example, by an opening clause.*[19] *This seems to be all the more advisable given that the proposed sanction for non-compliance with the quota is the nullity of the appointment of a director appointed in disregard of the quota rule*".[20]

13. *For the second category, that is to say listed companies*, the objections raised by the Council of State are more significant. It considers that the "*quota rule gives rise, having regard to the freedom of association guaranteed in particular by article 27 of the Constitution, to major reservations relating to the very operating philosophy of public limited companies as it is understood today, which translates this freedom into the Code of Company Law*".[21]

In its analysis, the Council of State begins by explaining the well-established rules of the organisation of powers within a public limited company, and in particular the rule whereby members of the board of directors are appointed by the general meeting and can be dismissed ad nutum by it. The general meeting is sovereign when it comes to appointing and dismissing directors, which is "*simply the implementation of the freedom of association guaranteed by article 27 of the*

18 Opinion of the Council of State, *op. cit.*, p. 10, no. 15.

19 In a footnote on p. 21 of its aforementioned opinion, the Council of State specifies that: "*Moreover, in this way, the text will respond more adequately to the observations made, at the time of the preparatory work, regarding the scope of the draft bill. In response to the question of what is to be understood by the equivalence of the persons concerned as one of the criteria of compatibility of a positive action with regard to European law, the representative of the Deputy Prime Minister and Minister for Employment and Equal Opportunities has explained that we must avoid lowering the bar for certain persons, by requiring them to be less qualified. It must be assumed that all people are equal and that they must therefore have comparable competences to be eligible for certain positions; moreover this has been confirmed by various members sitting on committees (House report, op. cit., pages 89 and 90).*" Moreover, it suggests "*seeing, in the same spirit, the aforementioned decree of the Flemish government of 13 July 2007 which, in its article 5, provides for the possibility of derogating from the quota of one-third when it is impossible to satisfy it. The Flemish government decree of 26 October 2007, establishing the exceptional procedure for a better gender balance on the advisory and administrative bodies of the Flemish government, specifies the procedure to be followed to obtain such a derogation.*"

20 Opinion of the Council of State, *op. cit.*, p. 11, no. 16.

21 Opinion of the Council of State, *op. cit.*, p. 12, no. 18.

Constitution. The right of association implies the right to choose the form of association and the members of its governing bodies".[22]

Obviously, certain restrictions are left to the freedom of choice of the general meeting; they may not however have the effect of denying the general meeting the opportunity to make an effective choice among various candidates.[23]

14. Nevertheless, for the Council of State, "*the question arises of whether by requiring the general meeting of shareholders of limited companies to comply with an absolute and unconditional quota of members of a given gender in the composition of the board of directors whereas they have, until now, been free to determine this composition, the present draft bill does not fundamentally call into question the current rules which govern public limited companies when their organisation is based on the principle of the sovereign power of the general meeting of shareholders, thereby giving concrete expression to the freedom of association. The legislator should examine the method used to introduce such a system in a set of rules which is consistent today as regards its foundations and the way in which it meshes. It would be advisable to base this review within the framework of a wider debate on the competence and effectiveness of the boards of directors of companies whose shares are listed on a stock exchange, given the rules of corporate governance, by ensuring that the composition of boards of directors is appropriate. In this context, it would be fitting to establish, in principle, the quota rule and to design it as an objective to be attained by accompanying it, as does article 3 of the draft bill which supplements article 96, §2, indent 1, of the Code of Company Law, by 6°, by the obligation to include, in the corporate governance declaration, an overview of the efforts made to promote a balanced gender representation on the board of directors of the company in question, and, consequently, to seek to achieve the target set.*"[24]

15. The Council of State also criticised the sanction proposed by the authors of the draft bill in the event of non-compliance with the legal quota within the allotted period of time.

The proposed Article 518*a*, §2 of the Code of Company Law provided for the nullity of resolutions adopted by a board of directors held to be irregularly constituted as a result of non-compliance with the quota requirements.

16. For the Council of State, "*It is immediately apparent that such a sanction would be likely to result in a serious malfunction if not the total paralysis of the company's operations, which could jeopardise the continuity of its activities, if all*

---

22 Opinion of the Council of State, *op. cit.*, p. 12, no. 19.

23 Opinion of the Council of State, *op. cit.*, p. 13, no. 20; see also J. Malherbe, Y. De Cordt, Ph. Lambrecht and Ph. Malherbe, *Précis de droit des sociétés – Droit communautaire – Droit belge*, Brussels, Bruylant, Bibliothèque de la Faculté de droit de l'UCL, 51, 4th edition, 2011, pp. 590 et seq., no. 941 et seq. and pages 694 et seq., no. 1046 et seq.

24 Opinion of the Council of State, *op. cit.*, p. 14, no. 21.

acts of administration are invalidated because the composition of the board of directors does not comply with the gender balance of the board of directors as required by law.[25] *Accordingly, a sanction which consists in invalidating the decisions of the board of directors of a listed company is a disproportionate interference with the freedom of association guaranteed by article 27 of the Constitution.*"[26]

17. Moreover, this risk of paralysis of the board of directors seems to infringe "*article 9 of Directive 2009/101/EC of the European Parliament and of the Council of 16 September 2009 on coordination of safeguards which, for the protection of the interests of members and third parties, are required by Member States of companies within the meaning of the second paragraph of Article 48 of the Treaty, with a view to making such safeguards equivalent (hereinafter the directive), which replaced the first Directive 68/151/EEC of the Council of 9 March 1968*".[27] The nullity of the decisions of an irregularly constituted board of directors "*would enable the company to invoke, with regard to third parties, the nullity of the decisions of the board of directors whose composition does not comply with the legal quota*"[28], which directly contravenes Article 9 of the directive.

18. The Council of State completed its review of the issue of sanctions by considering "*whether the nullity of the appointments of directors appointed in disrespect of the legal quota could not, as it is for economic public undertakings and the National Lottery, be envisaged as the only sanction to be applied*".[29] However, it qualified this proposal by pointing out "*the limited nature of the scope of such a sanction, which, in particular, would not apply to third parties acting in good faith*".[30]

C. AMENDED PROPOSAL

19. It was at its meetings of 31 May and 1 June 2011 that the House's Committee with responsibility for commercial and economic problems reviewed various amendments and, in particular, amendments intended to take account of the

---

[25] In a footnote on page 33, the opinion of the Council of State specifies: "*It is to be noted that, when drafting law no. 2011-103 of 27 January 2011, the French legislator had considered such a sanction before abandoning this 'succession of nullities' and providing expressly that the nullity of appointments 'does not result in the nullity of deliberations in which an irregularly appointed director participated'* (articles L. 225-18-1, indent 2 and L. 225-69-1, indent 2, of the French Commercial Code). See A. Charveriat, "*De quelques difficultés relatives à la nullité d'une décision sociale irrégulière*", *Rev. soc.*, 2010, p. 213."

[26] Opinion of the Council of State, *op. cit.*, p. 15, no. 23.

[27] Opinion of the Council of State, *op. cit.*, p. 15, no. 24.

[28] Opinion of the Council of State, *op. cit.*, p. 16, no. 24.

[29] Opinion of the Council of State, *op. cit.*, p. 16, no. 26.

[30] Opinion of the Council of State, *op. cit.*, p. 16, no. 26.

opinion of the Council or State which had been requested by the House at its plenary session of 31 March 2011.[31]

In this regard, amendment no. 19 tabled by Mrs Déom (PS) and others[32] proposed to replace the sanction of the nullity of the decisions of the board of directors by the suspension of "*all the financial and other benefits of all the directors in relation to the performance of their mandate*". This amendment was adopted, even if it is open to criticism, strictly speaking, on the ground that it is the board of directors which is sanctioned for a decision falling within the remit of the general meeting.

The amended text was adopted by the Committee on 1 June 2011[33] and adopted by the House at its plenary session of 16 June 2011.

20. Passed to the Senate on 17 June 2011, the text adopted by the House was discussed on 22 June 2011 by the Senate's Finance and Economic Affairs Committee and approved on 30 June 2011 at a plenary session of the Senate. The Senate's annals reproduce the plenary discussions and clearly show the divide between the political groups which supported the proposal and those which rejected it.

21. Thus, for the N-VA, MR, open VLD and Vlaams Belang, the proposal was a clear case of State interference in the organisation of the boards of directors of private companies. They therefore regarded it as a violation of freedom of association and a threat to the separation between public and private sectors. They also expressed their reservations regarding the constitutionality of the quota mechanism and the proposed sanction.

22. In this context, Senator Liesbeth Homans (N-VA) accused the parties supporting the proposal of imposing on private companies something which the State had been incapable of doing in the undertakings in which it held a majority stake: "*Political parties are now imposing on private companies requirements that they themselves cannot respect. Ironically, the State cannot even set a good example in economic public undertakings and enterprises with a public participation. Take the case, for example, of the political representatives on the boards of directors of two companies: the board of Belgocontrol has ten members: ten men. Apparently, the government is incapable of appointing 33% of women to its board. At Dexia, Jean-Luc Dehaene sits on the board of directors and is at the same time a member of a party which is one of the staunchest supporters of this law. However, only one woman has been appointed by the political parties to sit on the company's board. For the rest, it is always the same men: Patrick Janssens,*

31 *Parl. Doc.* House, DOC 53 – 0211/210.
32 *Parl. Doc.* House, DOC 53 – 0211/008, p. 2.
33 *Parl. Doc.* House, DOC 53K211.

Marc Justaert, Luc Martens, Tony Van Parys, etc. If we find a single woman ready to do so, she is forced to attend every board meeting. Yet, you now want to tell private companies how they should organise themselves. I find this misplaced, contradictory and ironic. Despite the overwhelming criticism of the business world, including from women, and worse, despite the damning opinion of the Council of State, you continue to cling to the law. The minor amendment made is in no way an adequate response to the criticism of the Council of State."[34]

23. The MR, in the person of Senator Richard Miller, opposed the proposal on the following grounds: "*The proposal, which aims to bracket State companies and private companies together for the same objective, under the same regulation, is clearly an attack on private rights. The MR group considers that it is legally open to criticism and is not fit for purpose. Moreover, it is detrimental to the economic interests of our country, our region and companies in the Walloon region to which I am particularly attached.*"[35]

24. Senator Bart Tommelein (Open Vld) expressed the substantive concerns of his party as follows:

"*(...) Although Open Vld supports the objective of the draft bill, quotas are not, in our opinion, the appropriate instrument for achieving the objective. Gender diversity is essential, but it is very difficult for us to impose quotas for boards of directors of listed companies and to impose sanctions if these quotas are not attained.*

It is one thing for economic public undertakings to lead by example, and we do not have the slightest problem with this. On the contrary, it is good for these undertakings to guarantee diversity, thereby encouraging a change in behaviour in general, but the introduction of quotas for listed companies stirs up considerable feeling and positions of principle. The opinion of the Council of State is, however, fairly clear. It states that priority must not be given automatically and unconditionally to candidates purely on gender grounds. The Council considers that the qualifications and merits of each candidate must also be taken into consideration and it advises the use of opening clauses for this purpose. The authors of the text have taken little notice of this.

Moreover, there is a risk that the introduction of quotas for listed companies will violate the freedom of association guaranteed by the Constitution, since quotas may threaten the general meeting's freedom of choice. Some observers readily resolve the problem by asserting that we are limiting one basic right to promote another fundamental right, namely equality.

---

34 Senate plenary session, 30 June 2011, *Parl. Ann.*, doc. 5-28, pp. 37 and 38.

35 Senate plenary session, 30 June 2011, *Ann. Parl.*, doc. 5-28, p. 39.

Senate plenary session, 30 June 2011, *Ann. Parl.*, doc. 5-28, pp. 43 and 44.

Let us look at the sanction. In a previous version, the proposed sanction consisted of invalidating all the board's decisions if the specified quota was not reached. This idea has been abandoned in order not to paralyse companies. The proposal now involves suspending the compensation of board members. This also reflects a lack of any sense of reality. The board of directors is appointed by the general meeting of shareholders. It is not because a general meeting puts in place a board of directors which does not comply with the one-third rule that the board members should be penalised.

It is particularly complicated to establish sanctions in this regard. Open Vld supports freedom of choice. This will not surprise anyone. A legally imposed quota reflects a distrust of companies. Moreover, companies have already started voluntarily to evolve gradually, over a seven-year period, towards a proportional representation of women and men on their management bodies. In our opinion it would have sufficed to integrate the recommendation of the Corporate Governance Committee in the code of good conduct. The "comply or explain" principle is a very healthy principle. People often claim that it does not work. It is somewhat premature to make this claim, given that this principle was only given a legal base one year ago. My group is convinced that we will obtain results rapidly via the code and that we will respect at the same time specific characteristics of each company, which is crucially important. The 'comply or explain' principle also accommodates freedom of association."[36]

25. For Vlaams Belang, Senator Anke Van Dermeersch rejected the paternalism of the measure and its failure to address the underlying causes of an absence of women on boards of directors. In her opinion, the proposal: "*is above all yet another attempt to impose a form of paternalistic public supervision and a fresh obstacle to free enterprise. The diversity argument which is often used does not hold water. Diversity is a very vague politically correct concept. Diversity of what? Where does diversity end? Why not then establish quotas for disabled people, lesbians and gay people or perhaps even blondes? In addition, it is very difficult to determine whether diversity represents added value for companies. Perhaps it is even a case of a "down value"? A board of directors must simply be composed of competent directors. Nothing more. If companies really wanted women on their boards of directors, we would not be talking of quotas, since there are more than enough women capable of performing all a director's duties. The reality is that at the current time, for all directorships, directors are recruited from a cosy club of people who know each other. Jean-Luc Dehaene is a striking example of this. This cosy club is a group of handpicked individuals composed mainly of men, with the consequences which we know. If there are so few women on boards of directors, it is therefore more down to recruitment mechanisms in general.*

---

[36] Senate plenary session, 30 June 2011, *Ann. Parl.*, doc. 5-28, pages 43 and 44.

Imposing quotas of women is tantamount to combating the symptoms of a deeper malaise which in the end remains untouched. As in any medical treatment, if we treat only the symptoms, the complaint is likely to re-occur and may even deteriorate. Women who hold directorships or who will obtain a directorship belong to a club just as selective. Women such as Thatcher and Merkel are examples of this in politics. They are women who do not suffer from discrimination, whose talents are not derided, but they are not at all 'typical examples', they are above all members of this selective club.

If we really want to eradicate the core cause of gender segregation, it is more appropriate in the interests of improving the number of women representatives to stop the glass elevator. The latter explains why, at the beginning of their career, men are promoted more rapidly than women. Many very competent women are thus relegated to a background role. This is also detrimental to the burgeoning family life of the men in question. Moreover, it is precisely the family which drives women out of the labour market and caps their ambitions with regard to management positions in companies. Support measures such as improving environmental factors for the careers of women are at the current time far more necessary than quotas for women. It is only once the necessary measures have been taken to improve environmental factors for women, such as childcare facilities and leave systems to help them achieve a better balance between their private life and their career, that we will be able to introduce voluntary quotas or targets. It would therefore be preferable for the proposed quota policy to be set as an objective and not imposed by law."[37]

26. The positions of the parties in favour of the proposal were equally polarised. Highlighting the results of the policy of quotas for electoral lists, doubting the effectiveness of corporate governance and self-governance, considering the principle of "comply or explain" insufficient and asserting the right of the State and the public sector to impose on the private sector meaningful quotas governing the representation of women on the boards of directors of listed companies, the various parties all asserted the need to adopt the proposal forthwith.

27. In this regard, Senator Fabienne Winckel (PS) emphasised that "*women account for 53% of students in higher education. However, in 2008, there were fewer than 7% of women on the boards of directors of listed companies, 29% had only one and 62% did not have any.*

Moreover, certain studies, including one particularly interesting study published by McKinsey – who cannot be suspected of having a "left-wing" bias – show that companies having a larger proportion of women on their executive committees are also those that are the most successful.

[37] Senate plenary session, 30 June 2011, *Ann. Parl.*, doc. 5-28, pages 44 and 45.

For the record, it has been noted that companies having three or more women in their management teams are better rated in terms of operational excellence, return on equity and operating income!

More seriously – and this figure should reassure the MPs who are worried about the potential threat of offshoring if the proposal is adopted – in the event of quotas of 30% of women on the boards of directors of listed companies, we would need, according to initial estimates, between 100 and 150 women over the next three years to sit on these boards. Are we likely to be short of competent candidates?"[38]

28. Senator Güler Turan (SPA) declared that she was "*convinced that a woman feels humiliated when she learns that, despite the fact that she can prove that she is better than men, women represent only 8.5% of the board member of the BEL20 companies. We need to remedy this immediately.*

We have already introduced quotas at political level. Thanks to these quotas 39% of MPs and 42.5% of senators today are women. Do the opponents of the draft bill believe that this regulation has adversely affected the functioning of our parliament?"[39]

29. CD&V's position was explained by Senator Sabine de Béthune in the following terms: "*(...) Pippa Norris, Professor at Harvard, has compared the quantified data of the political representation of women and men in the world according to several parameters. Her research shows that a better representation of women is not linked to either gross domestic product or level of education or to their share of the labour market. The only link that she found was the amendment of the electoral law with a view to establishing a better balance in terms of gender representation in the electoral system. A significant body of research on the subject can be consulted on the website of the Inter-parliamentary Union.*

Why should the political arena be different from the other decision-making arenas from which women are significantly absent? The data on women holding management positions on the executive committees and boards of directors of public undertakings, universities, hospitals, cultural centres, etc. are not good.

They are even worse in the business world. With approximately eight percent of women on the boards of directors of large listed companies, our country compares very unfavourably with other European countries. All calculations show that it will take at least sixty years to achieve a balanced representation. Therefore, I believe that these private companies need a small helping hand to achieve this balance within a reasonable timeframe. Women are not less competent. It is not true that they do not want management positions. I am even less convinced that we will not be able to find women to fill these positions. These are merely specious

---

38 Senate plenary session, 30 June 2011, *Ann. Parl.*, doc. 5-28, pages 38 and 39.

39 Senate plenary session, 30 June 2011, *Ann. Parl.*, doc. 5-28, pages 39 and 40.

arguments. The number of women graduates is very high, and for many years female graduates have outnumbered male graduates. The fact that they do not gain access to management positions must be attributed to the glass ceiling effect; it must be shattered.

Companies and their boards of directors should reflect society. We cannot talk of gender equality as long as women continue to be under-represented at the most senior management levels.

I am convinced that nobody here can deny the added value of a board of directors on which men and women are represented. Numerous studies also demonstrate that self-governance, codes, charters, etc. do not contain enough obligations and are too slow to produce results. In its green paper 'The EU Corporate Governance Framework' of 5 April 2011, the European Commission raised the question of the quality of information given in annual reports in the absence of corporate governance rules.

The imposition of quotas is the only way of speeding up the elimination of the glass ceiling. The proposal which has been submitted to us has been examined and discussed in depth by the House. The arguments of the business world and the opinion of the Council of State have been taken into account.

The public authorities must lead by example. For all public undertakings, the legal obligation entered into force last year. Listed companies have five years to conform. The specific characteristics of listed companies that have less than fifty percent of their capital listed on a stock exchange have also been taken into consideration, since they are granted a longer adaptation period. During this transitional period, companies must explain every year the efforts made by them in this regard. (...)"[40]

30. For Ecolo, Senator Jacky Morael defended the proposal on the following grounds:

"*Some of you suggest doing nothing; you want to let matters follow their natural course. If we were to go down that route, it would take at least half a century before women are adequately represented on the management bodies of our major financial and industrial companies.*

We note first of all that the arguments in favour of this option are outdated, tired old arguments. We have heard them since the early 1990s, when we first debated quotas for the electoral lists for municipal, provincial and legislative elections.

What were we told at that time? First, that we should let matters follow their natural course, which meant doing nothing. Secondly, that the idea of quotas was contrary to the free choice of citizens – how dreadful! And, thirdly, that quotas were an insult to the intelligence of women who, if they were elected on this basis, would be permanently subject to name-calling and insults. These women would be

[40] Senate plenary session, 30 June 2011, *Ann. Parl.*, doc. 5-28, pages 40 and 41.

derided on the ground that they had been elected solely because of inescapable quotas rather than on the basis of their intelligence, competences and political commitment. Quota creatures, as it were.

Today, now that these provisions are in force, nobody is interested in finding ways of subverting them. It is fortunate that parliaments can guarantee equitable gender representation. The group formed by Groen! and Écolo even has five women for two men – perhaps one day we will have to call for quotas for men (Smiles) – and I am proud of it. Would it still occur to anyone, within our assemblies, to deride an elected woman, on the pretext that she owed her election to a quota? Obviously not.

This argument is no more acceptable in the political arena than it is in the business world. The text submitted to us is the meeting point of two debates.

First of all, the debate on the place of women in society. The introduction of quotas for electoral lists has proved that quotas are a way of accelerating the famous natural course of things, so as to reflect a normal situation more in line with the diversity of our society, without causing the slightest problem as regards mutual respect or competences, whether in assemblies or governments.

The second more recent debate concerns the legislator's role with regard to companies. Some observers recommend a laissez-faire approach, relying on gentlemen's agreements in the business world, the whims of directors who, as we know, are men who more often than not tend to co-opt other men.

The legislator needs to intervene and legislate to produce the same undeniably positive results as those achieved in the political arena.

In fact, the question is simple: who is the guardian of civilisation in our society? The private sector? Definitely not. Its role is to do business and make profits. It is the legislator who is the guardian of civilisation.

That is our role. We cannot afford to wait for companies to address the issue. We must lead by example!"[41]

31. The Groen! Senator Freya Piryns disputed the idea that the proposal runs counter to the opinion of the Council of State: "*(...) The Council of State has not declared that quotas are unacceptable, it asked whether the parliament was aware what it was undertaking. The answer is yes, we are perfectly aware of what we are doing. It goes without saying that quotas limit the sovereignty of the general meeting; moreover, this sovereignty is not absolute at the current time. All those who have taken the initiative have carefully examined the question of limiting these sovereign powers in the face of the powerful argument of ensuring adequate gender representation.*

Contrary to what has been claimed in certain quarters, the proposal submitted to us today is balanced and reasonable. Companies have seven years to get used to the idea and take the necessary steps to comply with their obligations.

41 Senate plenary session, 30 June 2011, *Ann. Parl.*, doc. 5–28, pages 45 and 46.

Quotas alone will not resolve the problem but they are part of the solution (...)".[42]

32. Senator Dimitri Fourny spoke on behalf of CDh. He asserted that "*this draft bill and the proposals are fair, necessary and equitable since their aim is to ensure the representation of women on boards of directors.*

Fair and necessary since, for more than ten years, during which time an initial draft bill tabled by Mesdames Willame and de Bethune has never been adopted, we note that nothing has really changed in companies, despite the code of best practices. It is therefore indispensable to enact a law that can impose such provisions in order to further the cause of women in business life. More and more women have the necessary competences and knowledge. Their intelligence must be given the recognition it deserves in the business world.

Equity and representativeness demand that women should be better represented in companies, in formal and informal business networks and in economic activities. Their inadequate presence on decision-making bodies means that they are also under-represented in companies. This is confirmed by statistics on representativeness.

It is therefore useful and essential for the legislator to intervene. The examples given regarding the representativeness of electoral lists set the tone. It is time for our society to evolve and for women to be able to exercise their talents and competences, share their knowledge and contribute their know-how in our companies. This is a major step forward for our society and our group will therefore give its unreserved support to this initiative."[43]

33. Senators Marie Arena, Olga Zrihen and Hassan Bousetta, on behalf of the PS, explained why they supported the proposal. Madame Arena declared that it was necessary to uphold the pre-eminence of the principle of gender equality over the principle of freedom of association: "*Finally, I feel particularly challenged by the principle of a hierarchy of rights. For you, freedom of association – therefore entrepreneurial freedom and economic freedom – is more important than the right to gender equality. I do not agree: this right of equality is superior to the freedom of association. That is why we will give our unreserved support to this proposal.*"[44]

34. Mr Bousetta underscored what he described as stark numbers: "*Women have a seat on only 7% of the boards of directors of listed companies and 62% of boards of directors do not have any women. We should be ashamed of such a situation.*

The text proposes a measure which Mrs de Bethune has described as the only solution possible. It is an important means which must however be accompanied

42 Senate plenary session, 30 June 2011, *Ann. Parl.*, doc. 5–28, p. 47.

43 Senate plenary session, 30 June 2011, *Ann. Parl.*, doc. 5–28, p. 46.

44 Senate plenary session, 30 June 2011.

by other measures. We must pursue our regulatory and legislative work, but also we must develop incentives. We must set an example as regards representation. The entire career question also needs to be addressed.

I would remind you that we even organised a conference here within the framework of the Belgian Presidency of the European Union. Representatives of all the committees charged with gender equality in the European Union participated. We adopted a text which states that legal quotas are necessary to ensure balanced gender representation. We all took part in that conference. It is important to avoid adopting one position in international forums and another in the national debate.

We must be consistent and take the lead by proposing a very firm commitment to improving the representation of women on corporate boards of directors.

Moreover, this approach must be accompanied by other measures covering the entire career of women."[45]

35. The overriding impression after reading the preparatory work is one of a profound antagonism between the positions defended by the two camps. For those who are against quotas, the proposal demonstrates a lack of trust in the business world. They see it as a fundamental calling into question of corporate governance, despite the fact that this concept was enshrined in law by the recent law of 6 April 2010.[46] Although they consider that the State is perfectly entitled to regulate the public sector and therefore impose quotas on economic pubic undertakings and the National Lottery, they consider on the other hand that the proposal affects entrepreneurial freedom and the freedom of association by imposing compulsory quotas for private companies.

Moreover, they criticise a certain Poujadism of the measures and accuse the supporters of the proposal of wanting to impose on private companies something which the State has been incapable of doing for itself to date. They also rely on the opinion of the Council of State to denounce the absolute nature of the quota imposed and the lack of an opening clause in the adopted text. For the record, the opening clause is described in the case law of the Court of Justice of the European Union as the "*clause whereby women are not to be given priority in promotion if reasons specific to an individual male candidate tilt the balance in his favour*".[47]

Finally, they regret that the solution adopted is that of a binding law, rather than adapting the Belgian Code of Corporate Governance, and call into doubt the legality of the sanction provided for in the event of non-compliance with quotas.

---

45 Senate plenary session, 30 June 2011, *Ann. Parl.*, doc. 5–28, p. 50.

46 Law of 6 April 2010 to strengthen corporate governance in listed companies and autonomous public undertakings and to amend the system of professional disqualification in the banking and financial sector.

47 CJEU, 28 March 2000, no C-158/97, Badeck *et al.*, *CJEU case law*, 2000, I, p. 1875 and other references mentioned in note 17, p. 10 of the opinion of the Council of State, 26 April 2011, no 49.473/AG, Doc. 53–0211/07.

36. For their part, the parties that support quotas consider that enough is enough and that quotas are the only means of putting an end to the unacceptable under-representation of women on the boards of directors of listed companies. They believe that self-governance and the "comply or explain" mechanism of corporate governance are ineffective. They consider that it is for the legislator to impose a better representation of women on the boards of directors of listed companies and that it is normal for the law to require the private sector to comply with norms intended to put an end to a form of discrimination which they consider unacceptable.

The intensity of the debates and the nature of the arguments exchanged clearly demonstrate the fundamental opposition between the conflicting approaches. At the end of the day, everyone seems to agree on the objective to be achieved – to increase significantly the presence of women on boards of directors – the disagreement concerns the way of achieving this objective. The supporters of a more liberal concept of society consider that the best way is to encourage companies and shareholders to achieve this objective by voluntary means by following the recommendations of the Belgian Code of Corporate Governance. The supporters of a more social or more legalistic vision of society do not believe in the effectiveness of such an approach. They consider that progress has been far too slow and that it is absolutely necessary to legislate. They sometimes have over-simplistic, black and white views of the respective roles of the public and private sectors. Thus, for Senator Jacky Morael, "*Who is the guardian of civilisation in our society? The private sector? Definitely not. Its role is to do business and make profits. It is the legislator who is the guardian of civilisation.*" In other words, he does not believe in corporate governance and corporate social responsibility, which is surprising in a country where the social dialogue is as developed as it is in ours.

37. In conclusion, a close examination of the preparatory work for the law shows the importance of the debate on the type of society we want which took place regarding compulsory quotas for women on boards of directors. Could we incentivise companies to adopt this principle by standards of good conduct and a voluntary approach, or was it necessary, on the contrary, to impose legal quotas? The choice of compulsory quotas won the debate, although the adopted text has not cleared up all the uncertainties noted by the Council of State in its opinion.

III. NEW PROVISIONS INTRODUCED BY THE LAW

38. The law of 28 July 2011 consists of six chapters: the general provisions, the amendments to the law of 21 March 1991 reforming certain economic public undertakings, the amendments to the Code of Company Law, the amendments to the law of 16 April 2002 on the streamlining of the operation and management of the National Lottery, the evaluation and the entry into force.

39. In the general provisions, Article 1 simply indicates, as the Constitution requires, that it concerns a matter governed by Article 78 of the Constitution.

A. CERTAIN ECONOMIC PUBLIC UNDERTAKINGS AND THE NATIONAL LOTTERY

40. Chapter II, devoted to certain economic public undertakings, and chapter IV, devoted to the National Lottery, contain the same provision, Article 2 and Article 5 respectively of the law. The legislator has treated the National Lottery, governed by the law of 19 April 2002 on the streamlining of the operation and management of the National Lottery[48], and economic public undertakings referred to by the law of 21 March 1991 reforming certain economic public undertakings[49], in the same way.

41. Article 2 of the law supplements article 18 of the law of 21 March 1991 by a §2*a* worded as follows, and Article 5 supplements Article 8, §1 of the law of 19 April 2002 by an indent 2 worded identically as follows:

"At least a third of the members of the board of directors appointed by the Belgian State or by a company controlled by the Belgian State shall be of a different gender from the other members. For the application of this provision, the statutory minimum number of these members of a different gender shall be rounded to the nearest whole number. If the number of directors of a different gender does not reach the minimum laid down in this provision, the next director appointed shall belong to this gender, failing which the appointment shall be invalid. The same shall apply if an appointment results in the number of these directors of a different gender falling below this statutory minimum number."[50]

This concerns the following undertakings: Belgacom[51], S.N.C.B. Holding, Infrabel, Société nationale des Chemins de fer belges[52], bpost[53], Belgocontrol[54] and the National Lottery.[55]

42. The statutory quota applies only to the "*members of the board of directors appointed by the State or by a company controlled by the State*". It does not apply

---

48 Hereinafter "L. 19 April 2002".
49 Hereinafter "L. 21 March 1991".
50 Article 18, §2a, L. 21 March 1991 and Article 8, §1, indent 2, L. 19 April 2002.
51 Article 1, §4, 1°, L. 21 March 1991.
52 Article 1, §4, 2°, L. 21 March 1991.
53 Article 1, §4, 3°, L. 21 March 1991.
54 Article 1, §4, 4°, L. 21 March 1991.
55 Article 8, §1, indent 2, L. 19 April 2002.

to the representatives of other shareholders. If the State is the sole shareholder, this quota will apply to all Board members. If, as is the case for Belgacom, there are also private shareholders[56], this quota will not apply to the directors not appointed by the State. On the other hand, since Belgacom is a listed company, a double quota will be applied to its board of directors: the "public undertakings" quota for the Belgian State's participating interest and the "listed companies" quota for the Board as a whole.

43. To clarify the calculations, the following rule has been adopted: "*The statutory minimum number of these different-sex members shall be rounded to the nearest whole number.*" Take the case of a board of directors composed of 17 members. Pursuant to the quota rule, at least a third of this board must be of a different gender from the other directors. Seventeen divided by three equals 5.66. The nearest whole number is 6. The board must therefore have at least 6 members of a sex different from the 11 others. With 13 members, dividing the number of board members by 3 produces 4.33. The nearest whole number to 4.33 is 4. In this case, the board must include at least 4 members of a different gender from the 9 other members.

44. The system chosen provides for only one sanction for non-compliance with the quota, namely the nullity of the appointment of the director who is not of the statutory gender in accordance with the following stipulation that: "*If the number of directors of a different gender does not reach the minimum laid down in this provision, the next director appointed shall belong to this gender, failing which the appointment shall be invalid. The same shall apply if an appointment results in the number of these directors of a different gender falling below this statutory minimum number.*"

It is therefore advisable for the State to comply with the 33% imposed on it for the appointment of its directors. If an appointment is necessary for the quota to be reached among the directors appointed by the State, any new appointment by the State must concern a candidate of the necessary gender, otherwise the State will be unable to replace or change the directors whom it appointed before the entry into force of the law if the quota were not reached. If a new appointment would result in the quota falling below the statutory level, the appointment would be invalid.

45. The new provision entered into force on the first day of the company's fiscal year starting after the publication of the law in the Belgian Official Journal.[57]

---

56 As at 31 August 2011, the Belgian State owned 53.51% of Belgacom's shares. The free float represented 43.43% and treasury stock represented 5.40% of the shares. See web page www.belgacom.com/be-fr/annex_investors/Inv_Shareholders_structure.page consulted on 11 September 2011 at 10:25.

57 Article 7, §4, L. 28 July 2011. Although not all companies start their fiscal year on the 1st of January, the 1st of January 2012 will generally be the starting point for the entry into force.

B. LISTED COMPANIES

46. Chapter III amends the Code of Company Law and contains Articles 3 and 4. Article 3 of the law requires companies, with effect from the first day of the company's fiscal year beginning after the publication of the law in the Belgian Official Journal[58], to insert in the management report for the said fiscal year "*an overview of the efforts made to ensure that at least a third of the members of the board of directors are of a different gender from the other members*".[59]

This overview is added as no. 6° of the list of compulsory information in the management report contained in Article 96, §2, indent 1 of the Code of Company Law.

This overview will be particularly useful to assess every year the efforts made by the companies concerned to achieve the statutory quota on the expiry of the transitional period provided for by law.

47. Article 4 of the law inserts in the Code of Company Law a new Article 518*a* worded as follows:

> "*Art. 518a. §1. In companies whose securities are admitted for trading on a regulated market referred to in article 4, at least a third of the members of the board of directors shall be of a different gender from the other members. For the application of this provision, the statutory minimum number of these members of a different gender shall be rounded to the nearest whole number.*
> *§2. If the number of directors of a different gender does not reach the minimum level specified in §1, the next general meeting shall form a board of directors in accordance with the provisions of this paragraph. In the event of non-compliance with this provision, any financial or other benefits of the directors in connection with the performance of their mandate shall be suspended. These benefits shall be restored when the composition of the board of directors complies with §1.*
> *§3. For companies whose securities are admitted for the first time to a regulated market referred to in article 4, the obligation specified in §1 must be respected with effect from the first day of the sixth fiscal year which begins after the said admission.*
> *§4. If the statutory minimum number of directors of a gender different from that of the other directors, specified in §1, is not reached, the next director appointed shall be of this gender, failing which the appointment shall be invalid. The same shall apply if an appointment results in the number of these directors of a different gender falling below this statutory minimum number.*"

48. The companies referred to are the "*companies whose securities are admitted to trading on a regulated market referred to in article 4*".[60] In accordance with Article 4 of the Code of Company Law, this concerns "*companies whose securities*

[58] Article 7, §1 L. 28 July 2011.
[59] Article 3 L. 28 July 2011.
[60] New Article 518*a*, §Code of Company Law.

are admitted to trading on a regulated market within the meaning of article 2, 3°, of the law of 2 August 2002 on the supervision of the financial sector and financial services".[61]

49. Listed companies must, at the end of a transitional period fixed by law[62], ensure that "*at least a third of the members of the board of directors are of a different gender from the other members*". Here too, the law provides for a rounding mechanism to determine the statutory minimum number of members of a different gender.[63]

During the parliamentary work, the issue of the rules for determining the gender of a director when the said director is a legal entity was raised. In this regard, "*the representative of the Justice Minister referred to point 30 of the opinion of the Council of State (DOC 53 0211/007) concerning the question of the gender of a legal entity which might be a director, as well as to its first intervention on this aspect (DOC 53 0211/004, p. 15). It pointed out that it is the gender of the permanent representative, within the meaning of article 61 of the Code of Company Law, which is taken into consideration for the calculation of the quota rule; moreover this is provided for in justification for amendment no. 11 (DOC 53 0211/003).*"[64]

50. The objective of gender diversity on boards of directors is reinforced by two separate rules.

The first, inserted in a new Article 518*a*, §4 of the Code of Company Law, requires companies to ensure that, as soon as the quota enters into force and where it is not reached, the next director appointed is of the necessary gender in order to comply with the quota. Thus, if on the day that the new Article 518a, §1 of the Code of Company Law enters into force, the board of directors of a listed company consists of 3 women and 9 men, the next director appointed must be a woman since the quota has not been reached. The company may either replace a male director at the end of his term of office by a female director, in which case the board would then consist of 4 women and 8 men, or appoint an additional woman. With 4 women and 9 men, the board would have 13 members. A third of 13 members being 4.33, a board of 13 members made up of 4 women and 9 men would comply with the legal quota.[65]

The appointment of a director who is not of the right gender in accordance with the legal quota would be invalid. This now involves only the nullity of the

61 See J. Malherbe, Y. De Cordt, Ph. Lambrecht and Ph. Malherbe, *Précis de droit des sociétés*, Brussels, Bruylant, 2011, 4th edition, p. 222, no. 433 and p. 1334, nos. 1938 and 1939. For ease of reference, we will refer to them as "listed companies" in the rest of the text.

62 See below no. 52.

63 See above no. 43.

64 *Doc. Parl.* House, DOC 53 – 0211/010, p. 6.

65 See above no. 43.

appointment of the last director appointed in violation of the one-third quota rule, whereas the proposal submitted to the Council of State for its opinion provided for the nullity of the board's resolutions.[66]

This sanction also applies in the case of the appointment of a director of a different gender from that which would have made it possible to reach the quota and that of a director whose appointment would result in the quota no longer being respected. Thus, for example, if, in the case of a board of directors consisting of 12 members, including 4 women and 8 men, the general meeting were to appoint a male director in replacement of a female director, such an appointment would be invalid.

51. The second rule intended to ensure compliance with the one-third quota rule has been inserted in the new Article 518a, §2 of the Code of Company Law. The next general meeting after the entry into force of this provision must form a board of directors complying with the quota of at least one-third, failing which all the benefits of the members of the board of directors of the company concerned, in connection with the performance of their mandate, will be suspended. This suspension will last until a board of directors has been put in place in compliance with the one-third quota.

This raises the question of the parties targeted by this sanction, since it is the general meeting not the board of directors which appoints directors. However, it should be noted, first, that these benefits are suspended only for the time needed to put in place a board of directors that respects the quota and, secondly, that it is the board of directors which proposes to the general meeting candidates for election to the board of directors. Obviously, the meeting of shareholders does not have to validate the board's nominations, but the suspension of the benefits of directors should be a powerful enough incentive to encourage the board to nominate candidates in accordance with the legal quota requirement.

52. The entry into force of the new Article 518*a* of the Code of Company Law depends on the execution phase of the objectives fixed by law. The legislator has provided for a transitional period to enable listed companies to achieve, at the end of this period, the quota of at least one-third of directors of a different gender from that of the other directors.

As regards the effective date of §1 and 4 of the new Article 518*a* of the Code of Company Law, that is to say the requirement to comply with the one-third quota and the requirement to appoint a director of a gender that would enable the company to reach the quota if that is not the case, the legislator has chosen the 1st day of the sixth or eighth fiscal year beginning after the publication of the law in the Belgian Official Journal, depending on the size of the company concerned.[67]

---

66 See opinion of the Council of State, *op. cit.*, p. 12, no. 19.

67 Article 7, §2, L. 28 July 2011.

The rule for the largest listed companies is therefore five years from the 1st day of the fiscal year following the publication of the law in the Belgian Official Journal, but two additional years have been granted to listed companies "*whose free float is less than 50%*"[68] and to listed companies "*which, on a consolidated basis, satisfy at least two of the following three criteria:*

a) average workforce of less than 250 employees during the fiscal year concerned;
b) total assets of less than or equal to 43,000,000 euros;
c) net annual turnover of less than or equal to 50,000,000 euros".[69]

As regards the sanction of the suspension of the benefits of directors provided for in the new Article 518a, §2 of the Code of Company Law, this sanction will enter into force on the "*first day of the seventh fiscal year beginning after the publication of the (...) law in the Belgian Official Journal*"[70] for the largest listed companies, while an additional period of two years is granted to other companies having a free float of less than 50% or which, on a consolidated basis, meet two of the three criteria indicated in the preceding paragraph.[71]

53. Finally, the legislator has taken into account the situation of newly listed companies, since the mechanism of the new Article 518*bis*, §1 applies to existing companies. They therefore have a transitional period to enable them to reach the minimum quota of one-third. This period will be six or eight fiscal years from the first day of the fiscal year beginning after the publication of the law in the Belgian Official Journal.

In order to cover the case of new companies admitted to trading during this transitional period and at the end of it, the law provides that the quota must "*be respected from the first day of the sixth fiscal year which begins after such admission*".[72] If a company is admitted to trading on 1 June 2016 and its fiscal year begins on 1 January, the composition of its board of directors must comply with the one-third quota by no later than 1 January 2022, i.e. the first day of the sixth fiscal year beginning after 1 June 2016.

IV. CONCLUSION

54. The law of 28 July 2011 has introduced into Belgian law the legal requirement to ensure that the composition of boards of directors respects gender diversity. The parliamentary pathway to the adoption of this law was

68 Article 7, §2, indent 2, L. 28 July 2011.
69 Article 7, §2, indent 2, L. 28 July 2011.
70 Article 7, §3, indent 1, L. 28 July 2011.
71 Article 7, §3, indent 2, L. 28 July 2011.
72 Article 518*a*, §3, Code of Company Law.

complicated and highlighted the different approaches which exist in this area. Supporters of a legal approach, wanting to impose mandatory quotas, prevailed over those who would have preferred a more liberal approach, paying greater heed to the diversity of situations existing within listed companies.

Although no one questions the State's right to lay down rules that must be followed regarding the composition of the boards of directors of economic public undertakings or the National Lottery, it is legitimate to question whether it is not exceeding its role when it decides, in the place of the general meetings of listed companies, that in the future their boards of directors must comply with a minimum quota intended to ensure gender diversity.

It would undoubtedly have been more comprehensible and more stimulating for the business world to have been able to achieve the same result by way of corporate governance. In addition, this would have provided flexibility as and when necessary.

55. The parliamentary majority has decided otherwise, and the system of legal quotas will also apply to listed companies, provided that its constitutionality is not challenged by a company which considers that it has been prejudiced. In this regard, it is important to note various observations of the Council of State which have not been taken into account in the finally adopted text. For example, the text does not address the criticism regarding the absolute nature of the quota adopted[73], the absence of an opening clause in the system[74] and its incompatibility with freedom of association.[75]

56. It is perhaps regrettable that the Belgian legislator now seems disposed to involve in its action both autonomous public undertakings and listed companies.[76] It is not because a private company has raised funds from the public and has applied for a stock market listing on a regulated market that the State must interfere in its management and organisation as it would do if it were a public undertaking.

57. We will nevertheless conclude on a positive note, since the law should result in a significant increase in the number of women on the boards of directors of listed companies.

---

73 See above no. 11.

74 See above no. 12.

75 See above no. 14.

76 See for example the law of 6 April 2010 to strengthen corporate governance in listed companies and autonomous public undertakings and to amend the system of professional disqualification in the banking and financial sector.

CHAPTER 5

ROLE OF SELF-REGULATION IN LISTED COMPANIES RECRUITMENT OF WOMEN INTO TOP POSITIONS IN FINLAND

Anne Kovalainen* and Linda Hart**

I. INTRODUCTION[1]

Representatives of business and industries in Finland are eager to point out that when comparing the largest listed companies in EU countries, Finland comes first (or, in different years, at least among the top few) with its percentage of women as board members in listed companies. In 2012, women constituted 28 per cent of board members of largest Finnish listed companies (large-cap, that is, with market value over 1 billion €).[2] When looking at Finnish listed companies as a whole (large-cap, mid-cap and small cap, 123 companies in total in 2012), as researchers and statisticians often do, the picture is more varied. Roughly one in five of these companies did not have women on their Board of Directors according to annual reports of 2011. Indeed, the share of listed companies with no women on their boards was much greater a few years earlier, and this change is due to the introduction of self-regulation, recommendations from Corporate Governance Finland, an association of listed companies in Finland. In 2008, when the earlier part of the research project reported in this article was carried out about one third of listed companies in Finland had no women on their boards.[3]

---

* Academy professor, University of Turku, Finland.

** PhD Candidate in Sociology, University of Helsinki, Finland.

1 Academy of Finland Gendered Economy Project funding is gratefully acknowledged for support of the research.

2 L. Linnainmaa, *Lasikatto säröilee – Itsesäätely päihittää kiintiöt*, (Helsinki: Central Chamber of Commerce, 2012), p. 8. See also, "Selvitys: Naisten osuus...", *Helsingin Sanomat* 23 October 2012.

3 L. Hart, A. Holli and A. Kovalainen, "Gender and Power in the Nordic Countries: Report on Finland" in K. Niskanen and A. Nyberg (eds), *Kön och makt I Norden – Del I Landrapporter*, TemaNord 2009: 569, (Copenhagen: Nordic Council of Ministers, 2009).

About 50 per cent of the 123 companies listed in the Finnish stock exchange in 2011 had one woman board member. About 27 per cent of these companies had more than one woman on their Board of Directors. 15 companies, or 12% of this group of companies, had three or more women on their boards. The most common denominator between these 15 companies is that about half of them have a significant share of state ownership or the companies have a background in former state-owned businesses.[4] According to Konrad et al., three female board members seem to constitute a critical mass where the negative effects of "tokenism" tend to disappear. Tokenism refers to being the only one in the group, and for that reason, being singled out in the group or organisation.[5]

The companies listed in the stock exchange vary a little from year to year, the majority of them remain the same. New companies emerge mostly to the small cap list.[6] Presently, more companies than before, about 80 per cent, have one or more women on their boards now than a few years ago when the new recommendation had not been applied yet. What has changed and what does the situation look like? How does this change relate to the structures and history of Finnish business and industries and to the debate in Finland about introducing gender quotas in business? The article is structured as follows: First we have a look at the historical background of Finland as it pertains to gender and power in the field of business, as well as at how to conceptualise and analyse the kind of change that has taken place due to introducing soft, self-regulatory measures. Then we go through the numbers shortly before and after the introduction of this recommendation took place. After that, we reflect on the case of Finland and what kind of conclusions might be drawn from it.

II. HISTORICAL/CONCEPTUAL FRAMEWORK

The long industrial history of Finland, based on paper and pulp on the one hand, and on iron and metals in the Finnish economy has given a strong flavour for business competencies of managers as well: one had to study civil engineering to become manager in companies of those sectors. The strong segregation in the educational sector prevailing, it also meant that the progress for women was

---

4 In alphabetical order: Aktia, Finnair, Fortum, Huhtamäki, Kemira, Kone, Neste Oil, Nordea Bank, Outokumpu, Rautaruukki, Sampo, Sanoma, Stockmann, TeliaSonera, Tikkurila.

5 A. Konrad, V. Kramer and S. Ekrut, "Critical mass: The impact of three or more women on corporate boards" (2008) 37 *Organisational Dynamics* 145 at 147. Also S. Poutanen and A. Kovalainen, "Gendering Innovation Process in an Industrial Plant – Revisiting Tokenism, Gender and Innovation" (2013) 5 *International Journal of Gender and Entrepreneurship* 257 at 274.

6 There are several large and/or prominent family firms that have stayed outside of the stock exchange markets, as the capital funding has been sufficient for them and they wish to keep their control over the company.

slow in the 1960s and 1970s to the managerial positions. It could be argued that the growth of the public sector in the 1970s and 1980s structurally created new managerial positions for the highly educated generation.

When the economic structure began to diversify and open up in the 1980s and 1990s – much due to the collapse of the Soviet trade – the needs and qualifications of managers became very different rather suddenly. In addition to the technical skills, also other skills, such as several languages, and customer marketing, from those educational backgrounds women came from, were urgently needed by the businesses in the Finnish economy. The diversifying development has since continued, and emphasised different types of qualifications and competencies from top management as well.

The question of quotas for business positions is at its deepest a question of equality – whether political or regulatory – claims for equal rights for women and for men, and underlining the kinds of values which no longer belong to the vocabularies of businesses. Indeed, only few companies in Finland did follow the models of those US companies who set up pipelines for upwardly mobile women in the 1980s and in 1990s.[7] The business companies no longer focus on the exclusion of women but instead a focus on diversity is to be found in many companies' webpages, also in relation to HR functions. Hence, the aspects of gendered career paths and gendered work patterns exist even today. Research shows that several of the typical women's jobs ("behind-the-scenes jobs") are not favouring women in corporations, similarly as the lack of networks and sponsors. In Finnish culture the double bind that is the close linkage between masculinity and leadership has partly directed women in rather conventional positions in corporations.[8] Research has moved away from deliberate exclusionary actions against women, towards the analysis of the "second-generation" forms of gender bias as the cause for stalled development.[9]

Are the perspectives of descriptive and substantive representation, the bread and butter of discussing the representation of women and minorities in politics, worth also applying to the fields of business and private enterprises?[10] Does one woman mean "change" or is this comply-or-explain policy more a type of "window-dressing" for many corporations, thus representing descriptive

7 A. Kovalainen, *At the Margins of the Economy.* 1995. Avebury, Ashgate.

8 R. Ely, H. Ibarra, and D. Kolb, "Taking Gender into Account", *Academy of Management Learning & Education. 2011.*

9 C.L. Williams "The Glass Escalator, Revisited: Gender Inequality in Neoliberal Times", *Gender & Society* 2013.

10 L. Wängnerud and A. Sundell, "Do Politics Matter? Women in Swedish local elected assemblies 1970–2010 and gender equality in outcomes", *European Political Science Review* (2010) 4:1 at 97–120.

representation, corresponding to the minority position of women in the field of business more generally. Substantive representation would, in turn, mean that having women in the boardroom would affect the decision-making on the Board of Directors. For example, according to this line of argument the claim is that in a company where a great deal of the employees are women, having women in top positions might promote more understanding to the issues women tend to face in combining work and family life. On a concrete level, this might translate to work-related benefits such the company providing temporary childcare when a child is ill so that the employee does not have to take sick leave for taking care of his/her child. There are several even very concrete questions arising from this.

III. RECENT POLITICAL DEBATE ON QUOTAS FOR BOARDS OF COMPANIES

There has been debate over quotas on and off for a number of years in Finland, rather mild in tone, and diverse in arguments. The strong political actions have never taken place but for the state-owned companies or for those companies where the state had majority of shares, the target for equality at boards was set already in the 1990s with 30%, and later it was raised to the target level of 40% in the State owned companies in the Equality programmes of 2004–07 and 2008–11.

Even if mentioned in the equality programmes as one of the targets, it seems that neither State nor business has had strong vested interests in the matter. When Norway adopted the quota legislation, in 2006, the matter actualised in Finland as well on the polical level: the then Minister of Social Affairs, Ms. Tuula Haatainen (Social Democratic Party) joined the Prime Minister Matti Vanhanen (Centre Party) in writing a letter to the Chairs of Boards of the 100 largest listed companies with the plea for strengthening women's positions in top management and in boards. The letter did not activate changes in the Boards, and the topic was not an issue in the parliamentary elections either. The next Government did not take up the initiative by the former Government: the Minister for Equality affairs in the next Government, Mr. Stefan Wallin (Swedish People's Party) remarked in year 2007 that government is not preparing legislative actions for quotas.[11]

The question of quotas for businesses in Finland surfaced to the general political discussion in 2008 by Ms. Kiviniemi (Centre Party) who as Minister of Public Administration and Local Government took up the need for legislation on quotas for large companies' boards. The self-regulation through the Corporate Governance Code was introduced in Finland 2008, taken up in 2009 to be

[11] Demari 18 June 2007.

implemented in full from 2010. These steps were taken in close relation to the Swedish development. But as the change in the numbers has not been drastic, the demands from the political Left have increased recently, in 2011 both the Minister of Finance, Ms. Jutta Urpilainen (Social Democratic Party) and Minister of Culture and Sports, who is also responsible for the equality, Mr. Paavo Arhinmäki (Left Alliance) have raised the issue of quotas. Mr. Arhinmaki expressed the demand for the quota legislation to be put in place unless companies have not taken steps to have 40% of the board positions for minority gender by 2013. As of writing, there is not yet known preparatory steps are taken towards the quota legislation.

IV. BEFORE AND AFTER SELF-REGULATION: THE FIGURES

A. BACKGROUND

The first part of this research was carried out in 2008–2009 for within the framework of a larger, comparative research project on gender and power in the Nordic countries, administered by NIKK, the (former) Nordic Gender Institute (Hart, Holli, Kovalainen 2009). As comparative longitudinal data for women on the boards of listed companies did not really exist prior our study in any of the countries studies (Denmark, Finland, Iceland, Norway and Sweden), a lot of it had to be gathered manually. In the first phase of this research in 2008–2009, data the composition of the Boards of Directors and the Management Teams of Finnish listed companies was collected directly from the company websites: from the annual reports available on the web and the then-current situation from the websites themselves. In case the data was missing from the website, the companies were contacted for the purposes of data.

The follow-up data was gathered manually from the Internet in August-October 2012 following the previous procedure. The web pages of the 123 companies listed in the Helsinki Stock Exchange (Nasdaq OMX Nordic) were consulted to gather data on both the current Boards of Directors and Management Teams presented on the websites of the companies as well as from Annual Reports of these companies from 2008 to 2011. The figures in the Annual Reports for 2011 and on the websites were very close to each other, but some changes might have occurred. Some of these changes were clearly visible also in the 2012 data, which was not, however, final by the time this chapter was printed. However, how the composition of Boards and Management Teams was presented on the websites was more interesting from the point of view of investor communications and public relations: how the companies wanted to present themselves to investors, media and the greater public. We made several check-ups in order to get the data right. But of course, one person retiring or falling ill can actually make changes in the small numbers. In comparison to many other countries Finnish companies' boards tend to be smaller by numbers.

The recommendations of Corporate Governance Finland on the gender composition of boards of listed companies came into effect from the beginning of 2010.

> The number of the directors and the composition of the board shall make it possible for the board to discharge its duties in an efficient manner. The composition shall take into account the requirements placed by the company operations and the development stage of the company. A person to be elected to the board shall have the qualifications required by the duties and the possibility to devote a sufficient amount of time to the work. *Both genders shall be represented on the board.*[12] This formulation is slightly less imperative in comparison to the Swedish formulations, which puts forward the argument for the equality as the aim in board compositions: *the company is to strive for equal gender distribution on the board.*[13]

A further motivation for the succinct recommendation highlighted above is given under the same section: "One element of a diverse composition of the board is to have both genders represented on the board."[14] The formulation of "women and men" offers a basis for debate over whether this recommendation means that one woman is enough, or whether it refers to women in the plural – that there should be more than one woman on the board. In the annual reports for 2011, half of the companies had interpreted that one woman is enough.

A parallel from public administration and local politics may be found in a court case decided by the Highest Administrative Court in Finland. In the late 1980s, the first version of the Finnish Act on Equality between Women and Men (609/1986) stipulated that nominated or indirectly elected state and municipal bodies must have both women and men as members. The provision led to municipalities interpreting the provision so that one woman per body was enough. This led to legal disputes, and the Supreme Administrative Court in Finland ruled in 1990[15] that even though the preparatory works of the Equality Act spoke of women and men in the plural but that this was not of decisive

---

12 Finnish Corporate Governance Code 2010, Securities Market Association, 15 June 2010, p. 10. Italics added.

13 Swedish Corporate Governance Code 2010, Swedish Corporate Governance Board, 2010, p. 17. Italics added.

14 "Hallituksen monipuoliseen kokoonpanoon kuuluu myös se, että hallituksen jäseninä on molempia sukupuolia." Ibid.

15 Supreme Administrative Court in Finland: 1) KHO 1990-A-29, 21.1.1990, 2103/1/89, Edilex www.edilex.fi/kho/vuosikirjat/199000287; 2) KHO 1990-A-30, 21 Jan 1990, 2304/1/89, Edilex www.edilex.fi/kho/vuosikirjat/199000284.

significance and that one woman in each body was enough. In 1995, after much debate and lobbying from the women's organisations and women MPs, the Equality Act was amended to include a numerical, 40%–60% quota.[16] Obviously, this example is applicable to the public sector, but as it applies to state-owned companies as well, it provides a blueprint for how gender quotas in the private sector might be approached.

Figure 1. Share of women and men in boards of Finnish listed companies 2008–12

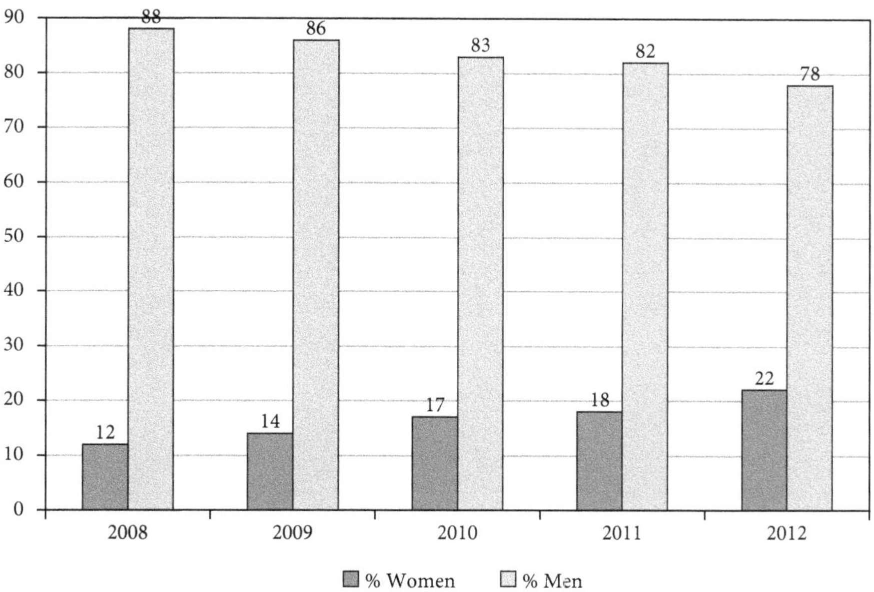

Source: Annual reports of Finnish listed companies, 2008–2012.

As we can see from the figure above, it is plausible that the debate around and knowledge about the forthcoming recommendation might have influenced the composition of the boards slightly already in 2009, as the share of women among board members has risen steadily since 2008, by 3–4 percentage points each year. What is especially interesting is that the growth has been largest in the biggest companies. The smallest companies (small cap) have either not followed the regulation, but explained it, or in rare cases, one or two individual company cases, have left the matter unexplained.[17] As no economic sanctions follow, only the loss of "reputation" for failing to fulfil the Governance Code, the problem of "cost" might not be so high for a specialised company not aiming for the

16 J. Lovenduski and P. Norris, "Westerminster Women: the Politics of Presence", *Political Studies*, 51(2003) at 84–102.K. Nousiainen, A.M. Holli, J. Kantola, M. Saari and L. Hart, "Theorizing gender equality: perspectives on power and legitimacy", *Social Politics: International Studies in Gender, State and Society*, 20 (2013) 41 at 55–56.

17 Linnainmaa, 2011.

consumer markets' credibility. The growth of the share of women in the boardroom kept on growing still in 2012, and it will be interesting to see if this growth goes on or if the figures settle at some point. The difference in the proportion of women between figures in the Annual Reports of 2011 (24%) and the websites in Autumn 2012 (29%) was five percentage points, showing that change was and probably still is occurring rapidly and that there was perhaps a heightened willingness to present to the public that women were indeed taken "on board".

Figure 2. Men and women in top management teams of listed companies, 2008-2011

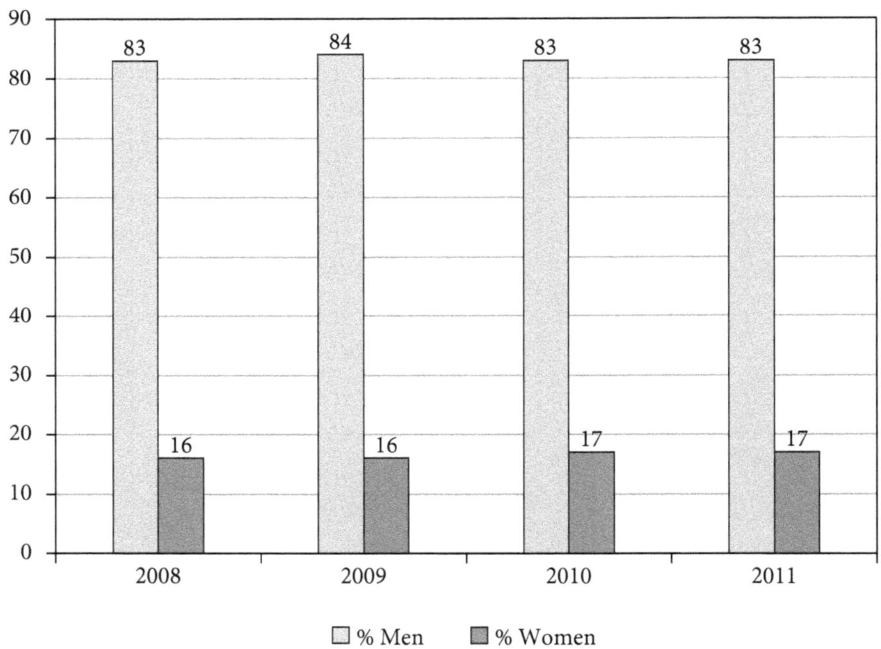

Source: Annual reports of Finnish listed companies, 2008–2011.

In contrast, the share of women and men in top management positions has remained rather stable. About 120 women hold full-time positions in Management Teams at the moment, and thus constitute a pool of potential Board Members. According to a survey by the Central Chamber of Commerce in Finland, women tend to be in charge of supporting functions such as human resources, finance, communications and marketing.[18] Women tend not to hold executive positions in the field of business operations as often as their male colleagues. The number of women CEOs in listed companies in recent years has been, one, two or none, depending on the situation. In a way, it is positive that

18 Ibid.

the share of women in top management positions has not dropped due to the growth of women in boardroom positions. The so called "golden skirt" phenomenon, described for example in the case of Norway after the introduction of quota legislation in 2006, means that when women are sought out as board members, woman board professionals tend to accumulate several positions. This might mean that the share of women in other top management positions drops. This phenomenon has not really taken over in Finland, as only about 20 women who are board members have more than one position as a board member.[19]

B. VARIATION BY BUSINESS SECTOR

The proportion of women among board members – and as managers – varies a great deal by business sector. According to the categorisation given by OMX Nordic, the largest business sector is Industrials, comprising over a third of all Finnish listed companies. In this largest sector, the share of women among board members is lower than average, 16% compared to 19% for all listed companies. Women made up over a quarter or even a third in categories such as Basic materials, Consumer services and Energy, Telecommunications and Utilities (a residual category made up of three different OMX categories due to a small number of companies spread over several categories). In Basic materials and Energy, telecommunications and utilities women's larger share than average of board seats is due to the presence of companies with significant state ownership in this category, as separate quota legislation applies to them. In Consumer services, the share of women (26%) is close to listed companies as a whole (24%), and probably due to women being more prominent in this sector culturally and socially.

Table 1. Number of women and men as board members by business sector, 2011

Business Sectors	Women	Men	Companies
Industrials	42	218	44
Technology	15	90	19
Financials	20	83	15
Consumer goods	14	76	14
Basic materials	22	55	11
Consumer services	20	56	11
Health care	5	33	5
Energy, telecommunications and utilities	11	20	4
Total	**149**	**631**	**123**

Source: Annual reports of listed Finnish companies in 2011.

19 Linnainmaa, 2012.

Table 2. Percentage of women and men as board members by business sector, 2011

Business Sectors	% Women	% Men	Companies
Industrials	16	84	44
Technology	14	86	19
Financials	19	81	15
Consumer goods	16	84	14
Basic materials	29	71	11
Consumer services	26	74	11
Health care	13	87	5
Energy, telecommunications and utilities	35	65	4
Total	**19**	**81**	**123**

Source: Annual reports of listed Finnish companies in 2011.

Compared to the situation of listed companies described in Hart et al. (2009), the percentage of women as board members has risen considerably between 2008 and 2011, from 12% to 19%. In Industrials, the largest business sector judging by the number of companies with high emphasis on production of industrial goods, the share of women on corporate boards has risen from 10% to 16%. This is partly explained through the fact that in 2011 there were six more companies in this category than in 2009. Energy, telecommunications and utilities, the smallest category, still has the largest share of women, 32% in 2009 and 35% in 2011. Women hold the largest shares, over 25%, in the categories of Basic materials and Consumer services, in sectors where there is or has been state ownership or which are somehow "identified" with women. Interestingly, Consumer goods and Health care, where women constitute a great deal of the consumers making spending decisions, women's share in the boardroom is among the lowest. This becomes very difficult – and very interesting – to explain, as there are competences among the professionals in this sector, and the education pipelines within the sector are female dominated.

V. ANALYSIS: THE CASE OF FINLAND

When not looking at the direct (political or business related) interests of the persons who have been active in the public discussion of the pro and against quotas, the arguments can be divided into two groups. Those who have been against the quotas, argue for the general trends of liberal market economy and loosening of regulation in the business sector, and relate the need to de-regulate rather than regulate to the growing global aspects such as global competition faced by the Finnish companies in an ever increasing way. The ethos of market liberalism with little or no need for the State governance is prevailing approach.

Those who are in favour for quotas in companies' boards relate the need for quotas for the equality issues in society at large, and to the need to make it even for women and for men through legislative manner. The arguments for the quotas relate to the general legislative regulations such as the equality legislation on the one hand, and on the experiences from the State-owned companies on the other hand. The argument used for the promotion of the quotas is interesting as it stems from the collectivist and universal claim for equality and at the same time is most often expressed jointly with the individualised capability claims: in the discussion the claim often made is that "the quotas promote equality and the best capabilities of women are lost if they are not selected on equal footing to the boards of the companies".[20] The collectivist notions of arguments for the quotas relate the issues of equality having higher priority in the business sector in comparison to profit making.

Those proponents that are against the quotas argue that greater self-disciplining within the business sector and within businesses themselves will do the trick, and no need to establish rigid quota system. However, against this argument it is possible to note that while the present situation with close to 28% of women in large-cap companies' boards has taken over 30 years to develop, the equal share is not close by.

It is plausible, however, that the Governance code has speeded up things: the comply or explain principle works effectively in those cases where companies' public reputation in the eyes of the investors, shareholders and public is on line: consumer business gets easily damaged through the bad publicity, and the importance of the public image management goes for any large cap company. For smaller companies who have been listed only a short while, with business logic building around the niche-market-type of thinking or business-to-business product range, it may well be that some of the comply or explain code do not necessarily make such a big threat to the reputation. Therefore, it is important to note that the companies differ according to their business logic, value creation logic and for most of the companies the reputation management and the control over the mediated image of the company is very important for the share price development.

---

20 A. Kotiranta, A. Kovalainen and P. Rouvinen, "Female Leadership and Company Profitability", in A. de Bruin, C.G. Brush, E. Gatewood and C. Henry, *Women Entrepreneurs and the Global Environment for Growth: A Research Perspective.* (eds.) Edward Elgar Publishing Ltd., Chapter 4, 2010.

VI. CONCLUSION

From the legal perspective, the main task of the boards is to take care of the shareholders' interests in the value creation, good governance and management of the company. Other tasks can – purely from the legal point of view – be seen inferior to this. However, mechanic legal perspective is seldom the only perspective, as the value creation of companies takes place in society, not in vacuum. The tensions between the political regulation and the companies' own self-management are crucial to be understood as the inherent context here.

We can justifiably ask, whether the companies in fact need to take into account any of the society's demands, as long as they do not break the law. And here is where the true dilemma arises: does the society need to have the quota legislation in place, and if so, will those arguments serve the best interests of the shareholders? The answer is not an easy one – nor one-dimensional one. On the one hand, the recent history – the last five years – show that the Finnish companies can be agile and nominate women in their boards without legislative actions. The nominations mean that the matter has been taken seriously to reach the nomination boards of the companies. The requirements for equality have not been met, but women have reached the minority position. On the other hand, the motives remain hidden: are the nominations of women occurring because companies are willing to shy away from the possible damages to their reputation, that is, they are sensitive to the possible image damage and for the reason nominate women, or indeed, do they think of the "greater good" in society as the main motivator. And interestingly, would those two lines of arguments that stem from very different traditions serve single one goal: that companies' values are reflected in their board nominations, and that these values are in harmony with societal values.

Overall, the discussion on the quota legislation in Finland has been taken up politically but with weak results and with no real agenda and its follow-up. No legislative initiatives have so far been taken in the Parliament, despite the comments by many politicians. It seems that none will be put forward either. The described development needs to be seen in relation to other regulatory mechanisms that are imposed to corporations in lesser amount than earlier (financial restrictions), and other mechanisms that are growing (environmental legislation). In that perspective, quota legislation may seem to some to be an "old fashioned" agenda, while the Corporate Governance Code is more flexible, modern and agile way to govern. As the case is in Finland, the Code regulates the companies in similar manner: Companies may deviate from individual rules, providing they report each deviation, describe their own solution and explain why deviation took place. In Swedish Code the argument is explicit: the aim of the Code is to provide an alternative to legislation. For many companies it seems that self-regulation is often preferable to legislation. But is the self-governing Code the best instrument for the societal changes, we may well ask.

The aim with the self-governance through soft regulation, the corporate governance introduced in many countries by the business community itself is to ensure that companies are run as efficiently as possible on behalf of their shareholders. The corporate governance thus serves the interests of the shareholders and gives agility and more flexibility in comparison to legislation. It may well be that the economy has cut off the king's head: the politics does not seem to have the hold over the economy in today's global economic climate. This may be especially true in current European economic situation where the national interests such as the national economic growth and stability for companies' national business environment clearly have a strong political priority over the equality in society. Issues such as lower taxation and loosening of legal regulations that relate to nation's competitiveness over other nations become important in the austere global economy of the 21st century.

REFERENCES

DEMARI 18 June 2007. "Hallitus ei valmistele naiskiintiölakia". Uutispäivä Demari. Helsinki. 2007.

ELY, R., HIBARRA, H. and KOLB, D., "Taking Gender into Account". Academy of Management Learning & Education, 2011.

Finnish Corporate Governance Code 2010 (unofficial English translation), Securities Market Association, 15 June 2010, http://cgfinland.fi/files/2012/01/finnish-cg-code-2010.pdf. Accessed 26 July 2013.

HART, L., HOLLI, A. and KOVALAINEN, A., "Gender and Power in the Nordic Countries: Report on Finland" in K. Niskanen and A. Nyberg (eds), *Kön och makt I Norden – Del I Landrapporter*, TemaNord 2009: 569 (Copenhagen: Nordic Council of Ministers, 2009). Also a web publication at www.norden.org/en/publications/publikationer/2009–569.

KOTIRANTA, A., KOVALAINEN, A. and ROUVINEN, P., "Female Leadership and Company Profitability", in DE BRUIN, A., BRUSH, C.G., GATEWOOD, E. and HENRY, C. (eds.), *Women Entrepreneurs and the Global Environment for Growth: A Research Perspective*, Edward Elgar Publishing Ltd., Chapter 4, 2010.

KONRAD, A., KRAMER, V. and EKRUT, S., "Critical mass: The impact of three or more women on corporate boards", (2008) 37 *Organisational Dynamics* 145.

KOVALAINEN, A., *At the Margins of the Economy*, 1995, Avebury, Ashgate.

LINNAINMAA, L., *Miehet johtavat pörssiyhtiöiden liiketoimintoja – Naiset päätyvät tukitoimintoihin* ("Men lead business operations in listed companies – Women end up in support functions") (Helsinki: Central Chamber of Commerce, 2011). http://

kauppakamari.fi/wp-content/uploads/2012/01/Naisjohtajuusselvitys_20111.pdf. Accessed 28 November 2012.

LINNAINMAA, L., *Lasikatto säröilee – Itsesäätely päihittää kiintiöt* ("The glass ceiling is cracking – Self-regulation beats quotas") (Helsinki: Central Chamber of Commerce, 2012). http://kauppakamari.fi/wp-content/uploads/2012/10/Lasikatto-s%C3%A4r%C3%B6ilee_Itses%C3%A4%C3%A4ntely-p%C3%A4ihitt%C3%A4%C3%A4-kiinti%C3%B6t.pdf. Accessed 1 November 2012.

NOUSIAINEN, K., HOLLI, A.M., KANTOLA, J., SAARI, M. and HART, L., "Theorizing gender equality: perspectives on power and legitimacy", *Social Politics: International Studies in Gender, State and Society*, 20 (2013) 41.

POUTANEN, S. and KOVALAINEN, A., "Gendering Innovation Process in an Industrial Plant – Revisiting Tokenism, Gender and Innovation", (2013) 5 *International Journal of Gender and Entrepreneurship* (2013) 5 257 at 274.

Swedish Corporate Governance Code 2010, Swedish Corporate Governance Board, 2010, Stockholm.

WILLIAMS, C.L., "The Glass Escalator, Revisited: Gender Inequality in Neoliberal Times", *Gender & Society*, 2013.

WÄNGNERUD, L. and SUNDELL, A., "Do Politics Matter? Women in Swedish local elected assemblies 1970–2010 and gender equality in outcomes", *European Political Science Review* 2012, 4:1, 97–120.

"Selvitys: Naisten osuus pörssiyritysten johdossa kasvaa yhä", *Helsingin Sanomat* 23 October 2012. www.hs.fi/talous/a1305609183891. Accessed 19 July 2013.

Supreme Administrative Court in Finland: 1) KHO 1990-A-29, 21.1.1990, 2103/1/89, Edilex www.edilex.fi/kho/vuosikirjat/199000287; 2) KHO 1990-A-30, 21 Jan 1990, 2304/1/89, Edilex www.edilex.fi/kho/vuosikirjat/199000284.

CHAPTER 6

FRANCE: THE MEASURES OF POSITIVE DISCRIMINATION WITHIN THE BOARDS OF DIRECTORS OF UNDERTAKINGS

Brigitte GRESY*

I. THE CONTEXT

It is as from the year 2005 that the issue of the underrepresentation of women in the positions of governance in the undertakings has become important in France. Until then, the law-maker, not really minding about introducing legal obligations in this area, relied on auto- regulation. But the slow speed of the evolutions, not to say the absence thereof, have modified the approach of this issue.[1]

Indeed, in the boards of directors, the part of the women was some 9% in 2008, a rate inferior to the European average, and significantly below the countries of the north of Europe. The percentage of women in the boards of directors and the supervisory boards was more or less 10% in the companies of the CAC 40 but fell to 8% for the 500 first French companies. More than half of them did not have a single woman in their board of directors. The evolutions were almost without any significance, some 0,4% from one year to another.

The management committee (CODIR) and the executive committees (COMEX) showed the same weakness of the female representation: 6.8% of women in the enterprises of the CAC 40 and 13.5% of women in the 500 first French companies but almost half of them did not have any women in their CODIR or COMEX.

However, this glass ceiling constituted a kind of paradox: the place of women in the labour market of France had, indeed, evolved a lot: an activity rate of some

* Secretary General of the High Council for professional equality in France.

83% for the women aged between 25 and 49, combined with a birth rate of some 2%, a strong increase of the population of female executives with almost 150% in 10 years and a good initial training of the girls since they represented two thirds of the degrees of the third cycle. Certainly, other signs pointed at strong inequalities on the labour market between men and women: a difference in remuneration of some 27% on gross yearly average and a growing precariousness of the female work since two thirds of the low salaries were occupied by women and women were twice as much on the SMIC (the minimal income for persons living in poverty in France) than men. But the gap between the place of women on the labour market and the conditions of their access to the positions of governance was obvious.

II. NUMEROUS OBSTACLES

Four categories of obstacles were counted:

- Organisational causes in the first place and notably the criterions of evaluation of the human resources, apparently neutral but in the facts copied on the male models of presence at work: presenteeism (politics of presence), linear career, detection of high potentials at the age when women have their children, etc. The time management and the working conditions in the enterprise also penalised the taking into account of a balanced parenthood;
- Furthermore, the role of the systems of representation that contribute to the sentiment of illegitimacy of women in the places of power as well as the small number of role models that lead them to refuse to occupy positions of power;
- A wrong orientation at school and at the university of girls that lead them to less promising outlets and also explains this exclusion of women from the places of power;
- Finally, the unequal division of household tasks that renders the balance between the family life and the professional life at very high level difficult in time-consuming functions that require a high level of mobility.

III. A LEGAL ARSENAL BUILT ON THE MODEL OF THE POLITICAL GENDER PARITY

The establishment of quotas has soon turned out to be an essential instrument having the advantage of being readable for the parties concerned. But the history of imposing quotas in the boards of directors of undertakings in France was made of advancements and regressions, illustrating the strong opposition both from the political power and the undertakings. To the difference of other great democracies, France has found itself prevented from having politics of positive discrimination in favour of women, including from a legal point of view, for a long time.

Despite this, France has an impressive legal arsenal in the field of professional equality. Not less than six laws have, since 1972, provided for the principle of professional equality in case of equivalent qualifications and responsibilities. So, the enterprises have the obligation to negotiate and sign an agreement both on the professional equality in the broad sense (recruitment, training, promotion, time management, compensation, working conditions) and on the removal of the differences in compensation, in the framework of an integrated negotiation in the annual negotiation on the salaries. A recent text has imposed a sanction that might go up to 1% of the sum of all salaries for the enterprises that do not meet their legal obligations.

However, not a single measure on positive discrimination for the positions of governance in the undertaking had been foreseen. These measures only existed in the field of the political elections since 2000.

A. THE MEASURES OF POSITIVE DISCRIMINATION IN THE POLITICAL FIELD

The constitutional principle of equality, as it results notably from the articles one, six and thirteen of the declaration of human and citizen rights of 26 august 1789, has indeed proven a crippling obstacle in a number of cases, and notably in favour of political parity. Already in 1982 and also in 1999, the constitutional council had banned lawmakers' initiatives in favour of political parity based on the argument that the quotas were incompatible with the sole consideration of the merit or the talent of the persons (decision No. 82–146 DC of 18 November 1982 and No. 99–407 DC of 14 January 1999). One therefore had to modify the constitution.

A first constitutional revision of 8 July 1999 has therefore allowed that *"the law favours the equal access of men and women to the electoral mandates and the elective offices"*. This opened the way to political parity, which came to being in the law of 6 June 2000 that imposed a compulsive equality of candidacies for the list systems, with the candidates of each gender alternating, and an optional equality for the voting for a single candidate for the elections for the law-making chambers but with an important financial sanction related to financing of the political parties.

B. THE ATTEMPTS TO BROADEN TO THE ECONOMIC FIELD

Strengthened by these advancements, the lawmaker has judged that he could also establish the equality in the bodies of governance of the economic world. Therefore, as from the year 2006, an amendment aiming at imposing 20% of the underrepresented gender in the boards of directors of the undertakings listed on the stock exchange has been deposited at the National Assembly during the examination of the Law on the compensation equality, but this measure has been rejected by the constitutional council in a decision of 16 March 2006 (decision No. 2006–533 DC of 16 March 2006) based on the motive that it was in contradiction with the constitution and that the search for a balanced access of women and men to responsibilities *"should not (...) let the consideration of gender have priority over the capacities and the common utility"*. The constitutional council has thus seen in the proposed measures of positive discrimination a breach of equality before the law since these would have the gender prevail over the competences of persons and the common utility.

Just as in the matter of parity in politics, the constitutional assembly has thus decided to draw the consequences of the case law of 16 March 2006 in the text itself of the constitution. The constitutional law of 23 July 2008 has therefore modified the first article of the constitution of 4 October 1958 in order to include that the law does not only favour the equal access of women and men to electoral mandates and to elective offices but also " *the equal access to professional and social responsibilities*". The road was thus open for the parity in the economic world.

In March 2009, a draft of law deposited by Marie José Zimmerman making the presence of 40% of the underrepresented gender compulsory in the boards of directors and supervisory boards stayed once more without effect.

It was then that the public authorities tried to have the mentalities changed by calling on expertise and programs of sensitisation. A request in that sense was made by the general inspection of social affairs. This report presented by Brigitte Gresy in July 2009 and proposing to impose 40% of the underrepresented sex in the boards of directors and the supervisory boards in the companies listed on the stock exchange, within a term of 6 years, had the effect of an electric shock both on the media and on the networks of women in undertakings. This proposal that was inspired by the Norwegian legislative package took away the violent reservations worded against the quotas still a few years ago, reservations often formulated by the women themselves, based on the argument that they wanted to be recruited for their competence and not by obligation. The quotas have massively been accepted in the public opinion, as a necessary evil in the absence of proven progress.

C. JANUARY 2011: THE VOTE ON THE LAW ON THE QUOTAS

As from December 2009, Jean-François Copé, president of the UMP group and Marie-Jo Zimmerman, seeing the opportunity of this shooting window opened by the impact of the proposals of the report in the public opinion and by the continuous treatment of the theme in the media, have deposited a new draft of law in that sense. The lawmaker of the two chambers needed less than one year to develop law No. 2011–103 of 27 January 2011 on the balanced representation of men and women within boards of directors and supervisory boards and on the professional equality.

The law therefore establishes two stages: 20% of the underrepresented gender within a term of 3 years, either in January 2014, and 40% within a term of six months, either January 2017, for all the companies whose shares are admitted to the transactions on the regulated market, in other words the companies having their shares listed on the stock markets, and the undertakings which, for the third consecutive year, employ an average number of at least five hundred permanent salaried workers and having a net turnover or a balance sheet total of at least 50 million Euros. The enterprises of public law are also concerned as well as the industrial and commercial establishments (EPIC). A draft of law deposited on 3 July 2013 broadens the field of the EPIC concerned to those having at least 200 salary workers.

The sanction foreseen is the nullity of the nomination, which does not imply that of deliberations and the non-payment of the directors' attendance fees. Not a single sanction has been imposed until today.

IV. A SATISFACTORY IMPLEMENTATION

A. NOTABLE ADVANCEMENTS BUT MONITORING IS REQUIRED

The feminisation of the boards has been made easier by two provisions of the Commercial Code in France: in application of Article L. 225–18 of the Code of Commerce, the duration of the mandate of the director is fixed by the articles of association of the company with a maximum of six years. Meanwhile, the Articles L. 225–21 and L. 225–77 of the Commercial Code limit the number of mandates as director or as member of the supervisory board of a limited company with anonymous shares having its registered office on French territory, that may be exercised simultaneously by the same physical person. These provisions may accelerate the renewal of the governance bodies.

In February 2013, the survey carried out by a consulting firm, on a sample of 450 undertakings with one quarter of big enterprises, one quarter of medium-sized enterprises and 50% of small enterprises, established that, in general, the undertakings had almost anticipated the call of 2014: the rate of feminisation was indeed situated between 19 and 21%, with the exception of energy where the number of women directors was only 16%. The enterprises of the CAC 40 had the best figures, up to 23.7%. In July 2013, the percentage of women directors elected in the general assembly in the companies of the CAC 40 reach 28%. In addition, the women directors do not have too many mandates as 87.1% of them, in the sample withheld, have only one position, 8.5% have two mandates, 2.9% have three mandates and 0.5% five.

The results of the companies of the CAC 40 are more mixed. Three groups, Publicis, Technip and Accor exceed on 25 June 2013 the threshold of 40% of elected women in the general assembly, but six companies are below the threshold of 20% and one of these, EADS, represents a percentage of only 8.3%.

Also, with regard to the SBF 120[2], of the 25 women elected in 2013, only 44% have the French nationality and more than half of the women elected already had at least one mandate in the SBF 120 before their appointment. The boards of the CAC 40 have accepted only four women in 2013 and 16 of the nomination boards have not a single woman as member.

In general, the increase of the rate of feminisation concerns essentially the positions of independent director and representative of the salaried workers. Furthermore, the proportion of male directors having a seat in a specialised committee at the end of 2011 is still significantly higher than that of the female directors and this whatever the type of committee (audit and risks, compensation & benefits, strategy, nomination etc.).

A watchful eye thus remains needed, at regular intervals. With this in mind, the results of the appointments in the board of directors and in the CODIR (BG: Management Committee) and COMEX (BG: Executive Committee) of the undertakings concerned by the law will be communicated yearly to the "Conseil supérieur de l'égalité professionnelle" (High Council for the professional equality).

2 BG: the SBF 120 consists of the companies of the CAC 40 and 80 companies with the other most traded shares in France.

B. CHALLENGES OF PERFORMANCE AND FAIRNESS AND CONSEQUENCES IN TERMS OF PROFESSIONALISING

The feminisation of the boards of directors meets in the first place an evident democratic need and a requirement to acknowledge the qualifications, competences and merits of the salaried workers whatever their gender. It's also a tool of economic performance. The capacity of a board of directors to meet the interests of enterprises depends, indeed, of its level of openness and thus the surpassing of the endogamous "little world" of the managing French class that practices types of co-optation among its members, more damageable to the renewal of the elites and to the taking of risks than the transparent quotas, fixed for a limited duration and favouring only persons with a comparable competence.

From another side, this reform has led to two notable advancements: a better use of available resources and a professionalising of the position of director. Indeed, as from the moment that the question of the recruitment ground of women available for such mandates has been raised, these of the contents of the function of director and the competences required have been raised at the same time, as well as that of the training adapted to this function. Consequently, men and women are from now on searched for according to formalised criteria and not a mere acquaintance or related interests. The companies had to search for women in other circles of excellence than those of company managers or capital holders: circles of lawyers, presidents of associative networks, economists, etc.

V. A DIFFERENT LOGIC FOR THE FEMINISATION OF THE CODIR AND COMEX

An initiative of imposing quotas could not be envisaged for the operational managerial functions in enterprises where only a contractual logic may prevail, in the shape of objectives of progression for example. On the boards of directors, however, an institutional logic is applicable since their rules of composition and functioning are governed by company law.

This approach by quotas, on condition that it is monitored during its implementation, and followed-up with attentiveness, constitutes without any doubt an instrument of equality, that serves the collective interest but also functions as an agent to transform the profession of director, benefitting both women and men.

CHAPTER 7
GENDER QUOTA IN COMPANY BOARDS: GERMANY

Bernd Waas*

I. INTRODUCTION

It is hardly disputable that Germany has considerable deficiencies as regards gender equality in the private sector. For many years the proportion of women in management positions has stagnated at a low level. No legal quotas apply. An agreement that was reached in July 2001 between the then Federal government and the umbrella organisations of German business associations to promote equality between women and men in the private sector so far has not led to significant progress. As before, supervisory boards and management boards (boards of directors) of large companies are firmly in the hands of men. In the thirty publicly listed companies which form part of the German stock index (DAX 30), women account for around 11% of all supervisory board members.[1] Very recently, however, there was a considerable increase in the number of female supervisory board members.[2]

Against this background the Federal government has stepped up its efforts to increase the proportion of women in the upper echelons of German companies by developing a phased plan that aims at reaching this goal.[3] In particular, the government achieved another commitment of German companies. On invitation of several government members the ceo's of DAX-companies promised in March 2011 to fix targets for increased women representation as well as timeframes

* Goethe University Frankfurt.

1 As regards management boards the situation is even more sobering as only 3% of all directors are women; see for more empirical data www.fidar.de/wob-index.html.

2 According to a study that was undertaken by PWC, one of Germany's leading auditing and consultancy organisations, the proportion of women on the boards of the DAX 30 companies increased by more than a third since the beginning of 2011.

3 The plan is called "*Frauen und Männer in Führungspositionen*" (Women and Men in Decision-Making).

within which to achieve them and to report regularly on the status of implementation. These targets relate to the levels below the management boards. However, most of the DAX 30 companies did also adopt individual targets regarding their supervisory boards. These targets are essentially based on a so-called "diversity-recommendation" that forms part of the German Corporate Governance Code.[4] Almost all DAX 30 companies by now followed this recommendation. Among them, 21 companies strive to achieve a quota of 20% or more while seven companies even try to reach 30% or more.[5] Nevertheless, there are wide-spread doubts whether voluntary agreements will be sufficiently effective. This may explain why there have been several legislative initiatives lately all of which aim at establishing a legal quota. The focus of these efforts is the supervisory board of big companies rather than the management board.

This paper will try to shed light on these plans. To this end the German legal framework that forms the "playing field" of all these initiatives will be outlined first. As will be seen, this framework consists of two pieces: corporate law and the law of workers' co-determination (II.). Thereafter the individual legislative plans will be presented in some detail (III.) before discussing the legal and in particular the constitutional concerns which these plans met with to a greater or lesser extent (IV.). At the end there will be a brief summary (V.).

II. THE LEGAL FRAMEWORK

A. CORPORATE LAW

In Germany two primary forms of companies exist. One is the so-called *Aktiengesellschaft* (abbreviated *AG*). An *Aktiengesellschaft* is a corporation that is limited by shares, i.e., owned by shareholders, and may be traded on a stock market. Liability to creditors with respect to obligations of the company is limited to the company's assets. The other is the so-called *Gesellschaft mit beschränkter Haftung* (abbreviated *GmbH*). A *Gesellschaft mit beschränkter Haftung* also forms a legal person. Again liability to creditors is restricted to the company's assets.[6] The *Gesellschaft mit beschränkter Haftung* was the world's first form of a limited liability corporation.

4 See 5.4.1 Deutscher Corporate Governance Kodex: www.corporate-governance-code.de/ger/kodex/5.html; see for more details Weber-Rey, "Gesetzliche Frauenquote?", in *Zeitschrift für Rechtspolitik* (ZRP) 2011, p. 127; Hüffer, in: Hüffer (ed.), *Aktiengesetz*, 10th ed. 2012, §100 note 2c.

5 See www.flexi-quote.de/ziele-der-dax-30-aufsichtsraete.html.

6 Section 13(2) ACLL.

The legal basis of the *Aktiengesellschaft* is the Stock Corporation Act (SCA) 1965 (*Aktiengesetz*).[7] Section 1(1) SCA – on the "character of the company" – states, that a stock corporation constitutes a separate legal entity. *Aktiengesellschaften* have a "two-tiered board" structure consisting of a supervisory board (*Aufsichtsrat*) and a management board (*Vorstand*). The supervisory board is generally controlled by shareholders, though seats may be reserved for workers' representatives depending on the size of the company.[8] The management board directly runs the company.[9] Its members may be removed, however, by the supervisory board,[10] which also determines the management board's compensation.[11] The legal basis of the *Gesellschaft mit beschränkter Haftung* is the Act on Companies with Limited Liability (ACLL) of 1892 (*Gesetz betreffend die Gesellschaften mit beschränkter Haftung*).[12] The *Gesellschaft mit beschränkter Haftung* is very common in Germany.

The supervisory board of an *Aktiengesellschaft* comprises three members. The articles of the company may provide for a higher number. Such number shall be divisible by three, however. The maximum number of members of the supervisory board for companies with a share capital of up to €1.500.000 is nine. The maximum number of members of the supervisory board for companies with a share capital of more than €10.000.000 is twenty-one.[13] In case of companies subject to the Co-determination Act 1976 (*Mitbestimmungsgesetz*) the supervisory board is composed of board members of the shareholders and the employees.[14]

As regards personal qualifications of members of the supervisory board it is stated in section 100(1) sentence 1 SCA 1965 that only a natural person with full legal capacity may be a member. According to section 100(2) SCA 1965 a person

---

7 *Aktiengesetz* of 06.09.1965 (BGBl. I S. 1089), last amended by Article 3 of the Act of 20.12.2012 (BGBl. I S. 2751).

8 *Infra* (II.2.).

9 See section 76(1) SCA: "The management board shall have direct responsibility for the management of the company"; see also section 78(1) sentence 1: "The management board shall represent the company in and out of court".

10 See section 84(1) sentence 1 SCA: "The supervisory board shall appoint the members of the management board for a period not exceeding five years".

11 Section 87(1) sentence 1 SCA. Recently, it has been increasingly discussed whether the position of shareowners in this regard should be strengthened.

12 *Gesetz betreffend die Gesellschaften mit beschränkter Haftung* of 20.04.1892 (revised version, BGBl. III, Gliederungsnummer 4123-1), last amended by Article 7 of the Act of 21.03.2013 (BGBl. I S. 556).

13 Section 95 sentences 1–4 SCA. There have been demands, however, lately to limit the maximum number of board members; see, for instance, Hüffer, in: Hüffer (ed.), *Aktiengesetz*, 10th ed., 2012, §95 note 2.

14 Section 96(1) SCA. The Act also makes provision for companies that are subject to other codetermination laws.

may not be a member of the supervisory board who (1.) is already a member of the supervisory board in ten commercial enterprises which are legally required to form a supervisory board; or (2.) is the legal representative of an enterprise that is controlled by the company; or (3.) is the legal representative of another corporation whose supervisory board includes a member of the management board of the company, or (4.) was a member of the management board of the same listed company during the past two years, unless he is elected upon nomination by shareholders holding more than 25% of the voting rights in the company. Nor may a member of the supervisory be at the same time a member of the management board, a permanent deputy member of the management board, a registered authorised officer (so-called *Prokurist*) or a general manager of the company (so-called incompatibility).[15] No board system exists in Germany. Instead, there is a clear separation of the duties of the management board on the one hand and the supervisory board on the other.[16] The members of the supervisory board shall be elected by the shareholders' meeting (*Hauptversammlung*), unless they are to be appointed to the supervisory board or elected as representatives of employees pursuant to the Codetermination Act (CA) 1976 or other Codetermination Acts.[17]

Supervisory boards are essentially monitoring bodies. Their main task is to supervise the management of the company.[18] In order to do so the supervisory board enjoys the power to inspect and examine the books and records of the company as well as the assets of the company, in particular cash, securities and merchandise. The supervisory board may also commission individual members or, with respect to specific assignments, special experts, to carry out such inspection and examination.[19] The supervisory board can call a shareholder's meeting whenever the interests of the company so require. A simple majority is sufficient for such resolution.[20] It must be seen in this context that the management board of the company is required to report to the supervisory board on various issues. According to section 90 SCA 1965 the supervisory board must report to the supervisory board on (1.) intended business policy and other fundamental matters regarding the future conduct of the company's business (in particular plans regarding financing, investment and personnel) responding to deviations of actual developments from objectives reported in the past and giving the reasons thereof; (2.) the profitability of the company, in particular the return on equity; (3) the state of business, in particular revenues, and the overall condition of the company; and, finally, (4.) transactions that may

15 Section 105(1) SCA.

16 See Hüffer, in: Hüffer (ed.), *Aktiengesetz*, 10th ed., 2012, §105 note 1.

17 Section 101(1) sentence 1 SCA.

18 Section 111(1) SCA.

19 Section 111(2) sentences 1 and 2 SCA.

20 Section 111(3) SCA.

considerably impact upon the profitability or liquidity of the company. The supervisory board may require at any time a report from the management board on the company's activities, on the company's legal and business relationships with affiliated companies, and on the circumstances concerning the business transactions at such enterprises as far as they have a significant impact on the condition of the company. Any member may also request such report, which shall, however, only be given to the supervisory board as such.[21]

Management responsibilities may not be conferred on the supervisory board. However, the articles of the company or the supervisory board have to determine that specific types of transactions may be entered into only with the consent of the supervisory board. If the supervisory board refuses to grant consent, the management board may request that a shareholders' meeting approve the grant. The shareholders meeting by which the shareholders' approves shall require a majority of not less than three-fourths of the votes cast. Neither may the articles provide for any other majority nor may they prescribe any additional requirements.[22]

As regards *Gesellschaften mit beschränkter Haftung*, there is no obligation under the according Act to establish a supervisory board. Companies are free, however, to form such board voluntarily. In this case the according provisions of the SCA 1965 essentially apply to the supervisory board of the GmbH *mutatis mutandis*, unless the partnership agreement (*Gesellschaftsvertrag*) provides otherwise.[23] As far as small companies are concerned, voluntary supervisory boards are exceptional, however.[24]

B. CO-DETERMINATION LAW

In Germany, co-determination of employees exists not only on plant but also on company level. While the co-determination rights on plant level as established by the Works Constitution Act (WCA) 1972 (*Betriebsverfassungsgesetz*)[25] are enjoyed by independent bodies, the so-called works councils (*Betriebsräte*),[26] co-determination on the company level is effected by securing representation of employees' interests in supervisory boards. The least extensive form of workers' representation is co-determination on the basis of the so-called One-Third

21 Section 90(3) SCA.
22 Section 111 (4) SCA.
23 Section 52(1) ACLL.
24 See Zöllner/Noack, in: Baumbach/Hueck (ed.), *GmbHG*, 20th ed., §52 note 1.
25 *Betriebsverfassungsgesetz* of 15.01.1972 (BGBl. I S. 2518), last amended by Article 9 of the Act of 29.07.2009 (BGBl. I S. 2424).
26 Whose members may or may not be trade union officials.

Participation Act (O-ThPA) 2004 (*Drittelbeteiligungsgesetz*).[27] Under this Act workers' representatives enjoy the right to occupy a third of the seats in the board companies to which the Act applies. The most far-reaching workers' representation is co-determination on the basis of the so-called Coal, Iron and Steel Industry Co-determination Act (CISICA) 1951 (*Montan-Mitbestimmungsgesetz*).[28] In these industries supervisory boards consist of shareholders and workers' representatives in equal numbers with further members and, in particular, a so-called "neutral member".[29] In between these two models is codetermination on the basis of the Co-determination Act (CA) 1976 (*Mitbestimmungsgesetz*).[30]

The One-Third Participation Act 2004 applies, among others, to stock corporations (*Aktiengesellschaft*) and limited liability companies (*Gesellschaft mit beschränkter Haftung*) if such company regularly employs more than 500 employees.[31] As a result limited liability companies may have to establish a supervisory board even if from a company law perspective the formation of a supervisory board is not required. The One-Third Participation Act 2004 is subsidiary to the other, more far-reaching Acts regarding co-determination. The Act, in other words, only applies if no obligation exists under other Acts to form a codetermined supervisory board.

In practical terms the Codetermination Act 1976 will apply in most cases, if one-third participation does not apply. As is the case with the One-Third Participation Act 2004 the Codetermination Act 1976 applies to stock corporations and limited liability companies. There is the requirement, however, that companies employ more than 2000 employees on a regular basis.[32] According to section 6(1) CA 1976 companies must have a supervisory board even if no such board is required by other Acts. With regard to the composition of such boards section 7(1) CA 1976 states that the supervisory board of a company which has as a rule no more than 10.000 employees shall consist of six board members each for shareholders and employees. If the company has as a rule more than 20.000 employees the board of such company shall consist of ten

---

27 *Gesetz über die Drittelbeteiligung der Arbeitnehmer im Aufsichtsrat (Drittelbeteiligungsgesetz – DrittelbG)* of 18.05.2004, last amended by Article 2 of the Act of 22.12.2011 (BGBl. I S. 3044).

28 *Gesetz über die Mitbestimmung der Arbeitnehmer in den Aufsichtsräten und Vorständen der Unternehmen des Bergbaus und der Eisen und Stahl erzeugenden Industrie* of 21.05.1951 (BGBl. III, Gliederungsnummer 801–2), last amended by Article 220 of the Regulation of 31.10.2006 (BGBl. I S. 2407).

29 See section 4 CISICA 1951. As regards the election of the "neutral member" see section 8 of the Act.

30 *Gesetz über die Mitbestimmung der Arbeitnehmer (Mitbestimmungsgesetz – MitbestG)* of 04.05.1976, last amended by Article 2 of the Act of 22.12.2011 (BGBl. I S. 3044).

31 Section1(1) O-ThPA.

32 Section 2(1) CDA 1976.

board members each. According to section 7(2) CA 1976, if a board must have six board members representing employees, four members must belong to company staff while two must be trade union representatives.[33] The respective numbers for a board that consists of eight/ten board members belonging to the employees are six/seven (company staff) and two/three (trade union representatives). Employee board members of a company employing more than 8.000 employees on a regular basis are elected through delegates as long as the employees eligible to vote do not decide to hold a direct election.[34] Employee board members of a company employing no more than 8,000 employees on a regular basis are elected in a direct election as long as the employees eligible to vote do not decide to hold the election through delegates.[35]

In co-determined companies the supervisory board elects from its ranks a chairman and a deputy with a majority of two thirds of the total members of which it is to consist.[36] In case that this majority is not reached a second ballot must be held. In this ballot, the board members of the shareholders shall elect the chairman of the board by majority vote and the board members of the employees shall elect a deputy by majority vote.[37] In other words: If a second ballot is needed a simple majority of votes of the shareholders is sufficient to get the chairman of the board elected. According to section 29(1) CA 1976 resolutions of the supervisory board require the majority of votes cast unless otherwise provided in the Act. Where the votes cast in the supervisory board result in a tie, a new ballot must be held on the same subject.[38] If this ballot results in a tie again, the chairman of the board enjoys two votes.[39] As a result, employees' representatives in supervisory boards are not exactly on a par with shareholders' representatives because the latter can ensure that one of their own is elected as chairman of the board.

III. LEGAL INITIATIVES TO ESTABLISH A QUOTA

As stated at the beginning no statutorily fixed quotas exist in Germany at present. There have been attempts, however, lately, to have quotas established in the future. These initiatives have been promoted at various levels: The Federal

---

33 As to the election of board members "belonging to the enterprise" and the election of union representatives to the board, see sections 15 and 16 CDA 1976, respectively. With regard to the former, specific provision is made in section 15(2) no. 1 CDA 1976 for the election of a representative of managerial employees (so-called *leitende Angestellte*).

34 Section 9(1) CDA 1976.

35 Section 9(2) CDA 1976.

36 Section 27(1) CDA 1976.

37 Section 27(2) CDA 1976.

38 Section 29(2) sentence 1 CDA 1976.

39 Section 29(2) sentence 2 CDA 1976.

parliament (*Bundestag*), the Federal Council (*Bundesrat*) and the Federal government (*Bundesregierung*).[40]

A. FEDERAL PARLIAMENT

1. *Initiative of Alliance 90/The Greens*

In 2010, the parliamentary group of *Bündnis 90/Die Grünen* (Alliance 90/The Greens) in the German Parliament tabled a draft Act on gender-neutral occupation of supervisory boards.[41] The bill foresees a 40% quota applying to shareholders. As regards employees' representatives, the draft Act tries to tie in with existing provisions: In section 4(4) of the One-Third Participation Act 2004 it is, for instance, provided that among employees' representatives there should be women and men in proportion to the numerical ratio in the company. As far as the Co-Determination Act 1976 is concerned, which does so far not provide for any gender quota, a similar provision is foreseen.[42] If the composition of a supervisory board is in breach of one of these provisions, it is provided that decisions of the board must be regarded to be null and void.

2. *Initiative of the Social Democratic Party*

More recently the parliamentary group of the Social Democratic Party (*Sozialdemokratische Partei Deutschlands*) in the German Parliament published a draft Act.[43] The bill aims in the long run for a quota of 40% for men and women in supervisory boards as well as in management boards. The quota would be implemented in stages. At the first stage a quota of 30% would be set for supervisory boards while a quota of 20% would apply to management boards. If the company fails to meet the quota the seats that are reserved for the under-

---

40 See also Bachmann, Zur Umsetzung einer Frauenquote im Aufsichtsrat, in: *Zeitschrift für Wirtschaftsrecht* (ZIP) 2011, 1131.

41 *Entwurf eines Gesetzes zur geschlechtergerechten Besetzung von Aufsichtsräten* of 13.10.2010 (BT-Drucks. 17/3296); see also the more recent motion "*Gleichstellung von Frauen und Männern im Lebensverlauf durchsetzen*" of 27.02.2013 (BT-Drucks. 17/12497).

42 In the context of workers' representation at plant level, there is a similar provision. Section 15 WCA 192 reads as follows: "(1) The works council should be composed as far as possible of employees of the various units and the different employment categories of the workers employed in the establishment. (2) The gender that accounts for a minority of staff shall at least be represented according to its relative numerical strength whenever the works council consists of three or more members". According to the Federal Labour Court (*Bundesarbeitsgericht*) this is in line with Article 3(2) of the Constitution; see Federal Labour Court of 16.03.2005, in: *Neue Zeitschrift für Arbeitsrecht* (NZA) 2005, p. 1252 (no "disproportionate interference with the principle of electoral equality which must be derived from Article 3(2) of the Constitution").

43 *Entwurf eines Gesetzes zur Förderung der Chancengleichheit von Männern und Frauen in Wirtschaftsunternehmen (ChGlFöG)* of 06.03.2012 (BT-Drucks. 17/8878).

represented sex must not be filled. The capacity of a board to take decisions is not immediately affected, however. Only after the lapse of one year the supervisory board becomes incapable to take decisions if its composition does not live up to the legal requirements.

B. FEDERAL COUNCIL

1. *Initiative of North Rhine-Westphalia*

In 2011 the State North Rhine-Westphalia put forward a draft Act fixing a quota of 30% that would apply to shareholders' representatives and employers' representatives alike.[44] This quota of 30% would apply as from 1 January 2017. It is foreseen, however, that after expiry of five years a quota of 40% would apply.

2. *Initiative of Hamburg and Brandenburg*

More recently the states Hamburg and Brandenburg presented a draft Act in the Federal Council (*Bundesrat*), the representative institution of the German *Länder*.[45] In September 2012 the Bill got a majority in the *Bundesrat*.[46] Even states that are governed by the ruling Christian Democratic Party (*Christlich Demokratische Union Deutschlands*), the majority party in the federal government, voted for it. The state North Rhine-Westphalia voted for it, too. The draft Act aims at publicly listed and co-determined companies. It contains long transition periods and two quotas (20% to be reached by 2018, and 40% to be reached in 2023). Sanctions foreseen in case of non-compliance are relatively mild. In addition, hardship clauses exist.

To be more concrete, the draft Act foresees for an amendment of section 96 of the Stock Corporation Act 1965 to which three new subsections would be added. Under the new provision the composition of supervisory boards should fairly reflect both sexes. If a supervisory board consists of members of the shareholders and the employees, both benches should separately form a fair reflection of both sexes. A fair composition of the supervisory board is assumed to exist if the following requirements are met: If the supervisory board or the respective part of the supervisory board (shareholders' bench/employees' bench) consists of three, four, five or six members, women and men must be represented by at least one representative. If the supervisory board or the respective part of the supervisory

44 *Entwurf eines Gesetzes zur Förderung der Gleichberechtigung von Frauen und Männern in Aufsichtsräten börsennotierter Unternehmen (FöGAbUG)* of 11.02.2011, BRats-Drucks. 87/11.

45 *Entwurf eines Gesetzes zur Förderung gleichberechtigter Teilhabe von Frauen und Männern in Führungsgremien (GlTeilhG)* of 11.09.2012 (BRats-Drucks. 330/1/12).

46 See BRats-Drucks. 330/12 Beschluss.

board consists of seven or eight members, women and men must be represented by at least two representatives. Finally, if the supervisory board or the respective part of the supervisory board consists of nine or more members, a quota of 20% applies. Shareholders' representatives and employees' representatives in co-determined supervisory boards each form a separate body with each body obliged to meet the legal requirements. As a result, there is no way of one body being allowed to fall short of these requirements just because the other body exceeded them. This is noteworthy because in practice there are currently more women among employees' representatives than among the representatives of shareholders.

According to one hardship clause a company is exempt from fulfilling its obligation to meet the quota if it can refer to an important reason. Such reason is assumed to exist, in particular, if a company, in spite of considerable efforts, failed to find suitable candidates among the underrepresented sex. Another hardship clause specifically aims at the composition of the employee bench of the supervisory board by providing that the legal requirements must not be met if a company regularly employs employees who together form 90% of company staff. Failure to meet the legal requirements will be sanctioned by the refusal of tax deductibility of payments made to members of a board that is not lawfully composed.

The bill was considered in the Federal Parliament[47] after the Federal Council decided to introduce the bill in the parliament according to Article 76(1) of the German Constitution.

C. FEDERAL GOVERNMENT

The Federal government for a long time struggled with the question of whether or not a strict quota should legally be fixed. Lately the position of the government has become clearer.[48] In particular, the Christian Democratic Party has made it clear recently that it prefers a so-called "Flexi-Quote" over a legally fixed quota.[49] "Flexi-Quote" means that companies would be legally obliged to make a commitment to reach a specific quota within a set period of time. Such commitment would have to be made with regard to supervisory boards and management boards alike. If a company were to fail the fixed target, sanctions would apply. There would also be sanctions if companies abstain from disclosing their targets.

After the federal elections, which took place in September 2013, the Christian Democrats (and their sister party, the Christian Social Union) and the Social

47 See BT-Drucks. 17/11270, 17/8878, 17/11139 and 17/12784.
48 Government press conference of 14 November 2012.
49 Such quota was determined in December 2012 at a federal party congress.

Democrats entered into negotiations to form a new government. In late November a "coalition treaty" was presented to the public.[50] This accord, which still needs to be approved in a referendum by the SPD's party members, provides for a quota of 30% in the boards of companies which are subject to co-determination. The quota would apply as from the year 2016.

IV. CONSTITUTIONAL FRAMEWORK

All attempts that aim at fixing a legal quota meet with doubts as regards their conformity with the German constitution (*Grundgesetz*, the so-called Basic Law)[51] and, in particular, the basic rights that are set out there.[52]

A. FREEDOM OF PROPERTY

Some commentators are of the opinion that a legal quota may violate Article 14(1) of the Constitution, the so-called freedom of property. Article 14(1) reads as follows: "Property and the right of inheritance shall be guaranteed. Their content and limits shall be defined by the laws."

Two questions arise in this context. First, there is the question whether a legal quota would conform to the constitutional protection of share ownership. Second, there is the question whether a quota would conform to the constitutional protection of the property of the companies affected by such regulation. The two issues cannot fully be discussed here. It should be noted, however, that there are many similarities between fixing a quota at supervisory boards for women under equality law and reserving seats for employees' representatives at such boards under the provisions of co-determination law. As a result, the judgment of the Federal Constitutional Court of 01.03.1979 on the conformity of co-determination with the Constitution[53] may provide some important "benchmarks".

In this ruling the Court pointed out that co-determination on company level was unlikely to considerably affect either the value of shares or the earning prospects of

50 "*Deutschlands Zukunft gestalten – Koalitionsvertrag zwischen CDU, CSU und SPD, 18. Legislaturperiode*", p. 102.

51 Basic Law for the Federal Republic of Germany (*Grundgesetz für die Bundesrepublik Deutschland*) which was approved on 8 May 1949.

52 See in this regard, for instance, the opinions that were expressed during a public hearing by the legal committee of the German parliament on 16 January 2013: www.bundestag.de/bundestag/ausschuesse17/a06/anhoerungen/archive.

53 Federal Constitutional Court of 1 March 1979, in: *Neue Juristische Wochenschrift* (NJW) 1979, p. 699.

shareholders or the "steering function" of capital. The same might have to be said about a legal quota. The story does not end here, however, because shares are no mere assets but also form the basis of membership rights. Against this background the question must be answered whether a gender quota system violates Article 14(1) of the Constitution because it would interfere with the "freedom of choice" of shareholders as regards the seats at supervisory board that they are allowed to fill. This question cannot be answered here either. However, in its ruling on the constitutionality of co-determination the Constitutional Court stressed several times that property is subject to limitations that arise from social considerations (so-called *Sozialbindung des Eigentums*). This reasoning may have to be taken into account in the context of a legal quota. With regard to the constitutional protection of the property of companies themselves the Constitutional Court in its ruling on co-determination law was of the opinion that a possible violation of Article 14(1) should be examined from the perspective of its possible impact on the "internal organisation and the process of decision-making of companies". Using this yardstick the Court stated, however, that co-determination could only be found unconstitutional if it would "lead to functional impairment of the company or to a situation close to the inoperability of a company as a result of, for instance, rendering the decision-making in companies too complicated resulting in making it (almost) impossible to take decisions". With regard to co-determination the Court was of the opinion that these requirements were not fulfilled. It looks even more doubtful that a gender quota could have such effect.[54]

B. FREEDOM OF ASSOCIATION

A legal quota would also have to be in conformity with Article 9(1) of the Constitution (freedom of association) which reads: "All Germans shall have the right to form corporations and other association". It is argued that a legal quota would breach this provision because of interfering with the internal organisation and decision-making of companies. Against the backdrop of the co-determination ruling of the Constitutional Court it looks doubtful, however,

---

54 The result may be the same as far as a possible inroad into the so-called freedom of entrepreneurship (*wirtschaftliche Betätigungsfreiheit*) is concerned. Such freedom is derived from Articles 12(1) and 2(1). Article 12(1) of the Constitution: "All Germans shall have the right freely to choose their occupation or profession, their place of work and their place of training. The practice of an occupation or profession may be regulated by or pursuant to a law". Article 2(1) of the Constitution: "Every person shall have the right to free development of his personality insofar as he does not violate the rights of others or offend against the constitutional order or the moral law". As regards freedom of profession (*Berufsfreiheit*) which is also guaranteed by Article 12(1) of the Constitution it would have to be asked whether membership in a supervisory board amounts to a "profession" within the meaning of Article 12(1). Even if this would be the case a legal quota might not constitute a violation of Article 12(1) because for an individual person there may be at best a *chance* of entering a board but certainly no hard and fast *right* (which could be breached by the legislator).

whether and to what extent Article 9(1) really applies to large corporations (as opposed to, for instance, political, cultural or social clubs). Apart from that it is widely acknowledged that, though freedom of association is guaranteed without express legal limits (there is no explicit so-called *Gesetzesvorbehalt*), the legislator enjoys ample freedom to fix the legal rules that apply to companies. As the Court stated in its ruling on co-determination: "Freedom of association is dependent to a greater or lesser degree on regulations that make associations and their life an element of the general legal set-up, that ensure legal transactions, that secure the rights of its members and which take into account the interests of third parties in need of protection as well as public interests".[55]

A legal quota would also have to conform to Article 9(3) sentence 1 of the Constitution (constituting the so-called *Koalitionsfreiheit* that is enjoyed by employers' associations and trade unions) which reads as follows: "The right to form associations to safeguard and improve working and economic conditions shall be guaranteed to every individual and to every occupation or profession. Agreements that restrict or seek to impair this right shall be null and void; measures directed to this end shall be unlawful". Violation of Article 9(3) sentence 1 by a statutory provision which fixes a quota for supervisory boards may seem improbable at first glance. It becomes less so if one considers the fact that trade unions play an important role in filling the seats that are reserved for persons representing workers' interests. As was mentioned earlier,[56] in supervisory boards of co-determined companies, dependent on the size of the company, either two or even three members must be trade union representatives. These representatives are proposed by trade unions represented in the company and they are elected by delegates by secret ballot and according to the principles of proportional representation.[57] As trade unions play a key role in the process it is a serious concern whether a fixed quota may interfere with their right to propose candidates. According to the dominating opinion in Germany, though co-determination has some roots in the German Constitution,[58] there is no constitutional *right* to co-determination in its present form.[59] This means that

---

55 Federal Constitutional Court of 1 March 1979, in: *Neue Juristische Wochenschrift* (NJW) 1979, p. 699 (701): "Vereinigungsfreiheit ist in mehr oder minder großem Umfang auf Regelungen angewiesen, welche die freien Zusammenschlüsse und ihr Leben in die allgemeine Rechtsordnung einfügen, die Sicherheit des Rechtsverkehrs gewährleisten, Rechte der Mitglieder sichern und den schutzbedürftigen Belangen Dritter oder auch öffentlichen Interessen Rechnung tragen".

56 *Supra* (II.B.).

57 Section 17 CDA 1976.

58 In particular having regard to the so-called principle of social justice (*Sozialstaatsprinzip*) as enshrined in Article 20(1) and 28(1) of the Constitution. Article 20(1): "The Federal Republic of Germany is a democratic and social federal state". Article 28(1) sentence 1: "The constitutional order in the Länder must conform to the principles of a republican, democratic and social state governed by the rule of law, within the meaning of this Basic Law".

59 See Scholz, in: Maunz/Dürig (ed.), *Grundgesetz*, 67th ed. 2013, Article 9 Abs. 3 note 289.

the legislator may interfere with the position of trade unions as far as the measure taken fulfils the requirements of the principle of proportionality.

C. EQUALITY BEFORE THE LAW

For obvious reasons a legal quota would have to be measured against the constitutional right establishing equality before the law. Article 3(1) of the Constitution states: "All persons shall be equal before the law." What it more, equality between the sexes is explicitly provided for in Article 3(2): "Men and women shall have equal rights. The state shall promote the actual implementation of equal rights for women and men and take steps to eliminate disadvantages that now exist". Finally, Article 3(3) states: "No person shall be favoured or disfavoured because of sex, parentage, race, language, homeland and origin, faith, or religious or political opinions. No person shall be disfavoured because of disability." Article 3(2) is the key provision as regards a legal quota. While sentence 1 enshrines an individual basic right, sentence 2 forms the basis of what is called a constitutional mandate of the state (*Verfassungsauftrag*) to promote women. Under these circumstances, a violation of Article 3(2) sentence 1 is out of the question if the legislator by taking a certain measure does not exceed the limits of the constitutional mandate.

This leads to the tricky question what the exact limits of this mandate are. Essentially, there is agreement that it must be possible for the legislator to tackle factual disadvantages which women typically meet. Beyond that it is far from clear, however, how far legislature can go in fulfilling its mandate to promote women. Opinions are divided, in particular, if the intended legislation responds to statistical evidence of under-representation of women in certain areas. Exactly this problem arises in the present context.[60]

In order to solve this problem, two questions may have to be asked. The first question is a rather factual one: Is under-representation possibly due to other reasons than discriminating against women? Or to put it differently: Can statistical evidence of discrimination following from under-representation of women be invalidated by sufficiently strong counter-evidence? The second question is a legal one: Does the fixing of a legal quota meet the requirements of the principle of proportionality which is to say that it must be regarded as the result of a fair balancing of the conflicting interests concerned?

As regards the first question it should be said that there is a wide-spread claim according to which there are not enough female candidates in sufficient numbers

60 Instructive reading: Ossenbühl, "Frauenquoten für Leitungsorgane von Privatunternehmen", in: *Neue Juristische Wochenschrift* (NJW) 2012, p. 417.

to fill the seats at supervisory boards.[61] Whether this is true is not to be discussed here. It should be noted, however, that the "pool" of possible candidates in reality is likely to be larger than it may appear under the current practice which is to choose candidates for supervisory boards manly from the management boards.

The second question may be more interesting. At the heart of it is the principle of proportionality which has been systematically developed by the German Constitutional Court with an aim of balancing the interests that are behind a certain legal measure and the interests that are protected by basic rights arising from the Constitution. Proportionality in that sense requires any state action interfering with basic rights to serve a legitimate public purpose (legitimate aim) and also to be suitable (suitability to achieve the aim), necessary (no less onerous way of achieving the aim) and proportionate in the strict sense (considering the competing interests of different groups at hand). While the aim as such and the suitability of a legal quota are scarcely disputed there are heated debates on whether or not such quota is necessary and proportionate in the sense described.[62]

Proponents of a statutorily fixed quota in Germany claim that there is no means of increasing the proportion of women on supervisory boards that would be equally effective. It is argued that indirect measures such as special programs for women or general measures to reconcile work and family life proved to be ineffective in the past. It is further argued that voluntary commitments so far did not lead to an increase of the number of women in supervisory boards. As regards proportionality in the strict sense the argument goes that a quota is only fixing a further eligibility requirement. In this context it is often pointed out that quotas of less than 50% would leave companies with a considerable measure of discretion. Finally, hardship clauses and "generous" transition periods are mentioned when claiming that a quota is reasonable.[63]

It should be mentioned in this context that the Constitutional Court in Germany is prepared to acknowledge a considerable "scope for legislative evaluation" (*Beurteilungsspielraum* or *Einschätzungsprärogative*). The judgment of the Court on workers' co-determination may serve as an example again. There it was held, inter alia, that "uncertainty about the impact of the law in an uncertain future (…) does not exclude the power of the legislature (…) to enact a law, even if it is

---

61 See in this regard, for instance, Redenius-Hövermann, Zur Frauenquote im Aufsichtsrat, Institute for Law and Finance, Goethe-Universität Frankfurt a. M., Working Paper Series no. 112, p. 5.

62 The principle of proportionality will be discussed here in the context of Article 3 of the Constitution only. It should be noted that the principle must also be observed by the legislator with regard to the basic rights that were mentioned earlier.

63 See, for instance, *Gesetzesantrag der Freien und Hansestadt Hamburg, Entwurf eines Gesetzes zur Förderung gleichberechtigter Teilhabe von Frauen und Männern in Führungsgremien (GlTeilhG)* of 29.05.2012 (BRats-Drucks. 33012), p. 22 et seq.

of great importance".[64] According to the Court the key question in this regard is whether the assessment of the legislator is "tenable". This standard requires the legislative measure be based "on a proper and reasonable assessment of the material accessible". The legislator "must have exhausted the sources of evidence available to him in order to assess the likely impact of the intended legislation as reliably as possible and to avoid a violation of constitutional law". All this leads to requirements applying to the legislative process rather than to material requirements. If they are fulfilled, the requirements of material "tenability" are met, the latter constituting the "scope for legislative evaluation" which the Constitutional Court must by all means respect.[65] Against this background a statutorily fixed quota might pass the test of conformity with the Constitution.[66]

V. CONCLUSION

A clear under-representation of women in management positions has prompted various legislative initiatives to remedy this situation. Most of these initiatives have their focus on the supervisory boards of companies. Framing legislation is tricky; not least because the specific rules of workers' co-determination must be taken into account. All attempts to arrive at a statutorily fixed gender quota have met to some degree with concerns as regards their conformity with the Constitution. If the legislator were to act the law would almost certainly land in the Constitutional Court. It is difficult to foresee how the court would rule on the matter. Drawing a parallel between gender quotas for supervisory boards and workers' co-determination on company level may be helpful in this regard.

---

64 Federal Constitutional Court of 1 March 1979, in: *Neue Juristische Wochenschrift* (NJW) 1979, p. 699 (701): "Ungewissheit über die Auswirkungen eines Gesetzes in einer Ungewissen Zukunft kann nicht die Befugnis des Gesetzgebers ausschließen, ein Gesetz zu erlassen, auch wenn dieses von großer Tragweite ist".

65 Federal Constitutional Court of 1 March 1979, in: *Neue Juristische Wochenschrift* (NJW) 1979, p. 699 (701): "Dieser Maßstab verlangt, dass der Gesetzgeber sich an einer sachgerechten und vertretbaren Beurteilung des erreichbaren Materials orientiert hat. Er muss die ihm zugänglichen Erkenntnisquellen ausgeschöpft haben, um die voraussichtlichen Auswirkungen seiner Regelung so zuverlässig wie möglich abschätzen zu können und einen Verstoß gegen Verfassungsrecht zu vermeiden. Es handelt sich also eher um Anforderungen des Verfahrens. Wird diesen Genüge getan, so erfüllen sie jedoch die Voraussetzung inhaltlicher Vertretbarkeit; sie konstituieren insoweit die Einschätzungsprärogative des Gesetzgebers, die das *BVerfG* bei seiner Prüfung zu beachten hat".

66 This was also the result of a working group of the states; see Bericht der Länderarbeitsgruppe "Teilhabe von Frauen in Führungs- und Kontrollgremien der Wirtschaft", p. 108 ("low risk of being not in conformity with the Constitution at best"): www.justiz.bayern.de/media/teilhabe_frauen_fuehrungs__und_kontrollgremien_1.pdf; see also Wieland, "Ist eine Quotenregelung zur Erhöhung des Anteils der Frauen in Aufsichtsräten mit dem Grundgesetz und Europarecht vereinbar?", in: *Neue Juristische Wochenschrift* (NJW) 2010, p. 2408. It must be stressed that opinions are divided on the issue; see, for instance, Spindler/Brandt, "Verfassungsrechtliche Zulässigkeit einer Gleichstellungsquote im Aufsichtsrat der börsennotierten AG", in: *Neue Zeitschrift für Gesellschaftsrecht* (NZG) 2011, p. 401.

CHAPTER 8

GENDER QUOTA ON THE BOARDS OF CORPORATIONS IN ICELAND

Gudbjörg Linda Rafnsdóttir*, Thorgerdur Einarsdóttir** and Jón Snorri Snorrason***

I. THE BACKGROUND

The economic crisis that has dominated the Western world since 2008 hit Iceland extremely hard. In October 2008 the Iceland's three major banks collapsed with serious consequences for the Icelandic economy. After the crises, lack of gender diversity in business leadership has been in the spotlight, both in Iceland as elsewhere in Europe. A discussion about how to increase the number of women on the boards of corporations is prominent, followed by a debate about if a mandatory legal framework or a voluntary regulatory framework is the best method to increase the gender balance in business leadership.

Iceland has a history of Gender Equality Policy. It passed the Act on Equal Status and Equal Rights of Women and Men (revised in 1985, 1991, 2000 and 2008), in an attempt to secure the equal influence of women and men in society, to work against gender-based discrimination in the labour market, and to enable both women and men to reconcile their work and family life. The Gender Equality Act in Iceland is quite labour-market oriented.

Iceland has the highest rate of women's participation in the labour market among OECD countries, 77% in 2011. However a significant gender imbalance is to be found on the boards of Icelandic corporations (OECD, n.d.). This has been

* Gudbjörg Linda Rafnsdóttir is a professor in Sociology, Faculty of Social and Human Sciences, University of Iceland. Address for correspondance: Gudbjörg Linda Rafnsdóttir glr@hi.is. Phone: + 354 525 4237.

** Thorgerdur Einarsdóttir is a professor in Gender Studies, Faculty of Political Science, University of Iceland.

*** Jón Snorri Snorrason is an assistant Professor, Faculty of Business Administration, University of Iceland.

met by childcare for pre-school children, a legal right for parents to return to their jobs after childbirth, and nine months paid parental leave, of which the fathers are entitled to a minimum of three months (Statistics Iceland, n.d. a; Gíslason, 2007; Gender Equality in Iceland, n.d.). This reflects the fact that at the same time as women in Iceland participate in the labour market to a larger extent than most women in Europe, they also tend to have more children. This can be seen in the picture below about fertility rate versus work among mothers in Europe in 2008.

Figure 1. Fertility rate versus working mothers

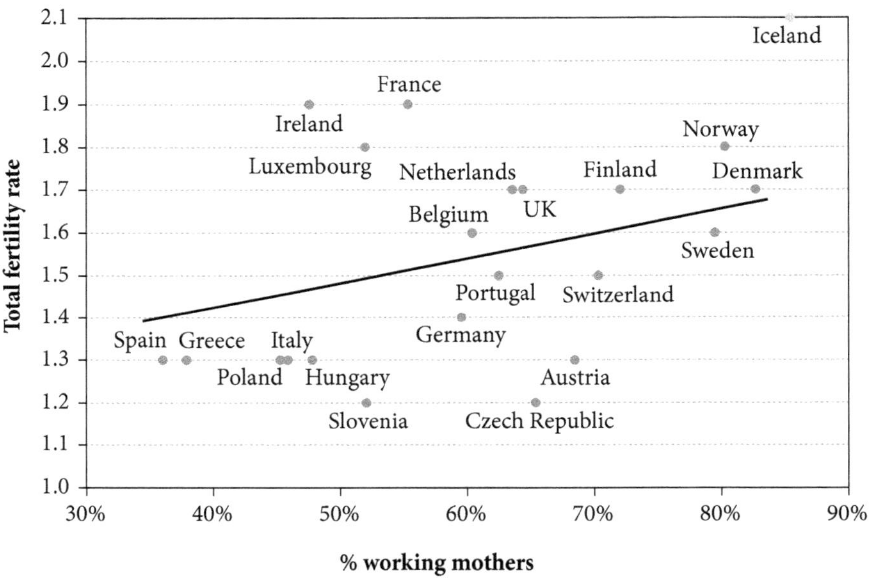

Reference: The European Social Survey [ESS]. Key Findings, 2008.

Iceland prides itself on promoting gender equality. According to the World Economic Forum's Global Gender Gap Index the country has been number one in gender equality in the world since 2009 (The Global Gender Gap Report, 2013). The Index benchmarks national gender gaps on economic, political, education and health-based criteria. Although Iceland has the top ranking in the overall score, this does not apply to economic opportunities in which Iceland's performance is far less prominent (Einarsdóttir 2010). The Icelandic labour market is highly gender segregated. Women and men often work in different sectors and women have been highly underrepresented in CEO positions, especially in private corporations. In 2011 women were 20% among CEOs, 24% among board members and 24% among chairmen (Statistic Iceland, 2012).

A survey by Creditinfo (2009) shows that 71% of all companies in Iceland had only men on their boards in 2009, 14% of the boards had only women and 15% had both men and women on the boards. According to unpublished information from Creditinfo no changes occurred in 2010 (Rafnsdóttir and Þorvaldsdóttir, 2012). In contrast to other European countries, the number of women on Icelandic business boards is higher in small companies than in the larger ones (Snorrason, 2011; Snorrason, 2012). This can be seen in Table 1.

Table 1. The proportion of women among CEOs, chairmen and board members in all companies and in companies with 50 employees and more

The proportion of female CEOs in all companies (20%)	
Size of companies (number of employees)	Proportion of female CEOs
50–99	13%
100–249	10%
250	11%

The proportion of female chairmen in all companies (24%)	
Size of companies (number of employees)	Proportion of female CEOs
50–99	18%
100–249	20%
250	9%

The proportion of female board members in all companies (24%)	
Size of companies (number of employees)	Proportion of female CEOs
50–99	19%
100–249	22%
250	26%

Reference: Statistics Iceland 2012; Rafnsdóttir and Þorvaldsdóttir, 2012

However, the majority of Icelanders see it as important to increase the gender balance in top management in corporations and in the public sector. A survey conducted by the Social Science Research Institute in 2011 shows that more women (85%) than men (71%) see it as important to equalise the proportion of men and women in top management of private companies and public institutions ($p<0.001$).

Table 2. It is important to equalise the proportion of men and women in top management of private companies and public institutions

	Those who reply: "I largely agree with" and "I strongly agree with" the statement
Gender ***	
Men	71%
Women	85%
Age*	
18–29	75%
30–39	81%
40–49	73%
50–59	76%
60 plus	84%

Significant difference between the groups;
* p<0.05, ** p<0.01, *** p<0.001 (Reference, Rafnsdóttir, 2011).

As seen by Table 2, the age groups 60+ and 30–39 years old are most positive towards increasing the proportion of women (84% and 81%). There was not a significant difference between the groups in terms of education, occupation, income and marital status. However, there is a correlation with political orientation. Those who support left-wing parties in Iceland are more likely to support increased balance than those who support right-wing parties (Rafnsdóttir, 2011; Rafnsdóttir and Þorvaldsdóttir, 2012).

Table 3. Female and male managers who agree or strongly agree with the following statements

Statements	Women	Men	P	R
It is important to increase gender equality among top managers in private companies and in the public sector	97%	74%	0.000***	0.268
I support legislation on gender quotas for the boards of private corporations	69%	25%	0.000***	0.417
The fact that fewer women than men hold top management positions in business and the public sector can be explained by institutional factors and the organisation of work (such as long and inflexible working hours, travelling and so on)	76%	66%	0.074	0.095
The fact that fewer women than men belong to the top leadership of business and public institutions can be explained by gendered stereotypes, traditions and customs about what suits best for women and men	78%	48%	0.000***	0.283

Statements	Women	Men	P	R
The fact that fewer women than men belong to the top leadership of business and public institutions can be explained by a lack of interest among women	33%	54%	0.000***	0.196
The fact that fewer women than men belong to the top leadership of business and public institutions can be explained by the fact that men are not interested in appointing women to these jobs	76%	31%	0.000***	0.407
Manager jobs are less suitable for women than for men because of physical facts that will not be changed	4%	10%	0.046*	0.106
Manager jobs are less suitable for women than for men because of social facts that will not be changed.	4%	12%	0.015*	0.129

Significant difference between the groups; * $p<0.05$, ** $p<0.01$, *** $p<0.001$ (Rafnsdóttir, 2011).

Table 3 present a study conducted in 2010 covering 218 managers in the largest companies in Iceland (response rate 50%; 65 women and 153 men). It showed a considerable gender difference in views on management and gender. This study aimed not only to analyse the attitude among managers in Iceland to gender quotas and gender equality in management, but also the main hindrances women meet on the way to top leadership (Rafnsdóttir, 2011).

As seen by Table 3 the majority of both female (97%) and male (74%) managers see it as important to increase gender equality among top managers in private companies and public institutions. The gender difference increases when asking if the managers support the gender quota legislation, where 69% of the female managers and only 25% of male managers agree with the statement "I support laws on gender quotas for the boards of private corporations". The majority of women, 78%, and almost half of the men, 48%, believe that the lack of women in business leadership is due to gendered stereotypes, as well as traditions and customs about what is considered appropriate for women and men. Slightly more than half of the men, 54%, but only one third of the women, 33%, believe the lack of women among top leaders in business can be explained by a lack of interest among women for this type of work. The gender difference increases, however, when the managers are asked to respond to the statement that men are not interested in appointing women to these jobs. A surprisingly large majority of female managers or 76% agree with the statement and almost one third of the male managers.

II. LAW ON GENDER QUOTAS IN ICELAND

Iceland is the 2nd country in Europe and in the world, after Norway, to implement quotas on gender in boards of corporations. On 15 May 2009 the Association of Icelandic Employers, the Association of Business Women in Iceland and the Iceland Chamber of Commerce signed an agreement in which they commit themselves to join forces in order to improve the situation of women on boards in Icelandic businesses. According to the agreement these parties intend to encourage and seek ways to get more women to the forefront of Icelandic business so that the proportion of either gender would not be under 40% by the end of 2013 (KPMG and the University of Iceland, 2013).

In December 2009 the Minister of Business presented a bill in which the gender ratio on the boards of public companies should be taken into consideration. In the parliamentary procedure in Althing, the wording was changed and in March 2010 legislation on a minimum of 40% of either gender on boards for companies with more than 50 employees on an annual basis was passed (Act on 40% Gender Quota on Boards of Directors no. 13/2010). Public limited companies, private limited companies and co-operative limited companies were all granted an adaptive period until 1 September 2013. In September 2011 Althing also passed legislation on a minimum of 40% of either gender in pension funds which will come into force 1 September 2013 (ACT on Gender Quota on Boards of Pension Funds no. 122/211; KPMG and University of Iceland, 2013). Two years earlier, in 2008, the Icelandic government adopted an article in the gender equality law introducing gender quotas in government committees, councils and boards (Act on Equal Status and Equal Rights of Women and Men no. 10/2008). In addition the Act contains a special clause on gender quotas which exceeds the existing requirements on public boards with detailed instructions for implementation.

The Icelandic legislation demanding a minimum of 40% of either gender on boards of companies and pension funds comes into force 1 September 2013. It applies to publicly owned public companies; public limited companies; private limited companies, and co-operative limited companies (where more than fifty persons are employed on an annual basis), and all pension funds. More specifically, the legislation covers the following:

Public limited companies which applies to companies where more than 50 people are employed on an annual basis. Each gender shall be represented on the board in cases where there are three members on the board. If there are more than three members it must be ensured that either gender makes up 40% of the board. The same applies to substitute board members, on the whole the gender ratio for board and substitute board should be as equal as possible (KPMG and University of Iceland, 2013).

Private limited companies which applies to companies where more than 50 people are employed on an annual basis. Each gender shall be represented on the board in cases where there are three members on the board. If there are more than three members it must be ensured that either gender makes up 40% of the board. The same applies to substitute board members, on the whole the gender ratio for board and substitute board should be as equal as possible (KPMG and University of Iceland, 2013).

Publically owned public companies which apply to companies where more than 50 people are employed on an annual basis. Each gender shall be represented on the board in cases where there are three members on the board. If there are more than three members it must be ensured that either gender makes up 40% of the board. The same applies to substitute board members, on the whole the gender ratio for board and substitute board should be as equal as possible. The law has already taken force concerning these companies (KPMG and University of Iceland, 2013).

Co-operative limited companies which applies to companies where more than 50 people are employed on an annual basis. Each gender shall be represented on the board in cases where there are three members on the board. If there are more than three members it must be ensured that either gender makes up 40% of the board. The same applies to substitute board members, on the whole the gender ration for board and substitute board should be as equal as possible (KPMG and University of Iceland, 2013).

Pension funds which applies to all pension funds regardless of number of employees. Each gender shall be represented on the board. If there are more than three board members the proportion of either gender shall not be lower than 40%. The same applies to substitute board members, on the whole the gender ratio for board and substitute board should be as equal as possible (KPMG and University of Iceland, 2013).

III. DOMESTIC DEBATE ON QUOTAS AND PRACTICAL INFLUENCE ON CORPORATE GOVERNANCE

According to the above mentioned survey conducted by The Social Science Research Institute in Iceland in 2011, the majority of both women and men in general supported gender quotas on the boards of corporations. However there was a significant difference between men's and women's attitude.

Table 4. I support the legislation on gender quotas for the boards of private corporations

	Those who agree or strongly agree with the statement
Gender ***	
Men	51%
Women	72%
Age*	
18–29	57%
30–39	66%
40–49	56%
50–59	59%
60 plus	67%

Significant difference between the groups; * $p<0.05$, ** $p<0.01$, *** $p<0.001$ (Rafnsdóttir, 2011).

As shown by table 4 more women (72%) than men (51%) support legislation on gender quotas for the boards of private corporations ($p<0.001$). There is not only a significant difference between women and men, but also between the different age groups ($p<0.05$). Those who were 30–39 years old (66%) and 60 years and older (67%), more often supported the gender quotas for corporate boards than other age groups. There was not a significant difference in attitudes when broken down by education, occupation, income and marital status. But those with left-wing political orientation in Iceland are more likely to support the gender quotas that those leaning more to the right (Rafnsdóttir, 2011; Rafnsdóttir and Thorvaldsdóttir, 2012).

The theoretical arguments for and against gender quotas in Iceland reflect similar themes as in Norway (Einarsdóttir 2007, Teigen 2011, Rafnsdóttir and Thorvaldsdóttir 2012). Those themes are democracy or justice arguments and profitability or utility arguments. The democracy or justice arguments emphasise that women have the right to equal representation to men and that their qualifications and proficiencies are currently undervalued in a male-dominated system. Therefore the quotas are a form of compensation for invisible barriers that prevent them from equal share of power. On the other hand the profitability or utility arguments refer to the opinion that women have special qualities in management that men do not have and that their capacities are underutilised which imposes loss on the firms in the long run (Einarsdóttir 2007). This is thought to be due to gendered socialisation or to inherent female talents. These female characteristics are believed to be empathy, carefulness, and cooperation, the opposition to the male characteristics that is competitiveness, initiative and power (Rafnsdóttir and Þorvaldsdóttir, 2012; Teigen, 2011). Dahlerup (2006) has found similar arguments when analysing gender quotas in politics.

The democracy or justice arguments may also be used to criticise the gender quotas. In these cases it is emphasised that the quotas go against the principle of equal opportunities and the principle of equal treatment. Thus the quota is seen as discriminating men by giving women preference over men; that women get chosen because of their gender and not their qualifications (Einarsdóttir 2007, Teigen, 2011; Dahlerup, 2006; Rafnsdóttir and Þorvaldsdóttir, 2012). It is also seen as discriminating women who have reached their position without being "quoted" into the boards. In addition it will disparage women board members, as they are here after seen as secondary board members, the ones that got their position just because of the gender quota (Rafnsdóttir and Þorvaldsdóttir, 2012).

A survey among board members of Icelandic corporations was conducted in 2012 by KPMG and the School of Social Sciences at the University of Iceland. The main goal of the survey was to explore the work methods and environment of boards; communication between board members, their education and experience, and their attitudes towards the composition of boards. Furthermore, the survey aims to map attitudes towards laws on 40% minimum membership of each gender on boards which came into force on 1 September 2013 (KPMG and the University of Iceland, 2013). A request for participation was sent to 265 companies and 31 pension funds. A total of 920 individuals received a request for participation, thereof 71% men and 29% women. The response rate was 43% (KPMG and the University of Iceland, 2013). According to the survey 76% of the women and 34% of the men were positive towards the gender quota legislation. Board members who are 50 years old or younger are positive in 47% of the cases, but 35% them are negative. Among board members over 50 years, the majority or 58% are positive, while 19% of them are negative. Thus the older the board member the more positive he/she is towards the gender quota legislation.

When asked about the effect of the legislation 68% of the men on boards and 49% of the women believed the law will not impact the board operation at all. Only 1% of the women and 7% of the men believed the law will influence board operation negatively. A large majority or 85% of the men on boards and 61% of the women believe the law will not influence financial outcomes for the company. On the other hand 26% of the women believe the law will have a positive influence on financial outcomes compared to only 2% of the men. As regards the issue of image 61% of the men and 40% of the women believe the law will not influence the company or the fund's image, whereas 56% of the women believe the legislation will have a positive impact on the image compared to 28% of the men. When asked about the corporate culture, 64% of the men on boards and 38% of the women believe the legislation will not influence the corporate culture of the company or the fund. However, 50% of the women on boards think the law will have a positive impact on corporate culture compared to only 19% of the men. No one believes the law will negatively impact corporate culture.

IV. DISCUSSION

Iceland is the 2nd country in the world to implement a law on gender quota in company boards. Women had for a long time been highly underrepresented in leadership in economic life in Iceland, and in fact, their representation was lower than in the other Nordic countries. This was considered unacceptable by the general public as reflected in the research. An agreement between the Association of Icelandic Employers, the Association of Business Women in Iceland and the Iceland Chamber of Commerce to join forces to improve this situation was signed in 2009. Before it was put to the test a law on gender quotas was passed by Althingi, to be enforced 1 September 2013. The chapter shows that even if managers and people in general see it as important to increase the number of women in economic decision-making, there is some scepticism towards gender quotas, especially among male managers. We also see gender differences in the view of what explains the fact that fewer women than men belong to the top management level of companies. This reflects that women and men have a different understanding of the hindrances against increased female representation. A survey from 2012 among Icelandic board members reveals considerable gender differences in views on the potential impact of the quotas. Women are much more positive than men and believe to a larger extent than men that the quotas will have positive effects. The law on gender quotas in Iceland and the practical consequences on economic life is a highly topical issue that will be in focus in future research.

V. REFERENCES

Act on Equal Status and Equal Rights of Women and Men no. 10/2008. (Lög um og jafna stöðu jafnan rétt kvenna og karla nr. 10/2008).

Act on 40% Gender Quota on Boards of Directors no. 13./2010. (Lög um breytingu á lögum um hlutafélög og lögum um einkahlutafélög (eignarhald, kynjahlutföll og starfandi stjórnarformenn) nr.13/2010).

ACT on Gender Quota on Boards of Pension Funds no. 122/211. (Lög um breyting á lögum nr. 129/1997, um skyldutryggingu lífeyrisréttinda og starfsemi lífeyrissjóða, með síðari breytingum (hæfi stjórnarmanna og framkvæmdastjóra, fjárfestingarheimildir nr. 122/2011).

Creditinfo á Íslandi. *Hlutdeild kvenna í íslensku atvinnulífi.* (Reykjavík: Höfundur, 2009). www.sa.is/files/CI%20-%20Hlutdeild%20kvenna%20í%20íslensku%20 atvinnulífi_1606926578.pdf.

DAHLERUP, D., "Introduction", in DAHLERUP, D. (eds). *Women, Quotas, and Politics,* (London and New York: Routledge, 2006), 3–31.

The Global Gender Gap Report. (Geneva: World Economic Forum, 2013).

RAFNSDÓTTIR, G.L. "Lack of Gender Diversity in Business Leadership. Potential Barriers and Solutions - Case of the Nordic Countries". In RAŠTICOVÁ M. (eds). *Diversity is Reality.* (Brno: *Vutium Press,* 2011), 97–105.

RAFNSDÓTTIR, G.L. and STYRKÁRSDÓTTIR, A. "Kön och makt i isländskt näringsliv". In Kirsti NISKANEN och Anita NYBERG (eds) *Kön och makt i Norden. Del 1. Landsrapporter.* (Copenhagen: TemaNord: 2009:569), 163–182. www.norden.org/da/publikationer/publikationer/2009-569.

RAFNSDÓTTIR, G.L. and ÞORVALDSDÓTTIR, M. "Gender quotas and possible barriers women face on the way to top-level positions" (Kynjakvótar og mögulegar hindranir á leið kvenna til æðstu stjórnunar). (2012) *Íslenska þjóðfélagið*, Reykjavík 3:57–76. www.thjodfelagid.is/index.php/Th/article/view/45/pdf.

SNORRASON, J.S. (2011). Kynjahlutföll í stjórnum fyrirtækja. In Ingjaldur HANNIBALSSON (ed.), *Þjóðarspegillinn 2011, Rannsóknir í félagsvísindum XII, Viðskiptafræðideild.* Reykjavík: Félagsvísindadeild. http://skemman.is/stream/get/1946/10259/25577/1/Rannsoknir_i_felagsvisindum_XII_Vidskiptafraedideild.pdf.

SNORRASON, J.S. (2012) "Yfirlit um stöðu og áhrif jafnari kynjahlutfalla við stjórnun og í stjórnum fyrirtækja", *Tímarit Stjórnmál og stjórnsýsla* 1:2012. http://skemman.is/stream/get/1946/12292/30677/1/a.2012.8.1.4.pdf.

KPMG and University of Iceland. *The Icelandic Board Member 2012. Survey on composition of boards, board tasks and board members' background and stance to pending gender quota.* (Reykjavík, KPMG, 2013)

EINARSDÓTTIR, T. (2010) "Kreppur og kerfishrun í ljósi kyngerva og þegnréttar" in *Íslenska þjóðfélagið,* Reykjavík 1: 27–48.

EINARSDÓTTIR, T. (2007) "Aumingjahjálp eða afbygging á umframvaldi? Sértækar aðgerðir, jákvæð mismunun og kvótar í íslenskri jafnréttisumræðu" in Gunnar Þór Jóhannesson (ed.) *Þjóðarspegillinn 2007, Rannsóknir í félagsvísindum VIII.* Reykjavík, Félagsvísindastofnun Háskóla Ísland, p. 391–402. http://skemman.is/stream/get/1946/8481/22580/1/F%C3%A9lagsv%C3%ADsindab%C3%B3k_2007.pdf.

OECD (n.d.) *OECD.Stat Extracts. Retrieved* 13 November 2012 from http://stats.oecd.org/Index.aspx?DataSetCode=STLABOUR.

STATISTICS ICELAND Kyn framkvæmdastjóra og stjórnarmanna eftir stærð fyrirtækja 1999–2011. Retrieved 28 May 2012 from http://hagstofa.is/?PageID=2595&src=/temp/Dialog/varval.asp?ma=FYR06101%26ti=Framkv%E6mdastj%F3rar+og+stj%F3rnarmenn+fyrirt%E6kja+eftir+kyni+og+aldri+1999%2D2011%26path=./Database/fyrirtaeki/stjornir/%26lang=3%26units=fjöldi, hlutfall.

SEALY, R., *The UK's Approach to Women on Boards. The Davies Report and Beyond. Exchange of good practices in gender equality.* (European Commission, Discussion paper, 2012).

TEIGEN, M., "Gender quotas on corporate boards". In NISKANEN K. (ed.), *Gender and Power in the Nordic Countries - with focus on politics and business* (Oslo: NIKK Publications, 2011), 87–111.

CHAPTER 9
THE DUTCH SOLUTION: NO QUOTA BUT LEGAL TARGETS

Chantal Remery

I. INTRODUCTION

Whereas the labour force participation rate of women in the Netherlands is among the highest in Europe, the share of female executive and non-executive board members is rather low. This low share and the slow progress is a topic of public discussion for years now and the government has implemented several measures to increase it. There is a strong emphasis on self-regulation; the position of women in top positions is the responsibility of companies themselves. The implementation of quota is therefore not an issue. In January 2013 legislation came into force obliging firms of a certain size to have at least 30% women (and also at least 30% men) in their executive and supervisory boards. However, as we will elaborate, this is a "legal target" and not a hard quota. This chapter describes the development towards this legislation. Attention will be paid to government policies, pressure of relevant stakeholders and the Dutch Corporate Governance Code. In addition, the current legislation will be analysed in terms of content and possible impact.

II. WOMEN IN TOP POSITIONS: PUBLIC POLICIES AND PUBLIC PRESSURE

Emancipation of women is a topic of Dutch public policies for several decades now; vertical segregation became a topic during the eighties of the last century. The point of departure has always been that improving the position of women in companies is primarily the responsibility of companies themselves; government policies are directed at stimulating and supporting companies to take initiatives in this respect. For example, during the late 1980s and early 1990s and inspired

* Utrecht University School of Economics.

by the approach of affirmative action in the United States of America, companies were stimulated to implement "positive action". Between 1988 and 1994, companies could apply for subsidies to develop a program of positive action to get more women in (top positions in) the organisation. However, the concept was not appealing to the majority of companies (Remery 1998). In 1996 a campaign called "Opportunity In Bedrijf" (Opportunity in Business) was launched, co-funded by the government, specifically aimed at increasing the number of women in higher positions. Organisations could participate voluntarily in this campaign. Participation implied that the organisation made a specific plan to improve the position of women (TK 1996–1997). Though several well-known private companies joined this campaign, again the interest of firms remained limited.

In the policy note on emancipation, published in 2000 and which focused on the short and medium term, for the first time a specific target for the share of women in top positions is formulated. The main target in the field of power and decision making was to attain a proportional representation of women at influential positions in society. This is translated in several quantitative targets. Regarding the profit sector the target was a doubling of the share of women in executive and supervisory boards in the top 100 largest firms in 2004, which implied an increase from 4% to 8%; in addition, the share should increase with 2 percentage points per year, so that in 2010 it would be 20% (SZW 2000). Though the targets were ambitious, proposed measures were rather soft, involving consultation with social partners, stimulating firms to develop specific targets and policies, creating networks of pioneers in the field, sharing good practices etc.

One of the measures was the instalment of an Ambassadors Network "Breaking the Glass Ceiling" in 2001. This Network consisted of 15–20 captains of industry and high administrators of public and non-profit organisations. Goals of the network were to keep the topic of women in top positions on the public agenda, to stimulate the implementation of measures to increase the number of women and to provide and spread good practices. There was a strong emphasis on the business case; more diversity in top management would result in better firm performance. Between 2001 and 2008 a total of five Networks, with different compositions, have been active. During those years, corporate governance became a topic of increasing attention; one of the issues focused on including diversity in the Corporate Governance Code. The fifth Ambassadors Network stimulated this; one of its goals was to increase the commitment of the top of Dutch companies by anchoring the topic of diversity in corporate governance (Ambassadeursnetwerk 2007–2008). At the end of May 2008 the network had its final meeting. At this meeting a publication was presented with good practices (EZ 2008).

The target of 20% women in executive and supervisory boards is confirmed in the Policy Note on emancipation concerning the period 2008–2011, published in 2007 (OCW 2007). This should be realised by implementing measures such as using specialised recruitment firms, development of a specific programme for female candidates, and setting targets regarding the share of women among new recruits and the presence of women in selection committees. In addition, the note made reference towards the Monitoring Commission Corporate Governance Code, which was evaluating the Code and had announced to do recommendations for including diversity (see section 3 for more details). Finally, the note announced a "Topbrainstorm" on diversity management with the Prime Minister and other members of the government, women in top positions, academic experts, social partners and captains of industry. As a result of this brainstorm, which was held in October 2007, the Charter Talent to the Top was initiated.

The Charter Talent to the Top was established in 2008 with the aim to increase the number of women in senior positions in organisations. In line with the "Dutch approach", it is a voluntary public commitment to increase the number of women in (sub-)senior positions. Signing the Charter is voluntary but organisations are expected to make a record of the actual situation, formulate targets and a plan to realise these targets. Organisations have to report progress and activities annually. The Committee Monitoring Talent to the Top monitors progress and provides feedback on these reports. The Charter does not specify a target for women. However, it refers to the findings of the famous study "Men and women of the Corporation" of Elisabeth Moss Kanter according to which there should be at least 30% of a minority group in order to be considered as "normal" (Talent to the Top 2008: 5). According to the Charter this finding is important to take into account when designing a company diversity policy. Since the founding 199 organisations have signed the Charter, covering a total of 700,000 employees (Merens et al. 2012).

In addition, several stakeholders have taken action to raise public attention for the issue of women in top positions. For example, in 2009 Woman Capital, an executive search agency specialised in finding women for top positions published the so-called "quota manifest" in national newspapers. Inspired by the Norwegian case and arguing that the number of women in top positions hardly increased despite all measures taken, this manifest asked for a legally binding quota of 40% women in all commissioner's posts and other supervisory positions. The legislation should apply to all listed firms, government agencies and other (semi-) public organisations and the quota should be attained within five years' time (that is 2014). The manifest was signed by more than 200 women in top positions (Women Capital n.d.). Another example is Neelie Kroes, EU

Commissioner. In reference to the general objection against quota that women do not want to be appointed in top positions based on their sex instead of capacities, she stated to be "proud to be quoted" (FD 2008).

The increasing attention for women in top positions had its impact on the Monitoring Committee Corporate Governance that was preparing a revision of the Corporate Governance Code. The development of this Code and the attention for (gender) diversity will be the topic of the next section.

III. GENDER DIVERSITY IN THE DUTCH CORPORATE GOVERNANCE CODE

In 1996 the first Committee on Corporate Governance (also called "Commissie Peters", referring to the chair of the Committee) in the Netherlands was installed as a result of an agreement between the Association of Securities Issuing Companies and Euronext Amsterdam (De Jong et al. 2005). Important reasons were the growing internationalisation and increasing international attendance for the role, position and influence of shareholders (Committee on Corporate Governance 1997: 9). This Committee formulated forty recommendations for "sound management, effective supervision and accountability" (p. 2), which are regarded as the first corporate governance code in the Netherlands (Akkermans et al. 2007). Diversity was not yet an issue at that time. Regarding the composition of the Supervisory Board recommendation two states that the composition should be such "that the Board Members should be able to operate independently of one another and of the Board of Directors and in a critical way" (p. 35). An important element of the report was self-enforcement; listed companies in the Netherlands were called upon to take the recommendations into account and report upon actions taken on a voluntary basis (De Jong et al. 2005). An evaluation in 2002 of corporate governance practices showed that progress was slow (De Jong and Roosenboom 2002).

The results of this evaluation study, and developments such as accounting scandals, resulted in the instalment of a new corporate governance committee in 2003. The chair of this committee was Morris Tabaksblat, a former CEO of the multinational Unilever. In the Summer of 2003 the Committee Tabaksblat presented the draft code, which in December 2003 became final: the Dutch Corporate Governance Code (Corporate Governance Committee 2003). As of January 2004 the code became effective. The code is anchored in the Dutch civil code (Article 2: 391, paragraph 4) as a code of conduct; listed firms should refer to this code in their annual reports and provide information on the extent to which the firm complies with the code and the reasons for not-complying (the so-called "comply or explain" principle). Tough there are several references to the composition of boards, diversity as such is not addressed. The Code includes a best practice provision (iii.1.3) that in the report of the supervisory board information shall be included on (among others) gender of each member. According to best principle III.3 "The composition of the supervisory board shall be such that it is able to carry out its duties properly" (ibid. p. 18).

To monitor compliance with the code, in December 2004 the Monitoring Committee Corporate Governance Code was established (also called "Commissie Frijns", after its chair Jean Frijns, a professor at the VU University Amsterdam). As illustrated in the previous section, during that time gender diversity in top management became more and more a topic of public debate. As a result, the Committee had to address the issue in its work. In 2007 the Committee recommended that boards of supervisors should strive for "mixed composition" (Monitoring Commissie Corporate Governance 2007: 11). This was clarified a year later in the evaluation report of the Code, which resulted in an update of the Code. In this evaluation report the Monitoring Committee referred to public debates on the Code and the pleas to extend it. One of the most salient themes in this respects proved to be diversity/position of women (Monitoring Commissie Corporate Governance Code 2008: 5). Research initiated by the Committee showed that the share of women in supervisory boards of listed firms proved to be rather low (at that time about 8%). According to the Committee it was of direct interest to stimulate women in top positions and companies should implement structural policy to attract, retain and promote female talent (p. 69). However, as the Committee emphasised, diversity not only refers to gender but also to nationality, age, expertise and background. As a result, the Monitoring Committee recommended for the updated Code "that supervisory boards strive for more diversity, in particular regarding gender" (ibid. p. 69). Despite pressure from stakeholders such as Parliament (see next section) to do so, the Monitoring Committee did not see reason to include specific quota for women in supervisory boards in the Code (Monitoring Commissie Corporate Governance 2007: 112).

The updated Corporate Governance Code was accepted in 2008 and became effective as of January 2009. Article III.3 of the current Code states that "the supervisory board shall aim for a diverse composition in terms of such factors as gender and age" (Monitoring Committee Corporate Governance Code, 2008: p. 22). In addition, Article III.3.1 states "The supervisory board shall prepare a profile of its size and composition, taking account of the nature of the business, its activities and desired expertise and background of the supervisory board members. The profile shall deal with the aspects of diversity in the composition of the supervisory board that are relevant to the company and shall state what specific objective is pursued by the board in relation to diversity. In so far as the existing situation differs from the intended situation, the supervisory board shall account for this in the supervisory board and shall indicate how and in what period it expects to achieve this aim (ibid, p. 22)". For the Dutch Parliament, the attention for gender diversity in the new Code was not far reaching enough, which stimulated the development of a legal target. This development and the details of legislation will be discussed in the next section.

IV. WOMEN ON BOARDS: LEGAL TARGETS

The reports of the Monitoring Committee on compliance with the corporate governance code are discussed in Parliament. In a debate in April 2008 (before the revision of the Code Tabaksblat of 2003 was finalised) the general opinion was that the Corporate Governance Code is too reserved regarding gender diversity. Paul Kalma, a member of the social democratic party (PvdA) therefore proposed to include targets for more diversity in boards in the Corporate Governance Code; more specifically, he formulated a target of 25 to 30% women to be attained within a couple of years.[1] If the Corporate Governance Committee was not willing to do so, he argued, legal quota should be introduced. In this context reference is made to the positive results of quota legislation in Norway. Other parties, including the liberal parties VVD and D'66, also emphasised the necessity for more women in top positions but were in favour of softer measures such as obliging firms to be transparent on diversity by publishing figures on the issue. The Minister of Finance argued that the Corporate Governance Committee was aware of the importance attached to diversity by the government and Parliament. However, as the Committee was established within the context of self-regulation, he was not in a position to instruct the Committee to include specific targets for diversity (TK 2007–2008a). In the end, Parliament accepted a motion of Paul Kalma and other members of Parliament to stimulate the Monitoring Committee Corporate Governance Code to include target figures for women in the Corporate Governance Code (Code Tabaksblat) (TK 2007–2008b). The motion was, however, not executed; the updated Corporate Governance Code did not specify targets. Moreover, developments of the share of women in boards went slow and the number hardly increased. Therefore, in 2009 Paul Kalma, together with a member of Parliament for the liberal party (VVD) and the Christian democratic party (CDA), introduced an amendment to Book 2 of the Dutch Civil Code stating that supervisory boards of (public) limited corporations should strive for a balanced composition in its board of directors and supervisory board. That is, at least 30% of the seats should be taken by

1 Initially, Kalma, referring to the Norwegian case, wanted to propose a target of 40%, but this proposal met too much resistance (De Pers 2008).

women and at least 30% by men (TK 2009–2010). The amendment applies to bigger firms and not to firms that meet two out of three criteria:

- The assets of the firm are less than € 17.5 million;
- The net sales in the fiscal year is less than € 35 million;
- Average number of employees is less than 250.

The liberal party VVD joined the amendment under the condition – as a concession to employers which were strongly opposed to quota – that no hard sanctions are envisaged. Therefore the "comply or explain principle" is applied; in case of non-compliance companies are obliged to explain why there is no balanced composition, what the company has done to realise a more balanced composition and what the company will do to realise a more balanced composition in the future. The amendment which was part of a larger revision of corporate law. Traditionally, Dutch corporate law was based on the two-tier system of corporations. As a result of the revision the one-tier system is now also regulated. An important reason was to make the Netherlands more attractive for foreign companies. The legislation was accepted in the Upper Chamber in May 2011 with a large majority. However, due to changes in the government, it lasted until January 2013 before the legislation became effective. The amendment expires per 1 January 2016. In the next section, the current situation regarding the share of women in top positions and the estimated impact of the legal target will be elaborated.

V. LEGAL TARGETS ON DIVERSITY: CURRENT SITUATION AND EXPECTED IMPACT

As elaborated in the previous section, the Dutch target figure of 30% men and women on boards in principle applies to all large firms. Due to a lack of information, it is not possible to determine the exact number of companies to which the target of 30% applies. Though companies are obliged to file company information, the Chambers of Commerce, collecting this information, do not have to enforce this. In addition, the information they have to provide is limited (SEOR 2012). It is estimated that the legislation applies to about 4200 to 6100 companies. As a result is not easy to give an accurate picture of the current share of women on boards in these firms. It is estimated that between 5 to 8 per cent of the executive board members are women, and about 10 per cent of the supervisory board members. Not surprisingly, there appear to be large differences between sectors with the highest shares found in the public sector and the lowest shares in agriculture, manufacturing and construction. A minority of 8–15 per cent of relevant companies already seems to meet the targets for the share of women among boards of directors and an estimated 9–10 per cent meets the target for supervisory boards. The legislation also specifies that the share of men has to be at least 30%. It is estimated that about 10% of the companies do not meet this target. These are mainly companies in non-commercial, female dominated services, including care, culture and education (SEOR 2012).

The share of women in executive and non-executive boards increases steadily but slow, as illustrated in Table 1. This table provides data on companies of different sizes. In the largest 25 companies, the share of women on boards has increased from almost 5 to almost 12% between 2001–2011, and the top 100 largest companies show a doubling from 5.1 to 10.2%. In the top 500 and 5000 the shares are lower. It appears that the share of women in non-executive boards is higher than the share of women in executive boards (not included in the table). Given the pace of development so far, it seems unlikely that the target of 30% women on boards will be attained in 2016.

Table 1. Share of women in executive and non-executive boards by size of the company, 2001–2011

Largest companies	Year			
	2001	2007	2009	2011
Top 25	4.6	8.9	10.6	11.7
Top 100	5.1	7.3	9.3	10.2
Top 500	3.9	5.6	6.8	7.5
Top 5000	3.1*	4.5	4.2	6.0

* estimation
Source: Elite Group; cited in Merens et al. (2012: 128).

Another source of information is the Female Board Index, which presents an overview of the presence of women in the executive and supervisory boards of all Dutch listed companies (Lückerath-Rovers 2012). The most recent Index represents the situation at the end of August 2012 and includes 96 companies. Of these companies, 48% have women on their boards; 44% have female non-executive directors and only 11.5% have female executive directors. The share of companies with female directors is increasing, albeit slowly; in 2009, the share was 41%. It appears that in 2012 seven companies have at least 30% women in the supervisory board and also seven do so regarding the executive board. However, only one company (TNT Express) complies with the 30% target for both boards. In the total sample, 4.6% of all executive directors is female, and 13.3% of the non-executive directors. Based on current growth, Lückerath-Rovers (2012: 16) estimates that the share of women is likely to be 5,2% among executive directors in 2016, and 18,4% among non-executive directors.

That companies do not seem to fully exploit opportunities for change is confirmed in the study of Van der Laan et al. (2010) on composition of non-executive boards of listed firms. Based on in- and outflow of non-executive board members, this study notes that the target of 30% could be realised within two book years. However, it also concluded that in the current pace, the target will not be attained in 2016.

A relevant question in this respect is to what extent companies have policies to increase gender diversity in top management. The Corporate Governance Code recommends listed companies to strive for more gender diversity. In practice, only about a third appears to have specific targets. A study on book year 2010 shows that regarding best practice iii.3.1 on diversity, the top three characteristics of diversity on which listed companies have defined targets are knowledge/expertise (69% of the sample), managerial experience (57%) and background (46%). Regarding gender diversity, 31% has a target in the profile sketch of board of non-executives. In about half of the companies in the survey (26 companies) new executives have been appointed. In six out of these 26 companies, targets regarding gender diversity have been formulated. In four of the six companies these targets have been realised. In more than half of the 26 companies (n=14; 54%) with vacancies, services of an intermediary, such as head hunters, have been used. The search criteria for these intermediaries are in line with the target regarding diversity; the top 3 are knowledge/expertise, managerial experience and background. In six of these 14 companies gender diversity was one of the search criteria. Additional in depth interviews showed that respondents perceive the supply of qualified female candidates as low (IVO 2012).

Another interesting source of information to assess the impact of the target legislation are the companies that have signed the Charter Talent to the Top. These companies are expected to set their own diversity targets and implement measures to attain these targets. Progress is monitored annually. It appears that the average target for women in top positions in these companies in the period 2008–2010 is 22%, which is considerably less than the target figure of 30% in the new legislation. In addition, developments are slow as the actual share of women in top positions in these firms increased from 17.8 to 18.5% between 2010 and 2011. Given this pace, it is not expected that the (self-chosen) target figures will be realised and additional efforts are necessary. Moreover, a comparison between the organisations that have signed the Charter and those that did not, shows that the signatories have a larger share of women in top positions. This also suggests that the target of 30% is rather challenging (Merens 2012).

Summarising, given the pace of development of the (general) share of women in top positions over the last years, and of the share of women in top positions in companies that actively pursue diversity policies in particular, it seems unlikely that the legal target of 30% women (and men) in executive and supervisory boards will be attained.

VI. RECENT DEVELOPMENTS: THE DUTCH RESPONSE TO THE EU PROPOSAL OF 40% WOMEN ON BOARDS

In the policy note on emancipation for the coming years, covering the period 2011–2015, more women in top positions is still included as an important objective, supported with the argument that a more diverse top results in better performance (OCW 2011). The government is, however, opposed to more strict regulation. This is clearly illustrated in the Dutch response to the EU developments on this issue.

In 2012 the European Commission launched a public consultation on Gender imbalance on corporate boards in the EU. In reply to this consultation, the Dutch government strongly emphasised that diversity is the responsibility of companies, employers and employees. It is argued that increasing diversity requires tailor-made solutions and that imposing quota and setting sanctions are not appropriate in the Dutch context (OCW 2012a). It is therefore not surprising that the Dutch government is not pleased with the EU proposal on mandatory quota for women on company boards. In September 2012, together with representatives of governments from eight other EU member states, the Dutch minister of Education (who is responsible for emancipation policies), sent a letter to President Barrosso and Vice-President Reding with objections against the proposal. While in this letter the importance of equal opportunities is emphasised, the signers adhere to the subsidiarity principle and declare that they do not support the adoption of this proposal (Mladena et al. 2012).

In October 2012 the Dutch minister of Education again sent a letter to Vice President Reding, re-emphasising that the Dutch government does not favour European quota and that tailor-made solutions are essential. The current policies of self-regulation and the legal target are considered as "ambitious" and it is argued that the legal target will be evaluated in three years' time, which "will provide an opportunity to re-examine the extent to which it would be advisable to implement additional measures" (OCW 2012b: p. 2). The letter (again) concludes that the government does not support an EU Directive on women on boards, and that it questions whether such a directive would be reconcilable with the principle of subsidiarity. However, the government would be in favour of a recommendation on the issue, as this "would create more opportunities to enter into dialogues intended to explore how we can join forces to increase the number of women in top-level positions." (OCW 2012). The majority of the House of Representatives and Senate is also opposed to the proposal of Reding. Together they have sent a letter to the European Commission arguing that it is against the principle of subsidiarity (information provided on the website of House of Representatives).

In addition, other stakeholders expressed their disapproval. The employer's association VNO NCW and MKB Nederland issued a press release that they are against the proposal of a EU quota of 40%, arguing that employers should be able to formulate their own targets and implement measures to realise these targets. They supported their objection with the Norwegian case where companies delisted from the stock exchange in order to avoid having to comply with the legislation and many companies had to find women abroad (VNO NCW 2012).

VII. CONCLUSIONS

The low share of women in top management in the Netherlands is a topic of public attention and public debate. The government has implemented several measures to increase this share. Point of departure is self-regulation, stimulating and supporting companies to take action on the issue. Coercive measures, such as the use of preferential treatment, are not discussed. The Dutch Corporate Governance Code is also rather noncommittal as it only recommends companies "to strive for more diversity on their boards, particularly regarding gender". Inspired by the Norwegian case, in 2013 legislation became effective which obliges firms to have at least 30% women and 30% men in their boards in 2016. This legislation applies to all larger (publicly) limited corporations. Legal targets seem useful, as they facilitate monitoring of the policy measures. However, in line with the Dutch emphasis on self-regulation, the legislation is based on the so-called comply or explain principle. No sanctions are applied in case of non-compliance. Given the slow pace of development of the share of women in top management in general and the limited results in companies that are openly committed to achieve more diversity in the top in particular, it seems unlikely that the target of 30% women (and men) in boards in 2016 will be attained. Implementation of more strict quota legislation after 2016 is not likely in the Dutch context. On the more positive side, it can be argued that public attention for women in top positions has clearly increased the pressure on companies to deal with the issue. As a result, diversity targets and measures increasingly seem to become a self-evident part of company policies.

VIII. REFERENCES

AKKERMANS, D., VAN EES, H., HERMES, N., HOOGHIEMSTRA, R., VAN DER LAAN, G., POSTMA, T. and VAN WITTELOOSTUIJN, A., "Corporate Governance in the Netherlands: an overview of the application of the Tabaksblat Code in 2004", (2007) *Corporate Governance*, vol 15 (6), 1106–1118.

AMBASSADEURSNETWERK, *Ambassadeursnetwerk 2007/2008; wie is wie*, (www.ambassadeursnetwerk.nl; accessed February 2013).

COMMITTEE ON CORPORATE GOVERNANCE, *Corporate Governance in the Netherlands. Forty recommendations*, (Report of the Committee on Corporate Governance, 1997).

CORPORATE GOVERNANCE COMMITTEE, *The Dutch Corporate Governance Code. Principals of good corporate governance and best practice provisions*, (2003). 9 December 2003. (Downloadable from: www.corpgov.nl/code-tabaksblat (accessed February 2013)).

CORPORATE GOVERNANCE CODE MONITORING COMMITTEE, *Dutch corporate governance code. Principals of good corporate governance and best practice provisions* (Den Haag, 2008). (Downloadable from: www.corpgov.nl/corporate-governance-code (accessed February 2013)).

DE PERS, *Vrouwen aan de top of bedrijf dicht* (*De Pers*: 18 april 2008).

EZ (MINISTERIE VAN ECONOMISCHE ZAKEN), *Benoemen en roemen; Benutten van vrouwelijk talent: good practices uit het Ambassadeursnetwerk 2007–2008*, (Den Haag: Ministerie van Economische Zaken/ Ministerie van Onderwijs, Cultuur en Wetenschap).

FD (FINANCIEEL DAGBLAD), Dwing vrouwen aan top af (*Financieel Dagblad*: 16 mei 2008).

IVO, *De samenstelling en het functioneren van de raad van commissarissen in het boekjaar 2011 alsmede het verslag van de raad van commissarissen*, (Groningen-Rotterdam: Instituut voor Ondernemingsrecht/Rijksuniversiteit Groningen/Erasmus Universiteit Rotterdam, 2012).

DE JONG, A., DE JONG, D., MERTENS, G. and WASLEY, Ch., "The role of self-regulation in corporate governance: evidence and implications from The Netherlands" (2005) *Journal of Corporate Finance* 11 473–503.

DE JONG, A. and ROOSENBOOM, P.G.J., "De balans na vijf jaar Peters" (2002) *Economisch Statistische Berichten* 84, nr. 4390, 924-928.

LÜCKERATH-ROVERS, M., *The Dutch Female Board Index 2012* (Nyenrode: Nyenrode University, 2012).

MERENS, A., HARTGERS, M. and VAN DEN BRAKEL, M., *Emancipatiemonitor 2012* (Den Haag: Sociaal en Cultureel Planbureau/Centraal Bureau voor de Statistiek, 2012).

MERENS, A. (ed.), *Monitor Talent naar de Top 2011* (Den Haag: Sociaal en Cultureel Planbureau/Commissie Monitoring Talent naar de Top, 2012).

MLADENOV, T., DRÁBEK, J., PEVKUR, H., BALOG, Z., VINELE, I., JANKAUSKAS, D., SAID, C., VAN BIJSTERVELDT-VLIEGENTART, M. and CABLE, V., Women on company boards (Letter sent to president J.M. Barosso and vice president V. Reding, 14 September 2012).

MONITORING COMMISSIE CORPORATE GOVERNANCE, Derde rapport over de naleving van de Nederlandse corporate governance code (Den Haag, 2007). Downloadable from: www.commissiecorporategovernance.nl/download/?id=412 (accessed February 2013).

MONITORING COMMISSIE CORPORATE GOVERNANCE, *Rapport over de evaluatie en actualisering van de Nederlandse corporate governance code* (Den Haag, 2008).

OCW (MINISTERIE VAN ONDERWIJS, CULTUUR EN WETENSCHAPPEN), *Meer kansen voor vrouwen. Emancipatiebeleid 2008–2011* (Den Haag: Ministerie van Onderwijs, Cultuur en Wetenschap, 2007).

OCW (MINISTERIE VAN ONDERWIJS, CULTUUR EN WETENSCHAPPEN), *Hoofdlijnen emancipatiebeleid: vrouwen en homo-emancipatie 2015* (Den Haag: Ministerie van Onderwijs, Cultuur en Wetenschap, 2011).

OCW (MINISTERIE VAN ONDERWIJS, CULTUUR EN WETENSCHAPPEN), Openbare consultatie "Ongelijkheid tussen mannen en vrouwen in ondernemingsbesturen in de EU", Beleidsbrief 20 april 2012 (Den Haag: Ministerie van Onderwijs, Cultuur en Wetenschappen, 2012a).

OCW (MINISTERIE VAN ONDERWIJS, CULTUUR EN WETENSCHAPPEN), *Women on Company Boards,* Policy letter 18 October 2012 (Den Haag: Ministerie van Onderwijs, Cultuur en Wetenschappen, 2012b).

REMERY, C., *Effecten van emancipatiegericht personeelsbeleid* (Rotterdam: Erasmus Universiteit Rotterdam, dissertation, 1998).

SEOR, *Nulmeting wettelijke streefcijfers vrouwen in the top* (Rotterdam: SEOR School of Economics 2012).

SZW (MINISTERIE VAN SOCIALE ZAKEN EN WERKGELEGENHEID), *Meerjarenbeleidsplan Emancipatie* (Den Haag: Ministerie van Sociale Zaken en Werkgelegenheid, 2000).

TALENT NAAR DE TOP, *Charter Talent naar de top* (Talent naar de top, 2008, downloadable from: www.talentnaardetop.nl/uploaded_files/mediaitem/Charter_Talent_naar_de_Top.pdf, accessed January 2013).

TK (TWEEDE KAMER), Emancipatiebeleid 1997 (Tweede Kamer der Staten-Generaal, vergaderjaar 1996–1997, 25 006 nr. 1).

TK (TWEEDE KAMER), *Corporate governance, hedgefondsen en private equity – verslag van een algemeen overleg* (Tweede Kamer der Staten-Generaal, vergaderjaar 2007–2008, 31 083 en 28 998, nr. 21).

TK (TWEEDE KAMER), *Corporate governance, hedgefondsen en private equity; verslag van een algemeen overleg* (Tweede Kamer der Staten-Generaal, vergaderjaar 2007–2008a, 31 083 en 28998, nr. 21).

TK (TWEEDE KAMER), *Corporate governance, hedgefondsen en private equity* (Tweede Kamer der Staten-Generaal, vergaderjaar 2007–2008b, 31 083, nr. 17).

TK (TWEEDE KAMER), *Gewijzigd amendement van het lid Kalma c.s. Afdeling 7. Evenwichtige verdeling van zetels over vrouwen en mannen* (Tweede Kamer der Staten-Generaal, vergaderjaar 2009–2010, 31 763, nr. 14).

TK (TWEEDE KAMER), EU-voorstel gender gelijkheid, (downloadable from www.tweedekamer.nl/kamerstukken/dossiers/eu_voorstel_gendergelijkheid.jsp, accessed in March 2013).

VAN DER LAAN, G., ENGELEN, P.J. and VAN DER BERG, A., *Samenstelling en functioneren van de raden van commissarissen van Nederlandse beursgenoteerde vennootschappen in 2009* (Groningen-Utrecht: Rijksuniversiteit Groningen/ Corporate Governance Insights Centre/Universiteit Utrecht School of Economics, 2010).

VNO NCW, *Europees vrouwenquotum gaat niet werken* (www.vno-ncw.nl, accessed December 2012).

WOMAN CAPITAL, *Quota Manifest* (information provided on the website www.womancapital.nl/campagnes/quota-manifest/het-manifest/, not dated; accessed February 2013).

CHAPTER 10

THE NORWEGIAN GENDER BALANCE LAW – A BENCHMARK?*

Morten HUSE**

I. INTRODUCTION

The world is looking to Norway to explore the effects of the gender balance law that was proposed in 2003. In Norway and internationally this law was by many groups applauded, by other groups this intervention was followed with curiosity or scepticism, and by many actors this was strongly opposed and criticized. The criticism came mainly from the financial communities and the international financial press. They argued that the Norwegian economy would be ruined, there would not be enough "board ready" or qualified women, and the law was a transgression of the rights of the shareholders.

Politicians and women activists in many countries wondered if similar means could or should be implemented in their own countries, and laws similar to the Norwegian were adapted in some countries. However, the interest shown in the Norwegian experiment has been growing exponentially in other countries. This interest developed further by proposals by the EU Commissioner of Justice and Equality–Viviane Redding. She proposed legal regulations in Europe for securing women representation on corporate boards. Recently the possibility of legal regulations is also considered in civil law countries.

In this chapter I will give some of the background and some of the lessons from the introduction of the Norwegian law. The chapter is divided into three main

* This chapter is built upon my empirical research on the topic. In this chapter I lean on, develop and supplement concepts and descriptions from several of my previous oral and written presentations, including in particular those in Huse (2007), Huse (2011) and Huse (2012).

** Reinhard Mohn Chair of Management and Governance, University of Witten/Herdecke. Professor of Organisation and Management, BI Norwegian Business School. Email: mhuse@online.no.

sections. First, there is a section about the Norwegian background and about how the law developed. Various programs to increase the number of women on board are presented including a presentation of the law. The section is summarized by a graph showing the development of the percentage of board members being women. In the second section I present observations about the development of multi-board memberships in Norway, including also how the "old boys' network" has disappeared and characteristics of the "golden skirts" that now have filled the boardrooms. Finally, there is a section with reflections about the success of the law.

II. HISTORY AND BACKGROUND FOR THE LAW

Some knowledge about Norwegian traditions may be important when trying to understand the Norwegian law about gender balance. Norway is a civil law country, and there is an egalitarian society with a large middle class and almost no upper class. Norway has also been known for an industrial democracy tradition based on collaboration and involvement, and employee representation on corporate boards has existed about forty years.

A. CORPORATE GOVERNANCE IN NORWAY

When understanding the Norwegian corporate governance arena it is important to understand the Norwegian history and the main actors (Rasmussen and Huse 2011). This includes that Norway is a small country with only a few large corporations. The state and public authorities are important actors. This will in practice mean that there are few large traditional family companies, but that even small companies have had active boards of directors, public policy initiatives have been of major importance, and recent movements of investor activism have received considerable attention.

The most common way to organise a business in Norway is by establishing a private limited company (AS). AS-companies represent 51.6% of the total number of companies registered in Norway. Of the 414 public limited companies (ASA-companies), 224 were listed on Oslo Stock Exchange including 41 foreign companies. Figures are from 2008. As limited companies (AS and ASA) represent the largest proportion of companies in Norway, both in terms of number and value creation, the main focus is usually related to these companies. There are two laws regulating the limited companies – one for private (AS) and one for public limited companies (ASA). In Norway there is a one-tier board system, but with a compulsory delegation of executive tasks from the board to the management. The Companies Act (AS) is developed based on the notion that there are relatively few shareholders, while the Public Companies Act (ASA) regulates companies with many shareholders. The main difference is that ASA-companies are publicly tradable, while the sales of shares in AS-companies require board decisions. Listed companies have thus to be organised as public companies (ASA). Although the regulations in the two different Acts are mainly identical, there are some important differences between them. The differences are mainly related to the formalisation of public information. Co-determination and gender balance are two core concepts in Norwegian corporate governance that are regulated by law.

The Norwegian authorities are as mentioned main players in the Norwegian corporate governance debate (Rasmussen and Huse 2011). Another main player is a group calling itself the Norwegian Corporate Governance Board (NCGB). The actors behind NCGB have largely a background in investor and shareholder groups, including the Oslo Stock Exchange. They have developed recommendations they call The Norwegian code of best practice for corporate governance. The stated purpose of the NCGB recommendations is to strengthen confidence in companies, and to help ensure the greatest possible value creation over time in the best interest of shareholders, employees and other stakeholders. The NCGB recommendations have adopted the "comply or explain" principle.

B. FOR ABOUT FORTY YEARS

The Norwegian law about gender balance in corporate boards was originally an equal opportunity issue. The Equal Opportunity Act that was introduced in 1988 had the following wording: "When a public body appoints a committee board or council, etc. with four members or more, then each gender must be represented with at least 40% of the members. Both genders must be represented in committees with two or more members. These rules are also valid for subsidiary members."

The requirement concerning gender representation was motivated by social justice and a societal need. It was argued that the particular interests of women would be better taken care of by women than by men, and that women had different background experiences from men. Institutionally the Norwegian government had tried to achieve gender equality by various means, including paternity as well as maternity leaves, a high kindergarten coverage, etc.

The objective with the Equal Opportunity Act was to accelerate this development by a quota system. This regulation had major effects. Between 1979 and 1987 the ratio of women members of public boards and councils increased from 22% till 40%. Since then this figure has been constant.

However, the effects on corporate boards were limited. In 1992 only twenty six of the 764 board member positions in companies listed on Oslo Stock Exchange were held by women. Since the beginning of the 1990s till 2002 the percentage of women on boards in Norwegian listed companies remained stable at around 4–6%. In some industries there were no women at all in the boards.

C. PROGRAMS TO INCREASE THE NUMBER OF WOMEN ON BOARDS

During the 1990's many activities and programs were developed to increase the number of women on corporate boards (Huse 2012). Networks of women activists and feminists had already existed for some time, and political argumentations in press increased. Research was also conducted, and results about the business advantages of having women on boards were presented. Around this time attention became focused, and input to this discussion came from the NHO (the Confederation of Norwegian Enterprises), the government's Equality Centre, various feminist groups and the debates in other countries and in particular from Sweden. The motivation for increasing the number of women directors changed from an equality and societal issue to a firm profitability issue.

Programs to increase the number of women directors continued to mushroom. Various programs and seminars to train women to become board members were offered. These included business training as well as training in the workings of boards. Programs to facilitate the selection of women were also introduced. They included mentorship programs, and databanks, registers or archives of "board ready women". A data bank provided by the Norwegian Equality Agency contained in 2000 the names and resumes of several thousands women aspiring for board memberships.

Since the mid-1990s the political situation in Norway has been quite volatile with frequent changes in government between a social democratic Labour Party administration and one conservative headed by Kjell Magne Bondevik from the Christian Democratic Party (Huse 2007). In 1999 the Ministry of Equality in Bondevik's first Cabinet submitted for hearing a proposed reform to have at least 25% women on the boards of all companies – private and public alike. The proposal involved a change in the Equal Opportunity Act, and it lead to a strong reaction from men as well as from women. No final law proposal was made as the first Cabinet of Bondevik shortly afterwards was replaced by the Social Democratic Cabinet headed by Jens Stoltenberg.

In 2000 the ratio of women on board in publicly tradable companies (ASA-companies) was still only about 6%. The change in the Equal Opportunity Act was then followed up by the new Social Democratic Labour Party Cabinet, but changes in the law were then implemented without requirements for board representation. However, a new proposal for quotas for women on boards in ASA-companies was submitted in 2001 by the Stoltenberg cabinet. In the new law the ratio for gender balance was as high as 40%. This proposal was also sent out for hearing, but the proposal got very mixed support in the hearing. The NHO and the financial community were those being the most negative.

The second Bondevik Cabinet (from the autumn 2001) continued working on developing a new law proposal, and the minister of Industry and Trade together with the minister of Equality were included in these preparations. In February 2002 the conservative middle-aged male minister of Industry and Trade (coming from the Høyre Party in Bondevik's coalition cabinet) announced that he was "fed up" with the lack of progress on the number of women on board, and that this now should be regulated by law. His argument was mainly related to the business case about women and gender balance on boards.

D. A SUNSET LAW

The law proposal was ratified by the Norwegian Parliament in 2003. Each gender should be represented by at least 40% on boards of ASA companies, for example in boards with three members there should be at least one of the least represented gender, in boards with four members half of them should be women, in boards with five members there should be at least two of the least represented gender, etc. There should be no exception, and gender balance should also include employee elected board members. It was presented as a regulation in the Law about ASA companies, and the law was proposed by the Ministry of Trade and Industry. Sanctioning followed the tradition from this ministry and most other regulations in the ASA law. Gender balance was an absolute requirement, and the firms not meeting the requirements needed to find another form of incorporation. This freedom to choose another form of incorporation was increased as financial companies from 2007 did not need any more to have an ASA-incorporation.

The Law about gender balance in boards was presented as a "sunset" law (Huse and Dysthe 2013). This meant that the law would not be implemented if the objectives of the law were reached without it. After the ratification of the law huge discussions about its implementation took place. The NHO was a core actor in presenting counterarguments to the law, and NHO tried to stop its implementation. NHO thus placed considerable efforts to achieve the objective by voluntary activities and voluntary quotas. The high profiled Female Future program was developed to reach these objectives, but the requirements were in 2005 far from being met. The law was thus implemented in 2005 and sanctioning would take place after two years. This would mean during the autumn 2007, but in practice during the spring 2008. About one out of four Norwegian ASA companies decided in 2007 and 2008 to change form of incorporation. Many of them were financial companies and subsidiaries. In 2008 about 400 companies were subject to the law.

E. A SUMMARY

The development of the number of women directors in Norwegian publicly traded companies is presented in figure 1 (developed from e.g. Huse 2012).

Figure 1

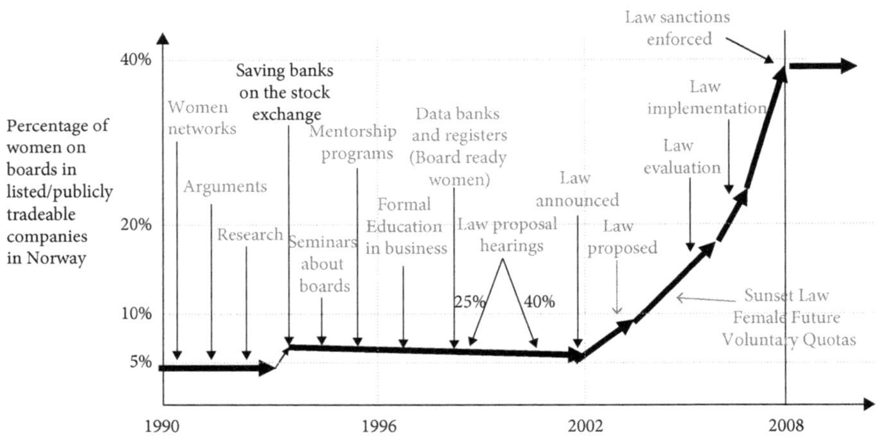

The figures reported are almost constant around 5% from 1990 till 2002. No increase took place even though considerable efforts were placed on a variety of initiatives. Two public hearings about law proposals also took place, but no increase in the percentage of women on corporate boards was achieved. The only change displayed before 2002 was around 1994. This change was caused by the fact that new types of companies (mainly saving banks) were introduced on Oslo Stock Exchange.

However, we see as a result of the law an immense increase from 2002 till 2008 – from 6% to 40%. The law has been directed to ASA-companies, but there has at the same time been a considerable increase in the women director ratio in large and medium-size AS-companies, and there are considerably more women CEOs in 2012 then it was ten years earlier.

III. CONSEQUENCES OF THE LAW

Norway has during recent years become a research laboratory that can help us understand various aspects about women on boards. In most cases studies of women on boards have been about demographic changes in the number of women on boards across different types of firms and among countries. Similar data from Norway was presented in the previous section. In the rest of this chapter I will present some observation from Norway that either are effects of the law or are based on the business case for women on boards. In this section I will present reflections about multi-board directors, the "old boys' network" and the "golden skirts". In the next section I will based on the business case make some reflections about the success of the Norwegian gender balance law.

A. MULTI-BOARD MEMBERS

The term the "golden skirts" have received considerable attention in the Norwegian and later also the international press, as well as in research, and studies have been conducted to explore who the women on boards in Norway are and how they have been selected (Seierstad and Opsahl 2011). Critical voices have in the international press been sceptical to the development of an elite group of prominent women that is replacing the "old boys' network".

The following figure shows that the majority of multi-board directors in ASA-companies in Norway are women. The figures used are means of the number of board positions in 2007, 2008, 2009 and 2010. The figure is an elaboration of a table in Huse (2012).

Figure 2. Multi-board directors in ASA companies: percentages (2007-2010)

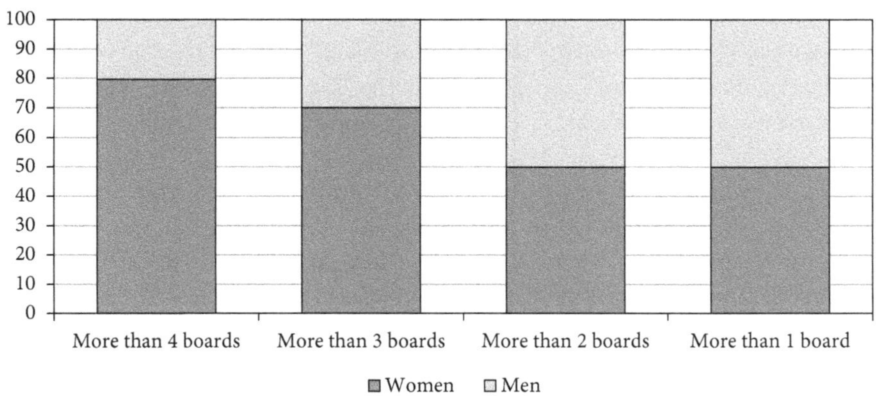

There are ten persons that in average (mean) in the years 2007–2010 had more than four board positions. Eight of them were women. There were thirty persons that in average had more than three board positions. Twenty-one out of them were women. One explanation to this situation may be the selection process. It has been a general criterion for becoming a board member to have previous board experience. This makes the few women having such experience more likely to get more. There were 96 persons with more than two board positions, and 314 that in averaged had more than one position in ASA-company boards.

B. REPLACING THE OLD BOYS' NETWORK

Multi-board memberships have moved from men to women, and the "golden skirts" have replaced the "old boys' network" (see Huse 2012 for more details). A "golden skirt" in Norway is typically defined as a woman that is making a living out of being a board member in ASA companies. Among the 21 women having more than three ASA company board memberships we found one being a major ship-owner. She was board member/chair also in her company's subsidiaries. Two of the women had major personal ties to the main owner of a financial company, and they were board members together in several of the subsidiary boards of this company. These companies disappeared later as ASA companies and became private. The remaining 18 were considered to be independent board members. Among them one had another main position, but for being a board members. In our studies we considered the remaining 17 women to be the "golden skirts". The few men remaining as multi-board members were mostly investors. Very few belonged to the group of men being professional board members who made a living out of these memberships. This indicates that that the "golden skirts" have replaced the "old boys' network" on boards.

One aspect of the "old boys' network" is interlocking directorates. Among the "golden skirts" no women were on more than one board together with another "golden skirt". This means that within the group of "golden skirts" there are very limited interlocks and no clear similarity to the "old boys' network". Some of the women even indicated that they did not know any of the others.

Based on the recent corporate governance literature we can identify three main types of board positions: insiders, investor and independent. The first group is held by persons having financial and psychological relations to the company leadership, including executive directors, consultants, family and friends and business partners. Included in the second group are owners or those having financial and psychological relations to main external stakeholders or ownership groups. These will often be investors, their representatives, family members and friends; sometimes also politicians. Members of neither of these groups are in the present corporate governance debates and recommendations considered to be independent. The last groups of board members will be those that are completely independent – with no relations to neither internal nor external actors.

When exploring the transition in Norway based on the gender quota law, we find that the board positions with insider or investor motivation are hardly replaceable. This means that the transition from men to women almost only has been in the group of independent directors. It is the women that in practice fill most of the seats as independent directors, and will fill most of the seats in important board committees as the auditing committee, nomination committee and compensation committee.

C. WHO ARE THE GOLDEN SKIRTS?

Who are then the "golden skirts"? Above we defined the concept and presented their general characteristics. I will here go beyond the surface level descriptions into a deeper level understanding of them. The descriptions are made based on portrait interviews with each of them. Detailed description of the study is found in Huse (2011). First, as above presented this group of women is very different from the "old boys' network". They hardly know each other, and we hardly see any interlocking directorates. Second, only the women making a living out of being a board member are included in the "golden skirt" definition.

And third, there are huge variations among these women as to background, selection processes and how they work on the board. The formal competencies and qualifications of these women were impressive – with respect to education as well as to practice, but we found that they differed in several ways. As a result of the interviews we categorised them based on a) experience and b) focus. The four categories are presented in the matrix.

Table 1

	Issue or process focused	Firm or system focused
Less experience	Advisors	Controllers
High experience	Decision-makers	Value creators

The advisors are characterized by being young, have strong analytical skills and having fact on the fingertips. The women in this group have also been called the McKinsey women. They contribute with lots of knowledge and skills. They have been trained together with men and learnt to compete with men. Often they have their spouses, partners or male schoolmates as mentors or sponsors. They have their identity in making a career, their field of work and their friends and network outside the actual board – often finance oriented.

The controllers are carefully doing the box-ticking when following corporate governance standards. This group of women seized the opportunity coming with the gender balance law requirements. They established themselves in their own private businesses to make a full time living of being board members even though their existing board experiences were limited. In this group we typically find lawyers and engineers, but we may also find women with management and leadership focus. They identify with being a board member. To prepare themselves for board positions they had training in board regulations and corporate governance requirements. The controllers have also been labelled the opportunists because of the way they seized the opportunity.

The decision-makers got their board invitations based on experiences from top-level politics. They typically had been ministers from some of the largest and most important ministries, i.e. the Ministry of Defence and the Ministry of Oil and Energy. Through politics they were trained in decision-making, and they typically have a large network that the firms and the boards normally appreciates. The iron-fists is a label having been used for this group, and they typically identify with their present or previous political career.

The last group is the value creators. They typically had heavy board positions long time before the gender balance law was introduced. As it is a main criteria for becoming a board member to have board experience, this group of women were the first being invited to take on more positions. These women are typically some older than the women in the other groups and they are characterized by being pragmatic and caring. They mostly identify with the firm and consider that their main tasks are to contribute to its long term sustainable value creation. We observed a tendency that those from the other groups when getting experience also moved over to this group.

IV. HAS THE LAW BEEN A SUCCESS?

In general I will argue that it is far too early to conclude whether the law has been a success. To respond to this question we need to get back to specifying measurement criteria. Should we evaluate the law based on what is best for the society, including elements of justice, democracy, participation, gender equality and conventions? It is not only a matter of counting the increase in the number of women on boards, but to understand the impact on underlying values. Should the law be evaluated based on what is best for women, including the breaking of the glass ceiling, furthering of career possibilities of women, etc.? Then we also need to consider the consequences this law have for men. Or should the law be evaluated based on what is the best for the company? Then we also need to specify how it impacts market values compared to company performance. We may conclude that in Norway the law and its consequences now in general are accepted even by people that were against it as it was introduced.

A. THE WARNINGS THAT WERE RAISED

There are some easily observable measures. The law increased the percentage of women directors from less than ten percent to about forty per cent. The law has not ruined the Norwegian economy, and neither the companies nor the investors have suffered. We have seen that a large number of highly competent women now have got the possibility to be board members in ASA companies without seeing any hoovering of women from CEO positions, boards in private firms or from other countries. And generally the women do not present that they experience being tokens on the actual board. But generally it is far too early to conclude. However, I will here in the end first bring in some observations and reflections about the business case and then how the law impacts other countries.

B. THE BUSINESS CASE FOR THE LAW AND WOMEN ON BOARDS

It is important to make a difference between the business case for women on board and the business case for a quota law. Is it good for businesses to have women on boards, and is it good to have a law requiring it? And if it is best for the business why then should the society need to intervene with regulations? The Norwegian minister of Industry and Trade that announced the law used the business case as the argument. The business case argument seemed for him easier to follow than the societal perspectives. He was obviously thinking that businesses did not know what the best was for them. However, there were in Norway some business case effects that came from the introduction of the law in addition to the general effects of having women on boards.

In about two decades I have been involved in studies about the business case for women on boards. Huse and Solberg (2006), Huse, Nielsen and Hagen (2009), Nielsen and Huse (2010) and Torchia, Calabro and Huse (2011) are some examples of recent empirical publications. They all use empirical evidence from Norway. Based on these I have made a ten point list important for understanding, evaluating and developing the business case for women on boards.

- Value creation: Who are defining value creation and how is it done? There may be differences for example between short term changes in market value on the stock exchange and long term sustainable value creating in the company.
- Board tasks: The impact of women varies with the tasks being focused. In some studies we have seen that there may be positive results related to women directors' contribution in strategy, but negative for networking and advisory tasks.
- Diversity: It is important to explore deep-level and not only surface-level diversity, and it is important to go beyond biological gender to understand women's contribution. Not all women aspiring for board positions have female values, a feminine behaviour or a feminist agenda.
- Using diversity: Good board leadership and good board structures can influence the use of diversity. However, boards are often set up for fast decision-making, and the knowledge and skills of board members are rarely fully utilized. We cannot expect to see any differences if the knowledge and skills of the women are not used.
- Gender role stereotyping: The impact of women depends on how they are being received. A male in-group in the board may reduce the impact of the women if they are excluded or just considered as tokens.
- Critical mass: The impact depends on whether the women are adapting to an existing culture. When there are only one or two women they tend to adapt to the existing board culture.
- Tokenism: Awareness about possible tokenism increases competence and preparations. Nobody wants to elect tokens or not-competent women, and the elected women do not want to be perceived as incompetent. The tokenism perspective thus leads to that the elected women are very highly competent and very well prepared. The tokenism discussion will be more related to the introduction of a law than most of the other points.
- Gender-related dynamics: Things may change when women and men are getting together. The behaviour of men often changes when a women is present. We can often observe a nicer atmosphere in a board with women than in those without women.
- Learning effects: Effects may change over time and place. We will in the future see more women with board experience filling the boardrooms.
- A new understanding of corporate governance is developing. A main focus in recent corporate governance debates has been on independent board members that can monitor the management. Transparency and value distribution have been the objectives. The discussion of women on board has a focus on competence, diversity and the use of knowledge and skills. Strategic decision making and long term sustainable value creation have become the objectives.

These points all shows the importance of understanding the dynamics of corporate governance, what a board is and how it is working, deep level diversity and gender related dynamics for concluding on the business case for women directors (Huse 2007, Huse 2008). This means that I am very sceptical to studies making clear conclusions about the business case without integrating these perspectives. Short term changes of the market value cannot be a reliable measure. One much cited study that I thus will have problems using as a benchmark for the success of the Norwegian gender balance law, uses changes in the market values of companies immediately after the announcement of increasing the number of women on board. Few studies are so extreme, but from finance scholars there are many studies about the Norwegian experience I do not trust. The board is in these studies considered as a black box, and research in the field of finance rarely considers studies from other disciplines.

C. IS THE NORWEGIAN EXPERIENCE RELEVANT FOR OTHER COUNTRIES?

A snowball has started rolling, and it is accelerating in speed and in size. Businesses, activists and political decision-makers are looking to Norway and want to learn from the Norwegian law about gender balance. Norway has been used as a benchmark, but what can be transferred to other countries?

Corporate governance and boardroom dynamics cannot be studied in the same way as physics or natural science. It is important to understand the actors and the context, including place and time. The core issues related to increasing the women on corporate boards will also vary across countries. In some countries it is a matter of meritocracy, and in some countries a matter of equal opportunity. Some will consider women and their contributions as different from those of men, while others will argue that when you are on boards there will be no differences. Institutional factors vary considerably across countries, and some countries like Sweden will probably achieve gender balance on boards without a law. This would probably not have been the case in Italy, Spain and the Netherlands. Politicians and businesses in some countries, as for example Germany and UK, still believe that they will get gender balance by voluntary actions. In other countries this is an issue of no importance. In Denmark will business leaders as long as possible avoid learning lessons from Norway.

The existing corporate law systems will be important for the adoption of quota laws and the following of the Norwegian example. Common law countries will for example most likely be more hesitant than civil law countries to introduce quota laws. Common law countries will have a larger belief in voluntary actions to change a system.

There are also variations in board and corporate governance systems across countries. In Scandinavia there is typically one board that delegates executive tasks to the management. In Germany and the Netherlands there are two levels of board. There is one supervisory board that the executive board reports to, and in e.g. Italy there is also two board, but with a vertical relationship. Finally, in USA and UK there is one board that used to be similar to the German executive board. What types of boards should then be compared, and will the effects be the same regardless of system?

In the beginning I introduced Norway as an egalitarian society. It has been possible for women from all classes of society to get to boards. This may be more difficult in for example UK, Italy or even from parts of Germany. The skewness in the distribution of women that will aspire for boards in these countries may have quite different societal impacts than when it is a more egalitarian based society.

V. REFERENCES

HUSE, M. 2007, *Boards, Governance and Value Creation: The Human Side of Corporate Governance*, Cambridge: Cambridge University Press.

HUSE, M. 2008, "Women directors and the "black box" of board behavior", in Vinnicombe, Singh, Burke, Billimoria and Huse *Women on Corporate Boards of Directors: International Research and Practice*, Cheltenham: E. Elgar, pp 140–151.

HUSE, M. 2011, "The golden skirts": Changes in board composition following gender quotas on corporate boards, Australian and New Zealand Academy of Management, Wellington December 2011.

HUSE, M. 2012, "The Golden Skirts: Lessons from Norway about Women on Corporate Boards" in Gröschl, S. und Takagi, J., *Diversity Quotas, Diverse Perspective: The Case of Genders*, Glower: Ashgate, chapter 1, pages 11–23.

HUSE, M. and DYSTHE, P. 2013, *Styrearbeid sett med nye briller: Loven om kjonnsbalanse, kvinner og mangfold i styrer*, Bergen: Fagbokforlaget.

HUSE, M., NIELSEN, S.T. and HAGEN, I.M. 2009. "Women and employee-elected board members, and their contributions to board control tasks" *Journal of Business Ethics* (2009) 89:581–597.

HUSE, M. and SOLBERG, A.G. 2006, "Gender related boardroom dynamics: How women make and can make contributions on corporate boards" *Women in Management Review*, (2006) 21 (2): 113–130.

NIELSEN, S.T. and HUSE, M. 2010, "The contribution of women on boards of directors: Going beyond the surface", *Corporate Governance: An International Review*, (2010) 18 (2): 136–148.

RASMUSSEN, J.L. and HUSE, M. 2011, "Corporate governance in Norway: Women and employee elected board members" in Mallin, C. (2011) *International Corporate Governance*, E. Elgar, (chapter 6), 121–146.

SEIERSTAD, C. and OPSAHL, T. 2011, "For the few not the many? The effects of affirmative action on presence, prominence, and social capital of women directors in Norway", *Scandinavian Journal of Management*, 27 (1): 44–54.

TORCHIA, M., CALABRO, A. and HUSE, M. 2011, "Women Directors on Corporate Boards: From Tokenism to Critical Mass", *Journal of Business Ethics*, 102: 299–317.

CHAPTER 11

THE BALANCED REPRESENTATION OF MEN AND WOMEN ON THE BOARD OF DIRECTORS OF COMPANIES LISTED ON STOCK EXCHANGES AND PUBLIC UNDERTAKINGS: THE *STATUS QUAESTIONIS* IN SPAIN

Reyes Palá Laguna*

I. INTRODUCTION

A. THE *STATUS QUAESTIONIS* IN PUBLIC LAW

1. *The Organic Act 3/2007 of 22 March for effective equality between women and men (Effective Equality Act, 2007)*

This Act has implied an unquestionable advance on the effective equality between women and men, at least in public administration and public undertakings. The Act is very ambitious[1] and goes beyond the transposition of the two main Directives on equal treatment, that is, Directive 2006/54/EC on the implementation of the principle of equal opportunities and equal treatment

* Professor of Commercial Law, School of Law, University of Zaragoza.

1 Article 1 of the Effective Equality Act reads as follows: *Purpose of the Act.*
1. Women and men are equal in human dignity, equal in rights and duties. The purpose of this Act is to ensure equal treatment and opportunities for women and men, in particular via the elimination of discrimination against women of whatsoever circumstances or background and in all areas of life, specifically in the political, civil, occupational, economic, social and cultural domains, so as to build a more democratic, fair and warm society, pursuant to Articles 9.2 and 14 of the Constitution.
2. To this end, the Act establishes the principles governing the action of public authorities, regulates natural and corporate persons' public and private rights and duties and lays down measures designed to eliminate and correct all forms of discrimination on the grounds of sex in the public and private sectors. (© Spanish Ministry of Justice).

between men and women (recast)[2] and Directive 2004/113/EC implementing the principle of equality of treatment between women and men in the access to and supply of goods and services.[3]

This Act acknowledges that the full recognition of formal equality before the law (s. 14 Spanish Constitution, 1978), indisputably constituting a decisive step, has proved to be insufficient. The still scant presence of women in positions of economic responsibility, stands as evidence of the fact that the attainment of full, effective equality between women and men, is even today an unfinished task, and further legal instruments are necessary to complete the task, to transform the principle of equality into effective practice.[4]

In general terms, the Act of 2007 imposes upon the Spanish Central Government a *balanced presence of women and men in the Central Government and its associated or subordinate public bodies.* Section 52 of the Act states that "Where appointment is incumbent upon the Government, it will honour the principle of the balanced presence of women and men in the overall membership of the management bodies of the Central Government and its associated or subordinate public bodies." More especially, in relation to the *appointment of Central Government representatives* (Section 54), the Central Government and its associated or subordinate public bodies will appoint their representatives in professional bodies and national or international expert or advisory boards in accordance with the principle of balanced presence of women and men, barring duly reasoned, justified and objective arguments to the contrary. As far as State-owned enterprises are concerned, the Central Government and its associated or subordinate public bodies will observe the principle of balanced presence in their appointments to boards of directors of companies in which the State has a holding. The Act defines "balanced presence" as "the presence of women and men, in the context in question, in a manner such that neither sex accounts for more than sixty per cent nor less than forty per cent of the total".[5]

Besides, the Sustainable Economy Act of 4 March 2011 sets forth the obligation for the public undertakings and enterprises in which the State exercises control, to adapt their daily management to the general principles of sustainability. These corporations and enterprises, in the elaboration of their Annual Corporate Governance Reports, shall pay special attention to effective equality between women and men. They must promote the adoption of social responsibility

---

2 Directive 2006/54/EC of the European Parliament and of the Council of 5 July 2006 on the implementation of the principle of equal opportunities and equal treatment of men and women in matters of employment and occupation (recast), OJ L 204, 26 July 2006.

3 Council Directive 2004/113/EC of 13 December 2004 implementing the principle of equal treatment of men and women in the access to and supply of goods and services, OJ L 373, 21 December 2004.

4 Preamble of the Effective Equality Act, 2007, part II.

5 See additional provision one of the Effective Equality Act, 2007.

principles and practices among their suppliers with special attention to the promotion of women integration and the effective equality between women and men.[6] The entry into force of the Sustainable Economic Act in 2011 implies new transparency requirements in corporate governance for listed companies and public undertakings.[7]

In spite of this legislation imposing the principle of equality in the composition of the boards of directors in public undertakings, in practice, it is proven that this is not the case, and that only in a few boards of directors of public undertakings there is an equal representation of men and women. However, in the State-owned enterprises the rule of equal representation of men and women on the board of directors is applied more effectively than in private companies; for example, the board of ENSA is composed by 6 men and 4 women.[8] But this is not a commonplace occurrence. Nevertheless, we highlight that equality is more respected in the public sector than in the private sector. The Government of Spain is formed by 4 female ministers and 10 male ministers, a proportion that is not present in any of the listed companies of the IBEX 35[9], in which the average of females on the boards is of 12.75% of the board members.[10]

B. THE *STATUS QUAESTIONIS* IN PRIVATE LAW

1. *The Effective Equality Act, 2007 and gender equality in mercantile companies' boards of directors*

a. Introduction. The inexistence of binding rules on gender equality on the boards of companies

There are no binding rules on gender equality on the boards of private companies as opposed to what happens in public undertakings. The Effective Equality Act,

6 Section 35 of the Act 2/2001, of 4 March, on Sustainable Economy.

7 This Act is in line with the legislative initiatives at an international level and non binding regulations in Spain. (*Dodd-Frank Act*, 2010, EU *Green Book on Corporate Governance*). See PWC, *Report on Boards of Directors of Listed Companies*, June 2012, pg. 4, www.pwc.es.

8 ENSA Annual Report 2012, p. 3, www.ensa.es. On the contrary, on the board of directors of the public company Corporation RTVE, there are 3 women and 6 men (www.rtve.es) in spite of the fact that in 2012 its Regulatory Act has been amended (Official Journal of 23 April 2012) and now its section 10.1 lays down the following "The board of directors of Corporation RTVE will be composed by nine members, all of whom will be individual entities with enough training and professional experience, trying to obtain equality between men and women in its composition". The State Company of Mail and Telegraphs (Sociedad Estatat de Correos y Telégrafos S.A.) has in its board 4 women y 12 men (*Corporate Governance Report*, 2012, p. 8, www.correos.es/comun/informacionCorporativa/1006.asp?n=1). The board of the parent company of the State holding, SEPI, is composed by 3 women and 13 men (www.sepi.es).

9 IBEX 35 (IBEX: contraction of "Indice Bursátil Español", Spanish Stock Exchange Index), is a capitalisation-weighted index comprising the 35 most liquid Spanish shares traded in the Continuous Market (SIBE).

10 *El peso de las mujeres en los consejos del IBEX 35*, Inforpress IESE, Madrid, 2013, p. 4.

2007 does not contain an obligation for private companies to observe the principle of gender equality (or at least a balanced presence of men and women) in the composition of the board of directors. Section 75 of the afore mentioned Organic Act just highlights that big companies[11]will endeavour to include a sufficient number of women on their boards of directors to reach a balanced presence of men and women within eight years of the entry into effect of the Act (that is, 2015). This provision will be taken into account when making appointments on the occasion of the finalisation of the terms of directors appointed prior to the entry into force of this Act (2007). But no sanctions are foreseen in case of breach of this regulation.

The measures in favour of equality observed by the Act fall within the framework of *moral suasion* through the award of marks to the companies which encourage equality within their labour force.

The Act of 2007, in an effort to promote gender equality, has created the Corporate Equality Mark (Section 50) to distinguish employers for outstanding achievements in the implementation of equal treatment and opportunity policies for their workers, which may be used in the company's commercial dealings and for advertising purposes.[12] The criteria to be taken into account for the award of this mark will include, among others, the balanced presence of women and men in the company's management bodies and occupational groups and categories, the adoption of equality plans or other innovative measures to further equality, and non-sexist advertising of company goods and services.[13]

---

11 The Act refers to this recommendation (Sec. 75) only for the companies that cannot prepare abridged income statements (not medium sized or small companies). Section 258 of the Corporate Enterprises Act, 2010, allows corporations to prepare abridged income statements if they meet at least two of the circumstances listed below on the closing date of two consecutive financial years: (i) total assets not over eleven million four hundred thousand euros, (ii) net annual turnover not over twenty-two million eight hundred thousand euros or (iii) average headcount during the financial year not over two hundred and fifty employees.

12 Royal Decree 1615/2009, of 26 October, regulates the obtaining and use of the mark "Equality at the Company (RD 1615/2009, of 26 October, which regulates the licence and use of the mark "Equality at the Company"). The mark is called on an annual basis and is in force for three years, though the distinguished companies shall send an annual report, that will be assessed by the Directorate-General for Equal Opportunities of the Secretariat of State of the Ministry of Health, Social Services and Equality, in order to prove that they keep the level of excellence in equality issues due to which they were awarded the mark "Equality at the Company". In 2011, several companies listed on the IBEX 35 have obtained the Mark [BBVA, Acciona, FCC, Indra, (see Ministerial Order SSI/499/2012, of 24 February, Official Journal 03/13/2011). In 2010, Banco Popular, Banco de Santander, Enagás, Endesa, Ferrovial, REE, Repsol (see Ministerial Order SPI/3138/2010, of 26 November, Official Journal 12/03/2010)].

13 The Ministry of Labour and Social Affairs will monitor the companies awarded the mark to ensure they implement equal treatment and opportunities policies on their workers on an ongoing basis, withdrawing the mark from non-compliant organisations (Article 50.5 Organic Act, 2007).

b. Companies' disclosure requirements

In relation to the notes of the companies financial statements, section 260.8 of the Corporate Enterprises Act, 2010[14], imposes on the companies the obligation to disclose, in their Annual Notes, the year-end distribution by gender of the company's personnel, broken down into a sufficient number of categories and levels, including senior management and directors, that is women members of the board. This rule applies to all the companies, listed and non listed companies, irrespective of their size.

It should be remembered that in Spain corporations follow the one-tier administration system (board of directors). The two-tier governance system (directors and a supervisory board) may be chosen by the European Companies (SE)[15] with registered offices in our country.[16]

II. CORPORATE GOVERNANCE OF LISTED COMPANIES AND OTHER BODIES WITH SECURITIES ADMITTED TO TRADING ON A REGULATED MARKET

A. CORPORATE GOVERNANCE RULES AND REGULATIONS

There are specific provisions for companies that issue debt securities and equity traded on a regulated market in any European Union Member State in the Corporate Enterprises Act, 2010 and the Securities Market Act, 1998.[17] These companies shall include their Corporate Governance Report in a separate section of their Management Report (Section 538 Corporate Enterprises Act, 2010).

Section 61*bis* of the Securities Market Act details the content of the Corporate Governance Report for listed companies. This Section does not make explicit reference to gender equality or the need of more balanced representation between men and women on the board of directors. Nevertheless, the Corporate Governance Report must contain, at least, the "degree of application of the

14 Royal Legislative Decree 1/2010, of 2 July, approving the consolidated text of the Corporate Enterprises Act (Official Journal 3 July 2010).
15 Council Regulation (EC) 2157/2001 of 8 October 2001, on the Statute for a European Company (SE).
16 See articles 455 to 494 Corporate Enterprises Act, 2010.
17 Law 24/1988, of 27 July, on Securities Market.

Corporate Governance Recommendations and an explanation, in any case, where the recommendations are not followed".[18] That is, the principle of comply or explain is implemented in our corporate governance legislation.

The Spanish Regulation on Corporate Governance has its origins in the voluntary codes of conduct adopted in Spain in the 1990s, following the model of the UK Corporate Governance Codes (for example, the Cadbury Report, 1992[19]). The first relevant Spanish corporate code, dated in 1996, did not include neither references to the promotion of the presence of woman on the board of directors, nor general mentions of woman participation in the management of a public company.[20]

The situation is similar in the Code of Good Governance of February, 1998 ("The Olivencia Code"), prepared by a Special Commission to consider a Code of Ethics for Companies' Boards of Directors.[21]

Almost five years later, the next Corporate Governance Code, prepared under the Government initiative, the Aldama Report, 2003[22], does not include references to gender equality on the board composition of listed companies.

The first reference to gender diversity on the board of directors of listed companies takes place in Spanish Law in 2006, when a Special Working Group was set up by the Spanish Government on 25 July 2005, in order to advice the

---

18 Section 61*bis*, paragraph 4, letter g) Securities Market Act.

19 Report of the Committee on the Financial Aspects of Corporate Governance, 1 December 1992, available at www.ecgi.org/codes/code.php?code_id=132.

20 *Una propuesta de normas para un mejor funcionamiento de los Consejos de Administración (A proposal of regulations for a best functioning of the boards of directors)*, Círculo de Empresarios, Madrid, October 1996, available at www.ecgi.org/codes/documents/empres.pdf.

21 On 28 February 1997, the Spanish Cabinet, at the proposal of the Second Vice-President of the Government and Minister of Economy and Finance, resolved to create a Special Commission to consider a Code of Ethics for Companies' Boards of Directors. By means of a Ministerial Order dated 24 March 1997, in compliance with the Cabinet's decision, the Second Vice-President of the Government and Minister of Economy and Finance appointed the members of the Special Commission, chaired by Manuel Olivencia, The final Report (The Governance of Listed Companies) is dated 26 February 1998 (available at www.ecgi.org/codes/code.php?code_id=110).

22 Report by the Special Commission to encourage transparency and security in the markets and in listed companies, of 8 January 2013, chaired by Enrique de Aldama y Miñón. On 19 June 2002, the Spanish Cabinet adopted a resolution by which a Special Commission is established "to study the criteria and guidelines that should apply to companies which issue securities and instruments admitted to listing on organised markets in their relations with consultants, financial analysts and other companies, persons or entities which assist them or provide professional services to them, and those which should apply among the latter, in order to increase transparency and security of the financial markets in the light of the structural changes, the current globalised economy and the trends in international markets. The Commission must also analyse the current status and degree of application of the Code of Good Governance for Listed Companies."

Comisión Nacional del Mercado de Valores (CNMV) on the elaboration of a new Corporate Governance Code.[23] This Special Working Group approved, in January, 2006, the draft of the Unified Code on Good Corporate Governance. This draft harmonises and updates the Olivencia and Aldama Report Recommendations for the good governance of listed companies. The Final Report of the Working Group was approved on May, 19th, 2006 and it is commonly quoted as the "Conthe Code" or *Unified Good Governance Code*.[24]

This Code means a significant advance in the recognition, for the first time, in Spain by a public body (the CNMV) of the importance of female presence on the boards of directors of listed companies. Three new Recommendations are introduced, on the matter, as we can read on the Draft of the *Conthe Code*. The new Recommendations "start from the conviction that a good gender mix is not just an ethical-political or corporate social responsibility question but also an efficiency builder, in the medium term at least: neglecting the potential business talent of 51% of the population – women – cannot be globally efficient for listed companies. Recommendations also assume that men domination of senior posts is, in some way, self-perpetuating, possibly fuelled by hysteresis and network externalities (the "old boys' network"). This makes it likelier that male appointments will continue to predominate, and suggests the diversity deficit will not go away without a directed effort".[25]

The Special Working Group also recognises that the gender diversity Recommendations of the Unified Code are aimed strictly at improving the performance of boards of directors, and do not address other changes that may be desirable from a "social responsibility" standpoint (for example, disclosure of salary differences or the company's adoption of policies to help reconcile family and working life).[26]

These ideas appear again in the final version of the Unified Code[27], in which Recommendation 15 says: "When women directors are few or non existent, the

---

23 Section one f) of Order ECO/3722/2003 of 26 December calls on the CNMV to publish "a single text with existing corporate governance recommendations" for listed companies to use as a benchmark when reporting their compliance or otherwise with corporate governance recommendations in their Annual Corporate Governance Report, as mandated by the Securities Markets Act. In the Government Agreement of 25 July 2005, on the creation of the Special Working Group, the Government orders the Group to take into account other recommendations made by the European Commission and International organisations (for example, the OECD).

24 The Unified Good Governance Code, the Appendix and other related documents are available at the CNMV web site www.cnmv.es/portal/Legislacion/COBG/COBG.aspx.

25 Unified Code on Good Corporate Governance (Draft), 18 January 2006, page 12.

26 Unified Code on Good Corporate Governance (Draft), 18 January 2006, page 13.

27 Under the Title "Gender Diversity", the introduction to Recommendation 15 reads as follows: "A good gender mix on boards of directors is not just an ethical-political or "corporate social responsibility" question; it is also an efficiency objective which listed companies might wish

board should state the reasons for this situation and the measures taken to correct it; in particular, the Nomination Committee should take steps to ensure that a) the process of filling board vacancies has no implicit bias against women candidates; b) the company makes a conscious effort to include women with the target profile among the candidates for board positions".

The reference in the Draft Unified Code to a section on Gender Diversity in the Annual Corporate Governance Report with detailed information on (i) the year-end gender distribution of company staff, with a detailed breakdown by occupational categories and levels, to include senior officers and directors and (ii) the changes occurring in the said distribution over the course of the year, had disappeared in the final version of May, 2006, probably because this recommendation turned into legal obligation by the amendment of the Companies Act, 1989 by the Effective Equality Act, 2007.[28]

A crucial point is the voluntariness of the Unified Code, subject to the *comply or explain* principle. Its recommendations are not binding for listed companies, but if they are not followed, the company must give a reasoned explanation for every deviation.[29] We will see *infra* some examples of explanations in relation to the lack of gender diversity on the board of directors.

Circular 4/2007, of 27 December, of the CNMV, adopted a new model of the Annual Corporate Governance Report for listed Companies.[30] Point B.1.27 of Annex I (model of ACGR) reads as follows: "In the event of few or no women directors, explain the reasons and the initiatives taken to correct this situation. In particular, indicate whether or not the Appointments and Compensation Commission has established procedures to prevent selection processes from being implicitly biased and raising obstacles for the selection of women directors and that it deliberately seeks candidates that meet the required profile indicating the main procedures". The listed company should fulfil this point B.1.27 even if the company complies totally or partially, or does not comply at all with the

to work towards in the mid term, at least. Neglecting the potential business talent of 51% of the population -women- cannot be an economically rational conduct for our country's leading corporate names. This is amply borne out by the experience of the last few decades which have seen women occupying a growing place in the business world. But more effort is required for this presence to extend into the senior executive and directorship spheres. With this in mind, the Code calls on listed companies with few women on their boards to actively seek out female candidates whenever a board vacancy needs to be filled, especially for independent directorships".

28 This obligation currently appears in Article 260.8 of the Corporate Enterprises Act, but without the reference included in the Draft Unified Code to the changes occurring in the gender distribution of company staff over the course of the year.

29 *Unified Good Governance Code*, p. 7.

30 Official Journal of 14 January 2008.

Recommendation on Gender Diversity on the board. If the company does not comply with the Recommendation, because there is no woman member on the board, the company should explain the reasons and the initiatives taken to correct this situation.[31]

The listed companies in the IBEX 35 that in 2011 had no woman representation on their board of directors were ENDESA S.A, GAS NATURAL S.A. and TECNICAS REUNIDAS S.A. They included, in their Annual Reports on Corporate Governance 2011, very general comments that avoided a clear and direct answer by the company.[32]

The approach of Spanish Law to the matter does not encourage the presence of women on the board of directors because it allows companies, if they consider it appropriate, not to provide details regarding the absence of women on the board of directors. But, at least, information about the presence or absence of women on the board of directors of listed companies is public and accessible to everybody on their web page (on which the Annual Corporate Governance Reports are published, s. 61*bis* Securities Market Act). This constitutes a first step

---

31 See Preamble of the Circular 4/2007.

32 In their *Corporate Governance Annual Report* 2011, ENDESA recognised that there were no female directors in Endesa. "However, Endesa does have an Equality Plan in place, reasserting its commitment to ensuring compliance with the gender equality principle". Article 15 of the ENDESA Board of Directors' Regulations stipulates that "the Appointments and Remuneration Committee will be entrusted with, among other functions, the functions of reporting and proposing the appointment of the members of the Board of Directors, whether in the event of co-optation or for proposal to the General Shareholders' Meeting guaranteeing that the selection procedures do not suffer from implicit flaws which impair the selection of female Directors" (ENDESA *Corporate Governance Annual Report* 2011, p. 20). The fact that this company (and the other two companies mentioned before) has a policy to encourage the presence of woman on the board of directors is questionable. It is unbelievable to think that, currently, there are no women that meet the professional profile that enables them to carry out the duties as members of the board in these companies. At least, as independent members of the board, if there are no women who can represent the quota of board members representing shareholders or executive members of the board. More briefly, GAS NATURAL only ticks the box "yes" to the question B.1.27 (In particular, indicate whether or not the Appointments and Remuneration Committee has laid down procedures to ensure that the selection processes are not subject to implicit bias that prevents the selection of female Directors and deliberately looks for female candidates with the required profile"). In relation to the main procedures it only says that "Article 31.2 of the Regulations of the Board of Directors lays down the Appointments and Remuneration Committee obligation to ensure that "[...] when covering new vacancies, selection processes shall apply that are not subject to implicit bias that prevents the selection of female Directors, where the potential candidates shall include, under the same conditions, women that meet the professional profile being sought" (GAS NATURAL FENOSA 2011 *Corporate Governance Report*, page 26). And more briefly, if possible, the answer to the point B.1.27 of TECNICAS REUNIDAS in their ACGR 2011 is "In the selection process of new members of the boards, the company follows procedures that are not subject to implicit bias that hampers the selection of female Directors". (TECNICAS REUNIDAS *Annual Corporate Governance Report*, 2011, p. 29).

to know about the representation of women on the boards of directors and to adopt measures that encourage their addition.

The Ministerial Order ECC/461/2013, of 20 March, which lays down the content and structure of the Corporate Governance Annual Report, the Annual Report on Remunerations, and other information instruments of listed companies, and of Savings Banks and other bodies that issue listed securities in official securities markets has been developed by Circular 5/2013, of 12 June, of the CNMV, that introduces a new model of Corporate Governance Annual Report.[33] This new model introduces the express obligation to refer, in the Corporate Governance Annual Report, to the number of women members on the board of directors and in the committees (executive, independent or external female directors); mentioning, as well, the evolution of this composition in the last four years. Besides, information regarding the implementation of measures shall be mentioned, if appropriate, in order to include in its board of directors a number of women that allows the achievement of a balanced representation of men and women. On the other hand, we can highlight that the requirement of explaining, in case of scant or null number of women directors, the reasons and initiatives adopted, where appropriate, is also met by the Appointments Commission so that when filling new vacancies the selection procedures are not biased hampering the selection of women members on the board of directors. The company shall deliberately search and include women who present the required professional profile among the potential candidates. This means an advance in favour of more information about the reasons why there is not a balanced representation of women and men on the boards of directors.[34]

Besides, the recent Report of the Experts Commission on Corporate Governance 2013[35] proposes an amendment of the Spanish Company Act by introducing a new article 529 bis, which imposes the duty of establishing procedures to prevent selection processes from being implicitly biased for the selection of women directors. This proposal has been included in the Draft Reform Companies Act, 2014.

---

33 The Minister of Economy and Finance (or, with his/her express authorisation, the CNMV) has the competence to establish the content and structure of the Corporate Governance Report (s. 61*bis* 4 Securities Market Act, 1988).

34 In this Circular there is the requirement to fill in a comparative chart showing the number of female members of the Board during the last four years, as well as their character: executive, independent or external female director.

35 Comisión de Expertos en materia de Gobierno Corporativo, *Estudio sobre propuestas de modificaciones normativas*, Madrid, 14 October 2013, p. 43.

B. THE PATH TO GENDER EQUALITY

1. *Some data of listed companies*

Currently, one of the aspects in which there has been most progress with regard to board composition is that relating to gender diversity, although this is an area of improvement which still has a long way to go (up to 40% of women on the board of directors). In 2011, 91.4% of the IBEX 35 companies had at least one woman on the board, an increase of 8.5 percentage points on the previous year. This continues the upward trend seen since 2007. In addition, the total number of women board members rose by 15.1% on 2010, with women accounting for 12.1% of board members in listed companies, compared with 10.6% in the previous year.[36] Nevertheless, as a counterpoint, we should note that the presence of women with an executive role remains unchanged since 2010.[37] In fact, there is only one woman chairperson of the Board in the IBEX 35 listed companies in 2012 (DIA). But the upward trend regarding the presence of women on the boards of directors seen in recent years was consolidated in 2011.

In 2011 a 66.4% of the boards of listed companies in official secondary markets had women presence. This means an increase of 2.3 percentage points in comparison with 2010.

But the 50,4% of firms reporting zero or near zero presence of female directors admit that they have taken no steps to remedy this situation. They do not comply with the *Unified Corporate Governance Code* Recommendations at this point. Most explain that their selection procedures are based on candidates' abilities and experience, and they do not make a conscious effort to find women with the target profile. Despite having improved from 35.6% in 2007 to 49,6% in 2011, full compliance with this recommendation still lags 32 points behind the average for the Code as a whole.[38]

Regarding issuers of traded securities other than shares, women directors occupied 8.1% of board places in 2011 (8,2% in 2010). One cooperative reported 66.7% of women membership and another from the industrial sector, 33,3%. If we exclude these two, the percentage of women directors drops back to 5.4% (4.1% in 2010). Twenty two companies, moreover, had not one woman on their

---

36 This percentage places Spain very close to the United Kingdom (13%), and close to the EU-16 (14%) and EEUU (16%). See PWC, *Report on the Boards of Directors of Listed Companies*, June 2012, p. 38, www.pwc.es.

37 CNMV *Quarterly Report* III, 2012, pp. 134 and 143 (available at www.cnmv.es/portal/Publicaciones/BoletinCNMV.aspx).

38 CNMV *Informe de Gobierno Corporativo de las entidades emisoras de valores admitidos a negociación en mercados secundarios oficiales* (IAGC), 2011, p. 87.

boards (it almost represents a 60% of the total). As in previous years, companies reported no female directors in the executive category.[39]

Women kept up their presence on company boards: 10.4% vs. 9.9% in 2010.[40] It accordingly urges companies with few or no women on their boards to deliberately cast round for female candidates whenever a director position falls vacant.[41] Women's share of board places averaged 10.4 in 2011, (11.9 among IBEX companies and 9.9% among those with market capitalisation above 1,000 million euros). The average percentage has risen in the IBEX 35 listed companies and fallen in the other corporations.[42]

Of the 164 women belonging to listed company boards in 2011 (158 in 2010), 15.4% also sat on the Executive Committee (16.5% in 2010), 37.7% on the Audit Committee (39.9% in 2010) and 32.7% on the Nomination and Remuneration Committee (30.4% in 2010). It bears mentioning, finally, that the number of women board members (36.4 of the total in 2011, 34.8% in 2010) who do not belong to any board committee has increased.[43]

2. *The codes of corporate governance as proof of the failure in the achievement of a balanced presence of women and men on the boards and the need to foresee sanctions both in the public company sector as well as in the private company sector to comply with the 40% objective*

Under the auspices of the self-regulation phenomenon in Spain with the first reports of corporate governance in the decade of the 1990s of last century, significant changes are taking place in Spanish Listed Company Law.[44]

Self regulation as a characteristic phenomenon of countries with Common Law tradition has conclusively influenced EU Law and by extensión Spanish Listed Companies Law not covered directly by EU Directives.

---

39 CNMV Informe de Gobierno Corporativo de las entidades emisoras de valores admitidos a negociación en mercados secundarios oficiales, 2011, pp. 106–107.

40 CNMV IAGC 2011, p. 30.

41 As remarks CNMV in 2010 (*Corporate Governance Report of Entities with Securities Admitted to Trading on Regulated Markets*, p. 38).

42 CNMV IAGC 2011, p. 290.

43 IACG 2011, p. 30.

44 Alonso Ureba interprets that there is an intention to reform the structural or organic regime of listed companies, without considering our system of sources, when the legitimate thing to do would have been that the work of these commissions present in these Codes would have constituted the base for regulation proposals of the General Commission of Codification that after a process of public information, is subject to the Parliament as a Bill [Alonso Ureba, A., "El gobierno de las grandes empresas (Reforma legal *versus* Códigos de Conducta)" ("The management of large companies (Legal reform *versus* Codes of Conduct))", in Esteban Velasco, G. (ed), *El gobierno de las sociedades cotizadas (The management of listed companies)*, Marcial Pons, Madrid, 1999, pages. 95–135, pages. 101–106].

The self-regulation phenomenon in countries with Roman Law tradition, within the sphere under study, is addressed due to the possible inadequacies of the Positive Law regulations for a correct protection of the interests at stake. These codes of voluntary compliance establishing a series of guidelines to be observed, on a voluntary basis, arise in order to compensate deficiencies in the balanced representation of women and men on the boards of directors.[45]

The idea that these codes are the result of the work of special commissions set up *ad hoc* and formed by experts on the subject and professionals in the sector as guarantee and legitimacy of its content trying to convey an appearance of neutrality and consensus in its elaboration; if to all this we add the presence of public administration representatives (the Conthe Code owes its name to the then president of the CNMV), the result is a polished text produced by experts that has undergone, on occasions, a public survey and has received opinions of other interested parties. And this is the text proposed to the listed companies in order to be voluntarily taken on.

In a first stage, as we have seen, the monitoring is not subjected to any company regulation, following a very British idea that what is at stake is the *reputational capital*[46] of the company which is the first interested party in complying with those Corporate Governance Codes. The concept of *moral suasion* appears here due to the fact that the underlying idea within the system is that the non compliance with the code without a justified reason will have a direct impact on the reputation level of the said companies within the market. The Securities Market Act only demands an explanation of the reason why these Corporate Governance Recommendations are not followed [s. 61*bis* 4 g)]. There is no doubt that there is an intention to influence the listed company since the moment it has to give explanations of why it does not follow a certain pattern of behaviour coming from a code drafted by the Government. The starting point – debatable from our point of view – is that the simple monitoring of the code recommendations produces a resulting effect of reinforcing the control and transparency of the decisions and the subsequent increase of the company

45 The reasoning can be summarised as follows: in a situation of crisis possible failures are detected in the way in which the board of directors works with empirical analysis that use, most of the times, economic techniques. For example, it is considered that different pieces of research show the convenience of counting with independent members on the board representing both the reference or control shareholders (that have representation on the board, directly or indirectly), as well as the executive board members. Thus, as it seems excessive to impose the presence of these board members by Law (we could think whether this fact breaches the right of association of art. 22 of the Spanish Constitution, 1978), the Spanish Corporate Governance Codes recommend their presence on the board of directors.

46 Concept that comes from economic science that has currently been strengthened due to the debate on Corporate Social Responsibility.

value.[47] Thus, the markets shall judge the monitoring or detachment from the regulations contained in the corporate governance codes.[48]

When companies voluntarily adopt these recommendations and they include them as part of their internal regulations we face regulations of conventional law originated from the will of the company.[49] Its efficiency derives from the exercise of the self-regulation powers of which the companies are invested.

In countries with Roman Law tradition the self-regulation phenomenon via codes of conduct of listed companies causes surprise. Reality is obstinate and Corporate Governance Codes voluntarily assumed by the companies in favour of a better reputation, at least in Spain, did not present signs of success in its first stages regarding the presence of women on the boards of directors. The encouragement of "voluntary" assumption has always been handled by the administration. The Conthe Code 2006 has regulatory consequences that became reality in the reform of the Securities Market Act made by Act 47/2007, 19 December. And it is not until the Effective Equality Act, 2007, when the draftsman refers to the convenience of the presence of women on the boards of directors.

Owing to the failure in Spain regarding the voluntary assumption of these Corporate Governance Codes, the Securities Markets Act is amended in order to introduce the principle *comply or explain* at a legal level to try to make the companies explain why they do not undergo or assume, in the composition of their boards of directors, the recommendations or guidelines approved in these Codes drawn up in Spain by encouragement of the State, as we have highlighted.[50]

---

47 These ideas brilliantly put forward can be found in Fernández de la Gándara, L., "El debate actual sobre el gobierno corporativo" ("The current debate on corporate governance"), in Esteban Velasco, G. (ed), *El gobierno de las sociedades cotizadas* (*The management of listed companies*), cit., pp. 55–93, pp. 71 to 75 (p. 73: "the zealots of corporate governance are convinced, summarising, about the fact that implementing a new company behaviour code will increase the financial value of the company and its position in the market").

48 "Every company must have its ideas, its philosophy, its beliefs and values, and transform them into commitments and the draftsman should not intervene", Masifern, E., "Gobierno Corporativo", in *Los Consejos de administración españoles en una economía globalizada*, Boletín del Círculo de Empresarios (News bulletin of the Circle of Businessmen), number. 62, 1997, pp. 289–324, p. 291.

49 Fernández de la Gándara, L, cit., p. 71.

50 The agreement of the Cabinet Meeting on 28 February 1997 by which a special commission is created to study an ethic code of the board of directors of listed companies, lays down that "in spite of the voluntary character for the governing bodies of listed companies to subject to the ethic code, the CNMV will be entitled to ask listed companies for information about whether the said ethic code has been assumed or not".

Thus, the Securities Market Act amended by Act 26/2003, of 17 July, Section 116 under letter f) renders compulsory, for listed companies, the introduction in the Corporate Governance Annual Report of a reference to the "degree of monitoring of the recommendations of corporate governance" or, if that is the case, an explanation for the absence of monitoring of the mentioned recommendations". Under Section 100 b bis of the Securities Markets Act it is considered a serious infringement not drafting or publishing the Corporate Governance Annual Report, or the existence of omissions in the mentioned report or false or deceitful data. The drawing up of the Report acquires legal status for listed companies and, step by step, some recommendations contained in these codes or in EU Recommendations are introduced in our Positive Law.

III. CONCLUSION

The scant presence of women on the board of directors of Spanish listed companies that issue equity and other securities shows relentlessly the failure of this self-regulation system and the failure to comply with good practices when there is no legal support.[51] Ethics and what can be legally demandable and what can be sanctioned must be separated. Regarding ethics, let us admit self-regulation and voluntary compliance.

But with the absence of the coercion of the law, self-regulation and voluntary compliance become simple behavioural guidelines that do not alter, in a significant way, the behaviour of private agents within the market. We consider appropriate, at this point, to remember the words of Hobbes "covenants, without the sword, are but words and of no strength to secure a man at all".[52]

---

51 In this sense the background of the Proposal for a Directive of the European Parliament and of the Council on improving the gender balance among non-executive directors of companies listed on stock exchanges and related measures (COM/2012/0614 final) "Member States and the EU institutions have undertaken numerous efforts in the course of several decades to promote gender equality in economic decision-making, notably to enhance female presence in company boards, by adopting recommendations and encouraging self-regulation. Two Council Recommendations (in 1984 and 1996) encouraged the private sector to increase the presence of women at all levels of decision-making, notably by positive action programmes, and called upon the Commission to take steps to achieve balanced gender participation in this regard. National self-regulation and corporate governance initiatives were aimed at encouraging companies to appoint more women into top-level positions. However, progress in increasing the presence of women on company boards has been very slow (...) The most significant progress was noted in those Member States and other countries where binding measures had been introduced. Self-regulatory initiatives in a number of Member States have not yielded any similarly noticeable changes. At the current pace it would take several decades to approach gender balance throughout the EU".

52 Hobbes, T., *Leviathan*, Part I, ch. 17.

Due to this fact we consider the approval of the Directive on improving the gender balance among non-executive directors of companies listed on stock exchanges and related measures, highly convenient. Particularly regarding command addressed to the Member States in order to lay down rules on sanctions applicable to infringements of national provisions related to the improvement of gender balance among non-executive directors of companies listed on stock exchanges (Article 6.1 of the Proposal Directive).[53] In Spain, more than a 60% of university students are women and 45% of the Spanish labour market is composed by women.[54] In the high Administration, most of those who become part of the last promotions are women (judges, notaries, registrars, economists of the state, state tax inspectors, etc.[55]). This reality does not appear reflected in the composition of the board of directors of listed companies. Neither the Effective Equality Act, 2007 nor self-regulation have achieved a balanced presence of women on the boards. Therefore, it is necessary to adopt compulsory and not merely voluntary laws considering penalties in case of the breach of a balanced presence of women and men on the boards of directors.

53 The Proposal makes reference to administrative fines and to the nullity or annulment declared by a judicial body of the appointment or of the election of non-executive directors made contrary to the national provisions that impose gender balance among non-executive directors. Recently on this Proposal, see González Bustos, M.A. and Fernández de Gatta Sánchez, D., "Luces y sombras sobre la propuesta de Directiva de 14 de noviembre de 2012 relativa al equilibrio entre hombres y mujeres en las empresas", *La Ley*, 12/2013, 01/24/2013, pages 6–12.

54 PWC and Isotés, *La mujer directiva en España, Women as Leaders*, Madrid, 2012, p. 6.

55 Indeed in the last years (2010 and 2011) the new judges and public prosecutors are women in a percentage of 74% www.manuelbagues.com/public_exams.html.

ABOUT THE AUTHORS

Philippe Culliford (Lic. UGent, MA HUB) is a PhD assistant at the social law department of the Law Faculty of Ghent University. Prior to his appointment, he has acquired 16 years of experience in employment law and related matters, including gender discrimination cases.

Marc De Vos (Jur.dr. UGent, Lic. ULB, LLM Harvard) teaches courses on labour and employment law, EU law, and the rule of law at Ghent University and at the Free University of Brussels. He has published extensively on issues of EU and domestic employment discrimination law.

Hans De Wulf (PhD in law Ghent, LL.M Tübingen) teaches various courses on Belgian and European company law and corporate governance at Ghent University and has published widely in these fields. His research currently focuses on shareholder suits, and on the constitutional aspects of the EU Banking Union.

Thorgerdur Einarsdóttir (professor of gender studies, University of Iceland) is specialised in gender issues with labour market issues as a central research area. She has published papers and articles on the topic.

Brigitte Gresy is specialised in the issues of equality between women and men since 15 years, as a top level civil servant and director of the cabinet of the minister for equality. She has originated the statute of 2011 in France on the quotas in the boards of directors and is nowadays secretary general of the High Council for professional equality, a body where the social partners and the State meet to evaluate and promote politics of professional equality.

Linda Hart (MA, E.MA) is a PhD candidate in sociology at the University of Helsinki, specialised in gender studies and legal sociology.

Morten Huse holds the Reinhard-Mohn-Endowed-Chair at the University of Witten/Herdecke. He is also a professor of organisation and management at BI Norwegian Business School. His work now focuses mostly on Value Creating Boards and Women on Boards. He has written several books and articles on these topics. The most recent book is *Getting Women on to Corporate Boards: A Snowball starting in Norway* (Edward Elgar 2013).

Anne Kovalainen (Dr. Econ. Sc.) is a Minna Canth Academy professor at the school of Economics, University of Turku. She is an economic sociologist by education. Professor Kovalainen's research interests range from gender, power and new economic sociology to social theories and methodological questions.

Philippe Lambrecht is a professor at UCLouvain, secretary general of the Federation of Enterprises in Belgium, and teaches corporate governance and financial law at UCLouvain. His main publications concern EU and Belgian corporate and financial law.

Reyes Palá Laguna (Jur.dr. University of Zaragoza) teaches courses on commercial law and company law at Zaragoza University and postgraduate courses at other universities in Spain. She has published extensively on company law, commercial law and securities law.

Gudbjörg Linda Rafnsdóttir (professor of sociology, University of Iceland) teaches courses on labour and employment law. She has published on issues of gendered working life such as work-life balance, lack of diversity in business leadership and occupational health.

Chantal Remery (dr.) is assistant professor in economics of the welfare state at Utrecht University School of Economics and is the Dutch member of the European Network of Experts on Gender Equality (ENEGE). She has written widely on gender (in)equality issues.

Jón Snorri Snorrason (Cand. Oecon et MA(Econ)) has been teaching microeconomics, corporate finance and organisational behaviour at Business Schools at Universities in Iceland. He has published on issues on gender quota laws, gender diversity on corporate boards and on corporate finance.

Andreas Stein is Head of Unit responsible for equal treatment legislation at the European Commission's Directorate General for Justice. He is a German lawyer (Dr. iur. University of Hamburg) and has a postgraduate degree in international relations (SAIS Bologna). After several years of practising as judge at a labour tribunal he joined the Commission in 2001 and has worked in the areas of private international law, gender equality and competition law before taking his current position.

Rosalinde van der Vlies is Deputy Head of Cabinet with Environment Commissioner Potocnik at the European Commission. She holds a Dutch law degree (University of Rotterdam) and has a postgraduate degree in European Law (College of Europe, Bruges). After several years of practising as a competition lawyer of the Brussels' Bar she joined the European Commission in 2002 and has worked in the areas of environment, gender equality and anti-discrimination before taking her current position.

Bernd Waas is a full professor of labour law and civil law at the Goethe University in Frankfurt. One of his main subjects of interest is discrimination law, on which he recently published two monographs dealing primarily with constitutional aspects and questions of EU law.

www.ingramcontent.com/pod-product-compliance
Ingram Content Group UK Ltd.
Pitfield, Milton Keynes, MK11 3LW, UK
UKHW051922100926
8556IPUK00021B/1328

9 781780 682297